9.95
75P

Invitation To Economics

D0920101

INVITATION TO ECONOMICS

A Friendly Guide Through the Thickets of "The Dismal Science"

Jim Eggert

Los Altos, California
William Kaufmann, Inc.

—

Cartoons by Robert Cavey.
Photographs by Jim Eggert

William Kaufmann, Inc.
95 First Street
Los Altos, California 94022

10-9-8-7-6-5-4-3-2-1
ISBN 0-86576-046-2

PREFACE

The purpose of *Invitation to Economics* is to combine into a single volume the essentials of macroeconomics and microeconomics. Much of the material was, in fact, drawn from my two narratives, *What is Economics?* and *Investigating Microeconomics*. Yet there is more here than just the marriage of two books. Of interest to those who teach Principles of Economics are new chapters on international trade—reflecting the greater role that the world economy plays in each and every nation, including our own. Note too, the microeconomics section containing a greatly simplified indifference curve and equal product curve analysis designed specifically for the beginning student. Also, I ought to mention one especially friendly guide. His name is Chester Olsen. We'll be watching Chester illustrate a number of important economic principles and ideas as he weaves in and out of the text.

As you read these pages, I hope to *encourage your curiosity* about economics. Indeed, my objective will have been achieved if this book urges the reader to dig deeper into principles and issues—to the point where he or she may feel confident to actively participate in the great economic debates of the day.

A warm thanks to my wife Pat and to my father Bob Eggert; and also to Dave Liu, Lou Tokle, Sunny Olds, Martin Giesbrecht, and the many other readers who, without doubt, made this a better book. And too, a very special thanks to James Pinto. Jim not only made helpful suggestions, but he also single-handedly prepared the supplementary Student Study Guide.

Finally, I wish to thank Dayle Mandelson (for the title suggestion), cartoonist Bob Cavey (whose cartoons always add a measure of fun and delight!), and, of course, all my "econ" students whose indirect contributions would be difficult to measure.

Jim Eggert
University of Wisconsin-Stout
Menomonie, Wisconsin

To my father,
Robert J. Eggert

TABLE OF CONTENTS

Part I

THE U.S. ECONOMY

Chapter 1

What Is Economics?

What Is Economics?

Unfortunately, there is no single or simple answer to that question. Originally, economics meant home management: economics was thus the study of how to organize and manage the resources of the home. What are these resources? They include things like money, time, working and living space, and so forth. What do all the items on our resource list have in common?

First, for any given household, the resources are limited. Very few people, for example, can honestly say that they "have enough." How often have you heard people say, "I wish I had more time," "I wish I had more money," or "I wish I had more space"? Limited resources are therefore a universal frustration. Second, these resources can be organized in many different ways; i.e., we can *choose* how these resources are used.

Families do have other resources, however, that aren't as easily manipulated, for example, love, family unity, good memories. These are also important in determining a person's welfare, but they, and other values as well (ethical, aesthetic, and religious values), are outside the realm of economics; you can't honestly put a monetary value on them, nor can you manipulate them to meet desired objectives as you can with your time or your money.

Thus, our definition of economics includes the idea of choice, that is, how a family (or company or nation) may choose to use its limited resources to best meet its economic objectives. These objectives can range from bare survival to high material comfort, depending on the available resources and how well or how poorly these resources are organized. This is what economics is all about.

Let us now extend our view from the household economy to the national economy. The basic economic problem is the same: the nation's resources are limited. Our material demands, however, tend to be unlimited, and the nation must learn how to best organize its resources to satisfy its material wants. Unwise use of resources—whether by consumers, businesses, or governments—can bring about unfortunate results such as unemployment, inflation, poverty, and (in extreme cases) hunger or starvation. The study of economics can help us understand how we might avoid such mismanagement of national resources.

National Resources

What exactly are our national economic resources? The first and primary resource is *labor*. This includes the millions of men and women in the U.S. labor force: the doctor, the farmer, the butcher, the assembly line worker, and so forth.

Next is *land*. America's land resources include every natural resource above, on, and below the soil. Air is a land resource, as is crop land. The mineral ores and petroleum in the crust of the earth are also land resources. These resources are distinguished by the fact that man cannot make more of them. The earth has only so much topsoil and so much oil. Once the topsoil has been destroyed[1] and the oil burned up, they will be gone forever.

The third major resource is *capital*. Many people think that capital means money; you often hear someone say "I need to raise so much capital for my new project." What is actually being referred to is financial capital. To the economist, capital means the physical tools that aid the worker in production. In other words, capital goods are man-made, can be reproduced or replaced, and tend to increase the productivity of labor. What are some examples of capital goods? The typewriter that I use is a capital good. It is a tool that increases my output; it's man-made (unlike land resources); and, once it wears out, I can replace it. The pen that you wrote your last check with is a capital good and so is the car that gets you to work. In fact, all machinery, tools, buildings, plants, and equipment are capital resources. (You can see now that there is much more to the meaning of capital than just plain money.) Capital goods are thus very important in determining the nation's level of wealth and economic growth.

Finally, we come to that elusive resource called *management*. The manager is quite special in our economy; it is he or she who coordinates and organizes all the other resources in order to produce and market the products and services that people want, thereby creating a profit. In the old days, the manager was called an entrepreneur; we think, for example, of Henry Ford or Andrew Carnegie as large-scale managers personifying this scarce resource. Perhaps the days of the great "wheeling-dealing" entrepreneurs are over, but whether you are talking about the bakery down the street or General Motors, some one person or group of people must still coordinate resources to produce saleable products and services.

Asking Questions, Making Choices

Thus, labor, land, capital, and management are the four major resources available to our economy to produce goods and services that people need and want.

To define a working economic system, however, we must ask further questions; for example, *How does an economic system determine what will be produced?* What will our economic output consist of, and who will determine its composition? Will our economy produce bombs and tanks or hospitals and homes? Small cars, large cars, or bikes and trains? Gas, oil, or solar heat? Who or what will decide for us? Of course, different economic systems will provide different answers to these questions. The Soviet Union or communist China determines what will be produced in a manner somewhat different from that of the United States or Brazil.

In addition, there are other important questions to ask, such as, *How does the economic system decide who gets the output?* Why are incomes, goods, and services distributed the way they are? Throughout U.S. history, dividing up the economic pie has always been a very controversial question. Will our economic system give a majority of the output to a few "super rich" families, will it try to divide the pie up more equally, or will it fall somewhere in between? Uneven distribution of incomes and wealth is often a result of differences in education, intelligence, skills, work habits, monopoly power, geography, family background, luck, and political or social savvy. More equal incomes, on the other hand, usually come about through government policies such as minimum-wage laws, progressive taxation, subsidized education, and welfare assistance.

And finally, there is the question, *How will these goods be produced?* At first glance, the answer might seem to be a purely technical one. Building an automobile, for example, is a problem for the engineer. And yet we know there are really many ways to produce a finished automobile. Ideally we want to build efficiently, using abundant, low-cost resources in place of scarce, high-cost resources. Assembling that car one way in preference to another returns us to the question of allocating resources. Choosing the correct techniques for production (conserving the scarce resources and using the abundant) is thus as much an economic problem as it is a technical or engineering problem. Economics is therefore the science (or art) of making choices—choosing the best way to organize our limited resources in order to meet our material needs.

Finding Answers

The method by which an economic system answers these questions varies from time to time and from country to country. Economist Robert Heilbroner in his excellent book, *The Making of Economic Society*, explains that there are in fact three basic systems for organizing economic resources.

The first is called *tradition*. The decision makers in a traditional system answer these questions by saying, "We will organize our economy the way we have always organized it." Tools and houses are constructed as they were always constructed. Junior goes into the same trade as his father. Output is allocated by custom, with few changes over the years and only with minute trial-and-error improvements over the centuries.

Economics by tradition certainly has some advantages: There is very little conflict, and there are few expectations that can't be met. But it is likely to be a stagnant system offering relatively low levels of economic well-being for its people. If you feel that having more choices moves you closer to the good life, then the traditional economic system is probably not for you.

Yet we certainly have elements of tradition in our so-called modern economy. For example, my own father is an economist, and he was once a teacher. Many instructors still use a lecture method that dates back to Plato in ancient Greece, even though some critics think that the lecture technique should have been dropped with the invention of the printing press. Whether the critics are correct or not, contemporary education certainly adheres to very traditional methods of performance. Women, too, have become more aware of the extent to which their lives are determined by social and economic tradition.[2] By discriminating on the basis of sex and thus eliminating a large proportion of our population from competing for highly productive and professional jobs, our economy has lost a potentially vast economic force. You can probably think of many more examples of how tradition subtly weaves in and out of our supposedly "modern" economy.

The second way to solve the economic problem is with a *command system*. A command system is characterized by the allocation of resources, incomes, prices, etc., by a centralized authority; in other words, a dictatorship. The command system invites no questions—either you follow orders or you take the consequences. This system is often the offspring of a despotic political system; they frequently go hand in hand. The economy of the Soviet Union is a good example.

European democratic socialists believe, however, that we can have a planned, state-directed economy without the terror. The combination appears to be difficult, and yet democratic state planning has been approximated in Scandinavia, Japan, and a few eastern European countries. The U.S. economy too has some elements of economic command. Our military services, for example, work on this principle, as does the government allocation of goods during wartime. When price-wage controls are in effect, we have a perfect example of government command. Furthermore, almost all government laws on economic affairs (including our tax system) constitute direction from above. By and large, however, our private enterprise system cannot really be called either command or traditional.

What we have in the United States is a *market economy*. The market system is a relatively recent phenomenon. Instead of using force to get things done (as in the command system), the market system motivates people by offering economic rewards within a process of exchange. Instead of government direction, decisions on resource use are made by millions of independent individuals and institutions attempting to do what is best for themselves or their businesses. Here the economic mule moves by carrot instead of stick. The U.S. economy is indeed a system of carrots.

If the command system is centralized, the market system is decentralized. A market economy churns out prices in countless markets of supply and demand, and these prices in turn act as guidelines in a new round of economic decisions; it is a competitive, interdependent, and self-regulating system. If you and I were not so accustomed to such an arrangement, we might find it somewhat strange, as we see in Heilbroner's little scenario:

> . . . assume for a moment that we could act as economic advisors to a society which had not yet decided on its mode of economic organization. Suppose, for instance, that we were called on to act as consultants to one of the new nations emerging from the continent of Africa.
>
> We could imagine the leaders of such a nation saying, "We have always experienced a highly tradition-bound way of life. Our men hunt and cultivate the fields and perform their tasks as they are brought up to do by the force of example and the instruction of their elders. We know, too, something of what can be done by economic command. We are prepared, if necessary to sign an edict making it compulsory for many of our men to work on community projects for our national development. Tell us, is there any other way we can organize our society so that it will function successfully—or better yet, more successfully?"
>
> Suppose we answered, "yes, there is another way. Organize your society along the lines of a market economy."
>
> "Very well," say the leaders. "What do we then tell the people to do? How do we assign them to their various tasks?"
>
> "That's the very point," we answer. "In a market economy no one is assigned to any task. The very idea of market society is that each person is allowed to decide for himself what to do."
>
> There is consternation among the leaders. "You mean there is no assignment of some men to mining and others to cattle raising? . . . What happens if no one volunteers to go into the mines, or if no one offers himself as a railway engineer?"[3]

The leaders argue on and on, unable to fully comprehend what motivates people in a market system—despite the explanation that it is in everyone's self-interest (more money, profits, etc.) to do whatever is necessary. Finally, the African representatives end the discussion saying, "We thought you had in mind a serious proposal.

But what you suggest is madness," and then with great dignity they take their leave.

Economic Sacrifices

Another way of looking at economics is to examine sacrifices. Economists call these *opportunity costs*. What exactly do they mean?

Let's say that you have spent half an hour reading this chapter. By spending this time reading, you have given up doing something else. In all likelihood you have given up a number of activities you would have enjoyed. Thus, when you use up one of your resources (an hour of time, a dollar, etc.) the cost to you is really the opportunities that you have forfeited. That hour is gone forever and so are the alternative activities you might have enjoyed. Sometimes we hear the question, "If you had your life to live over, would you do it any differently?" If you answer yes, then you are referring indirectly to your opportunity cost.

Although the above explanation of opportunity cost is somewhat philosophical, the economic concept is much the same. Economists look at the sacrifices that must be made when the economic resources of land, labor, capital, and management are used. If, for example, we commit our resources to producing 10 million automobiles, then these resources cannot be used for alternative goods and services such as housing or mass transit. Thus, the economist (unlike the business person) is not only interested in monetary costs but also in the question of what is going to be sacrificed when resources are put to use.

The idea of looking at economic costs as sacrifices can be seen quite dramatically in Figure 1–1.

Look, for example, at point A. We can assume that A represents an economy much like our own, i.e., it has directed most of its total resources toward the production of "butter" (private consumer goods) and comparatively fewer resources toward "guns" (military expenditures). As you move away from zero on either the "guns" or "butter" line, you are producing more and more of that good. Thus, point B represents a country that has chosen to produce more military goods than consumer goods (such as the United States during World War II). Given the fact that a country has only so many total resources, they are forced to choose some mix on the

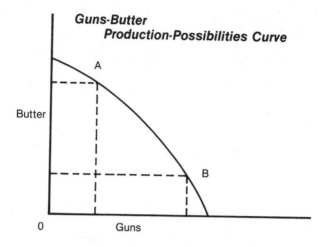

Figure 1-1

line between guns and butter. This line or curve is called the *production-possibilities curve.*

Our production-possibilities curve thus represents all the various choices open to society regarding consumer or military production. With our limited resources we may favor butter (A) or guns (B), but note that we cannot have a large amount of both goods—there are simply not enough total resources! In fact, to move from point A to point B means that the production of guns *must be sacrificed* to get more butter. Putting the opportunity cost idea slightly different, economists sometimes say, "There is no such thing as a free lunch!"

The true cost (opportunity cost) is, therefore, the measure of what is sacrificed. Thus we might view the true economic cost of a war as all the good things that could have been produced or accomplished instead. Or, the true cost of having so many cars is that the resources are not available to produce mass transit systems (see Figure 1–3).

Let's now take a look at another production-possibilities curve, this time representing a less developed country like China.

Curve A represents China at an early stage of development, with more agricultural potential than industrial potential. How-

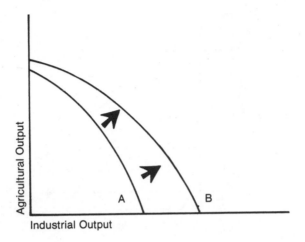

Figure 1-2

ever, an expanding production curve such as line B represents China after economic growth. The kind of economic growth that China chose in this example tended to favor industrial output over agricultural output. This is a typical pattern for economic development throughout the world.

Finally, there is an additional piece of information we can gather by examining a production-possibilities curve. Take a look at Figure 1–3.

Assume for a moment that the United States is producing a lot of cars and few mass transit systems; the country is therefore operating at point A. Suppose, though, that we decide to put more resources into mass transit and move down the curve a little way from A to A⁺. Note how much additional mass transit there is in relation to the relatively small amount of sacrificed cars. If, however, we are producing a lot in mass transit (point B) and want even more, we gain the same amount as before when we move to B⁺. Note the difference in the real cost of obtaining that extra mass transit; the number of sacrificed automobiles is much larger. We might say, then, that as we move to higher levels of mass transit, the opportunity cost of squeezing out yet *more* mass transit becomes greater and greater as more and more cars have to be sac-

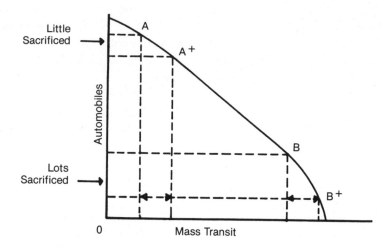

Figure 1-3

rificed. Obviously when a country is producing almost all mass transit, there are few interchangeable resources left to make the switch to even more mass transit; the sacrifice (or cost), therefore, must be very high to gain these additional trains, buses, etc. Economists call this phenomenon *the law of increasing costs.*

The Economist's Concerns

Let's return to our original question: What is economics? We might answer this question by simply saying that economics is "what economists study." Most economists, in fact, are not much concerned with broad generalizations such as "studying how to best allocate resources to meet our unlimited wants." They are more interested in the specific economic problems of society, such as unemployment, inflation, balance of payments, economic stagnation, and pollution. We could then say that economics is the study of how we solve economic problems.

Alternatively, we could view economics as the study of goals, i.e., how we move closer to specific economic objectives. These economic goals are more or less universal; i.e., most countries—capitalistic, socialistic, and communistic—are striving to achieve them.

The primary economic goal that seems to be universally desired is a decent material standard of living for all citizens, and thus much of our economic activity contributes toward this goal. But what exactly are the steps or intermediate goals that lead to a successful economic system?

The first of these objectives is *full employment*. All nations would like to see all, or nearly all, of their available resources being used. Men and women out of work or machines and factories idle can result in great economic suffering and social instability. It is foolish to have unused resources when there are the means to correct the situation. How we move an economy toward full employment will be explored later in the text.

The second goal of an economic system is *price stability*. Rapid price increases—or what is commonly called *inflation*—have the undesirable effect of grossly distorting income distribution. The victims include people on fixed incomes, savers, and lenders. While these groups lose, others win including borrowers and speculators. At best, mild inflation is merely irritating, if it is accompanied by full employment. At its worst, however, inflation invites panic buying and can lead to the eventual collapse of a monetary system.

Note the conflicts that arise in pursuing these various economic goals, such as with price stability and full employment. For example, when there is high unemployment, there is frequently lower inflation, and if there is high inflation, almost everyone is working. Thus as we struggle to achieve one economic objective, we sometimes lose our grip on another.

The third goal is *growth*. There are respected critics who argue that the United States is presently overdeveloped and who believe that we would benefit by not adding any more to our economic affluence. And yet, most Americans, and most other people in the world, seem to desire higher and higher levels of output and consumption. We feel concerned when the total economic output fails to rise; if output drops, alarms are sounded throughout government and business. Furthermore, when we talk about the poorest two thirds of the world, a lack of economic growth means hunger and possible starvation.

Fourth, we all desire a *quality environment*. The mounting evidence of the massive pollution problems that face this small planet compels economists to regard the environment as a major economic issue. But again note the potential conflicts that arise in pursuing these various economic goals. For example, strong enforcement of antipollution laws may well slow down economic growth. "Everything has a price," says one man jokingly to another in a newspaper cartoon. "To get a high standard of living we have to reduce the quality of life."

A fifth goal of an economic society is to move toward a *fair distribution of income*. This does not mean, however, an absolutely equal distribution; perfect equality would be unrealistic and probably undesirable for it would destroy healthy economic incentives. On the other hand, most economists would agree that a system which allows a large number of its citizens to live in poverty while others enjoy immense wealth is certainly unfair. What then can we do about a grossly unequal system?

Generally accepted methods of moving toward a more equal distribution of income include government taxation and redistribution of income (welfare, food stamps, Medicare, etc.) and also the enforcement of equal opportunity in education and job procurement. If the government became, as some have suggested, "the employer of last resort," then it would have even greater impact in this area. Although some people disapprove of government intervention, the policies and programs mentioned above are at least some of the ways we can break down the natural, social, and institutional inequalities that operate in all societies.

The last goal is *economic freedom*. Like our goal of fair income distribution, economic freedom is sometimes difficult to define precisely. To many Americans, economic freedom will thrive in a decentralized, free enterprise system. This includes freedom for the workers to choose occupations commensurate with their skills and experience. By this definition, twentieth century America may be one of the "freest" economies in the world. Yet the critic might ask what meaning that kind of freedom has for a consumer without income. Indeed, what occupational freedom does an unskilled, unemployed, ghetto resident have? In fact, what real freedom of enterprise would you or I have if we were to attempt to compete with IT&T, General Foods, or the Ford Motor Company? Clearly, the ideal goal of freedom has been greatly obstructed by barriers imposed by large, concentrated industries, as well as by restrictive policies and regulations of government agencies. But compare the United States with other countries, and it is clear that we would score quite high in meeting this objective.

Having read this far, you are hopefully getting a feeling for what economics is all about. However, before ending this chapter, let's briefly consider what economics is not. Our culture has many values. For many of us love is a strong value and so is religious faith. Great beauty has its place in the pyramid of values, as do ethics. As we mentioned before, however, the values of economics are primarily material values, and even though we must spend much of our lives pursuing material things (economic values), these probably fall somewhere below those values that are less tangible.

Yet unfortunately we often tend to confuse economic and non-economic values. This sometimes happens when someone is trying to sell us a product. For example, in a special CBS report called "You and the Commercial," the contemporary psychologist Erich Fromm was asked his reaction to TV commercials. His answer was that many of them were designed to instill fear such as fear of body odor. Even more chilling is "the general fear of not being loved and then 'finding' love by buying and consuming some particular product." Thus, love becomes confused with consumption. Here's an illustration:

> I walked around in the rain for hours after she said good-bye. It was sad enough, having her call everything off. But did she have to be so cruel? "Good-bye, Nick," she said. My name is Tom. Nick was what she called me, though, because I always nicked myself when I shaved. The rain was loosening the bandage on my face.
>
> It was late when I arrived at my apartment and found a small, plainly wrapped package at my door. I picked it up and went in. Exhausted, but unable to sleep, I sat down and opened the package.
>
> Inside was a Gillette Techmatic razor. The note carried her fragrance into the room, and memories flooded my dulled mind. The Techmatic, she wrote, is adjustable so I can change the setting to fit my skin and beard. . . . A smooth, safe shave, she wrote. But, best of all, she signed it, "Hello, Tom."

Funny? Perhaps, but such a tale is possible. According to Fromm, it is a sad reflection on our society that we're often seduced into meeting our need for love and acceptance through artificial means, such as buying commodities, rather than in more personal and lasting ways. We will therefore try to keep our subject in its proper place as we now move on to examine the U.S. economy.

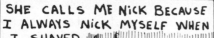

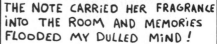

Chapter 2

THE U.S. ECONOMY

What is the U.S. economy like? What makes it tick? Suppose a foreigner asked you to describe our economic system. What would you say?

We learned in Chapter 1 that our economic system is basically a market economy. Let's now amplify this important idea. A pure market economy is self-regulated, interdependent, and competitive. Self-regulation takes place when supply and demand operate for every good and service that has economic value. There is a market for welders and secretaries, for wheat and bread, for toothpicks and plows. Each of these markets is constantly interacting with hundreds of others. This process churns out prices, and these prices in turn modify other markets and influence economic decisions. Let's look at an illustration.

We will begin by assuming that there is a shortage of milk, and, as a consequence, the price of milk goes up. In a market economy, buyers and sellers note this signal (high milk prices) and then respond in various ways. First, the existing dairy farmers demand more cows and farm land so that they can expand their operations and increase their profits. Soon, higher profits in milk production begin to attract more farmers into the dairy industry.

This growing number of farmers will now be demanding more milking machines and silos. Stainless steel for milking machines and cement for silos will be diverted into farming and away from other industries. Milking machine manufacturers, for example, will try to outbid steel-pipe manufacturers for the available steel. Plumbers may find that steel pipes are simply priced too high. They may discover that low-cost plastic pipes can do the job almost as well. Suddenly the plastic industry has a need for new people and raw materials: chemists and petroleum. The readjustments that could take place because of a milk price increase are almost endless. Note that in this example no economic dictatorship tells people what to do; everything takes place automatically in response to price signals in the marketplace.

In reality, our neat system of supply and demand is often not allowed to regulate itself. The government, reacting to special economic interest groups, is often the culprit. For example, when the federal government imposes price-wage controls, we find that prices are no longer flexible. If prices are not allowed to move upward or downward, the signals are thwarted. Shortages and black markets develop where the demand for certain products is great. We can see something similar happening when city governments impose rent controls. Rents that are artificially low create greater quantity demanded than is supplied, leaving many frustrated demanders. Other examples of governmental market regulation include farm subsidies, the setting of minimum wage laws, and tariffs. Each time the government interferes with the free movement of prices, market efficiency is usually reduced.

Specialization

Our economy can also be described as *specialized*. All of us specialize. You may specialize in programming computers, making handmade furniture, fixing cars, or tightening a bolt on an assembly line automobile. If we did not specialize, many of us would be forced to become self-sufficient—like the original settlers of the American frontier—and we would undoubtedly undergo a reduced standard of living.

Why does output increase when workers specialize? Some people, of course, simply have natural abilities in some specialties. Also, the more we work at our particular job, the faster and generally more efficient we become. We learn the shortcuts and how to use the special tools that increase our productivity. The assembly line operation is a good example of how specialization and division of labor can create greater output than a system of nonspecialized workers.

Specialization can be worthwhile even when an individual has superior skills in several areas. For example, Jim is a good plumber, but he is also a good auto mechanic. Bob is a plumber and an auto mechanic as well. Bob, however, is almost a genius at fixing cars, whereas Jim is just average. As plumbers their skills are about equal, but Bob is a little better here too. Even though Bob has an *absolute advantage* in both skills, he has a *comparative advantage only* in auto mechanics; that is, his advantage is bigger than Jim's in mechanics rather than plumbing. Jim is not as good in either skill, but his disadvantage is smaller in plumbing. We therefore say Jim has his comparative advantage in plumbing. If they lived in a town that had room for only one plumber and one auto mechanic, the economy would be more productive if Bob stayed with auto mechanics and Jim concentrated on plumbing. In short, specialization will bring about higher output in almost all situations.

Some economists feel, however, that we are overspecialized despite the gains from comparative advantage. One drawback of specialization is that we become highly dependent on our specialists. What would happen if the truck drivers and railway workers—only about 1 percent of the labor force—went on strike at the same time? Our economy would be paralyzed within a week. If the strike lasted a month, we might have starvation and mass panic. The slender threads of economic interdependence can easily be broken in a complex economy such as ours. There is also some evidence that overspecialization on the assembly line and in menial jobs takes its psychological toll.

> The man whose whole life is spent in performing simple operations which the effects to are, perhaps, always the same, or very nearly the same, has no occasion to exert his understanding or to exercise his invention . . . He naturally loses, therefore, the habit of such exertion and generally becomes as stupid and ignorant as it is possible for a human creature to become.

Adam Smith wrote this in his book, *Inquiry into the Nature and Causes of the Wealth of Nations* in 1776. Even today we see many people rebelling against such overspecialized, menial jobs. A surprisingly large number of individuals and families have moved out of the cities and into the country to set up "new homesteads" where they can operate their semi-self-sufficient farms with little specialization. Often they build their own homes, make their own clothes, and grow much of their food, as most of our nation's

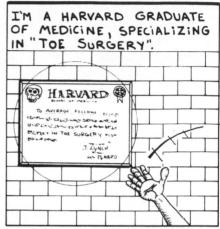

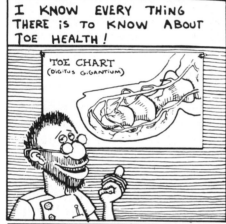

farmers did some generations ago. Even though their material standard of living is usually lower than average, they take great pride in their work and seem quite happy with their newly found independence.[4]

Finally, there is increasing evidence that many people would like to rely less on the services of others. Gardening, for example, is on the increase, as is doing one's own auto maintenance; "do-it-yourself" remodeling has always been popular in this country. This trend seems to defy the laws of comparative advantage and specialization. Still, by and large, we remain primarily specialists operating within a very specialized and interdependent American economy.

Self-interest

If much of our high productivity and efficiency in the U.S. economy comes from specialization and division of labor, the motivation to do all this work comes from self-interest. Why do some people go into hot, dirty mines or get up early on a cold winter morning to work on an outdoor construction site? Why does the barber cheerfully cut your hair even when he isn't feeling so hot? Why does GM make Chevrolets? Why do companies go to all the trouble of making safety pins to help you diaper your baby? There is no economic commander in chief telling them what to do, and they don't do it because of tradition. They perform their job *because it is in their own self-interest to do so*. Economists call this self-interest *income maximization*, others call it "just trying to make a living." Whatever it's called, it is the motor of our capitalist economic system. Things get done because each individual group or institution is constantly trying to enlarge its base of income, consumption, or profit.

The self-interest of businesses is to maximize profits. The self-interest of workers is to maximize their income. Finally, the self-interest of consumers is to maximize their material satisfactions from limited incomes. Surprisingly enough, in this very "self-centered" economic turmoil, the society as a whole benefits! This is what Adam Smith called the *invisible hand.* In *Wealth of Nations* he said that each individual (or business) pursuing his own interest is "led by an invisible hand to promote the end which was not part of his intention."

It was not the intention of the safety pin company to make it easier for parents to diaper their babies. Their purpose was to make a profit. The company therefore had to make something society wanted. That is where the safety pins came in. If the company did not make a product that society wanted, it would be eliminated by the laws of economics. You might recall an ad from the Sun Oil Company; it had a refreshing honesty about it:

> These days, I need all the friends I can get. This is a tough business I'm in. You really have to hustle to make a buck. And right now I need the bucks. I'm due for a new wrecker. A new car. And my wife's screaming for an avocado refrigerator. That's why, when you drive into my station, I'm going to come out smiling. I'm going to wash your front window. Your back window. Now to be honest, I'm not really crazy about having to work this hard, but I need that new wrecker, the new car, and like my wife says, what's an avocado kitchen without an avocado refrigerator? Try me, I can be very friendly.

Of course, not everyone is interested in maximizing their income. Henry David Thoreau once said, "None can be an impartial or wise observer of human life but from the vantage ground of what we should call voluntary poverty." And in James Park's thought-provoking article, "Four Reasons for Voluntary Poverty,"[5] Park explains that income maximization can lead to exploitation, pollution, compromises on personal freedom, and a tacit support of militarism (through taxes). Readers will have to decide for themselves whether voluntary poverty is a desirable path to follow. It seems safe to say, however, that if a majority of workers and businesses renounced income and profit maximization, the U.S. economic system would be radically different from what it is today.

Private Ownership

Another notable characteristic of the American economy is *private ownership*. If we were living under a socialistic instead of a capitalistic system, then the means of production—the businesses, factories, capital, and other resources—would be largely publicly owned.

The debate over socialism versus capitalism has been going on for years. Unfortunately, opinions are too often based on emotion rather than on factual information. Many people, for example, are convinced that socialism implies a political system that is totalitarian, ruthless, and nonlibertarian. The truth is that political des-potism can thrive in a capitalist state (South Africa, Brazil) as well as in a socialist one (U.S.S.R., Cuba). Again, the major difference between the two systems is the following: socialism means that businesses are owned and controlled by the public, whereas capitalism implies that businesses are owned and controlled privately. To say much more is to confuse the issue.

Which of these two systems then is "better"? Unfortunately there is no easy answer. Socialism can work well under certain conditions. For example, most observers of recent Chinese economic history are quite impressed by the progress socialism has made in upgrading the economic welfare of nearly a billion Chinese citizens. Yet, most economists will agree that historically the United States has done quite well under a free enterprise, capitalistic system. Particularly in newly formed small businesses, private ownership and the profit motive have made for energetic and efficient operations.[6]

Consider now the term "communism." How does it differ from capitalism and socialism? Karl Marx defined communism as a system where the production-distribution philosophy was, "From each according to his ability, to each according to his need." Surprisingly, our most "communistic" institution is the family. In most conventional family setups members receive an approximately equal distribution of goals and services. Consumption is based on "need" instead of productive effort (an infant, for example, doesn't work for its formula). Pure communism has been approximated by a few comparatively small groups (the Shakers and some North American Indian communities, for example), but on a national scale it doesn't appear to be as practical as the more common socialistic or capitalistic economies.

Competition

The next characteristic is *competition*. Perhaps no other quality of American capitalism draws as much praise.

Proponents of the capitalist system say that competition allows the most intelligent and skillful to prevail in a "dog eat-dog" battle for survival. This is a virtue, they say, because in a system where only the fittest and strongest come out on top, the economic organization itself will remain strong and healthy. Producers must make a cheaper, better product than their rivals, or they will find themselves out of business. A competitive economy is like a grand-scale pro-football game where, according to Green Bay Packer Coach Vince Lombardi, "Winning isn't everything, it's the only thing." It should be noted that some people feel this kind of "competition" can also be unhealthy. Educator George Leonard, for example, writes:

> The . . . argument for hot competition all the way down to nursery school is that competition makes winners. The argument is, at best, half true. It makes nonwinners, too—generally more nonwinners than winners. And a number of studies indicate that losing can become a lifelong habit.

What is perhaps even more interesting is a businessman's reaction to the suggestion that this kind of competition creates more problems than it solves. Leonard continues:

> I once spoke to a group of top ranking industrialists in a seminar session and argued that hot competition is far from inevitable in the future. As my argument developed I noticed a look of real anxiety on some of the faces around me. One industrialist finally spoke up, "If there is to be no competition, then what will life be all about?" We would probably be appalled to discover how many people in this culture have no notion of accomplishment for its own sake and define their own existence solely in terms of how many other people they can beat out.[7]

To beat out your opponent and to build a better product than your rival are thus common ways of defining competition. Economists, however, define it somewhat differently. A good example of a competitive industry in the United States is farming, with tens of thousands of producers who actually don't care about what the other producers are doing! In pure competition there are in fact no differences between the sellers' products. For example, grade A milk is the same throughout the industry. We never see advertisements claiming that Farmer Jones's milk is better than Farmer Brown's. Another characteristic of competition is that no seller is big enough to set prices or to control the market. A competitive industry is the *least concentrated* of all industries. (In contrast, a monopoly is the most concentrated.)

Obviously, to be a producer in a truly competitive industry is to operate at a disadvantage. For example, the farmer's inability to control prices and their low rate of return on investment are problems that have plagued U.S. agriculture for a long time. Even though competition may mean "hard times" for sellers it usually gives consumers the lowest possible price. Furthermore, the more sellers, the more potential choice for the buyer. Competition is therefore a kind of "insurance policy" against getting ripped off.

Since real competition can be threatening to businesses, we see all kinds of efforts to do away with it. Sellers can sometimes lessen competition by eliminating other sellers; by erecting barriers so that new firms have a difficult time entering; and, finally, by making products slightly different from other sellers in the industry. Keep in mind that even though a decentralized competitive market is a traditional American "ideal," it is a rare sight on our economic landscape.

To summarize, we can say that industry is purely competitive if it has the following characteristics:

- A large number of sellers of the same product
- No single seller with any control over price
- Easy entry into the industry
- Low profits in the long run
- No rivalry among sellers

Monopolies

Let's look now at the other extreme. If competition allows consumers the widest potential choice, a monopoly market structure gives the consumer the least choice. The monopoly seller has absolute control over his economic kingdom. If you are a consumer and want the goods, you must buy from him. He is, in short, a "one-firm industry."

Are there any good examples of monopolies in the United States? Well, your local telephone company has an effective monopoly on local telephone service. The government, too, holds a legal monopoly on first-class mail. The companies that sell you electricity and natural gas are also monopolies. We call them *natural monopolies* because the market is too small to accommodate more than one seller. If, for example, your local utility already has electric power lines leading to your home, it would obviously be inefficient (and also very costly) for another firm to do the same. We therefore tolerate natural monopolies. You might wonder, then, how the consumer is protected from profit-hungry utilities. The answer is by government regulation. Although their monopolies are legally protected, their prices and rates are subject to review by public commissions.

There are other monopolies, however, that operate without any restrictions. Imagine a small town with just one drug store or only one dentist. We call this kind of market a *regional monopoly*. We can't say they are pure monopolies because there may be another drug store twenty miles away. Yet for the retired residents of that town or for those without transportation, the one drug store becomes an effective monopoly operating without any competitive or regulatory restraints. Here, the buyer is at the mercy of the seller. Did you ever have a nightmare where your car broke down in the middle of nowhere, and you discover there is just one garage within fifty miles? You can just see the owner of the garage rubbing his hands together as his tow truck brings your car in. Unregulated monopolies can be bad news!

We can also see monopolistic behavior among the big industrialists. American Tobacco, Standard Oil, and Alcoa Aluminum were at one time considered monopolies. Others, such as General Electric and Westinghouse, simply conspired during the late 1950s to set prices on certain products and behaved as if they were a single monopoly. This arrangement is called a *cartel*.

However it occurs, such monopolistic behavior is illegal under the Sherman Antitrust Act of 1890. Section 2 reads:

> Every person who shall monopolize, or attempt to monopolize, or combine or conspire with any person or persons . . . shall be deemed guilty of a misdemeanor . . . .

The antitrust laws were written in an attempt to reverse the natural tendency for industries to become more concentrated. In capitalism, the big often get bigger; and if one firm begins to dominate a market, there is a natural tendency for that firm to attempt to eliminate (or merge with) rivals. General Motors, for example, could probably ruin Ford by simply lowering car prices below cost. What prevents GM from doing this? Primarily it is because of our antitrust laws.

Let's now review the conditions for a monopoly:

- Only one seller (i.e., one choice for the consumer)
- No close substitutes for the product the monopolist sells
- Great barriers of entry into the industry
- Usually higher prices than in a competitive market

There is one industry that fits all these conditions and yet is not ordinarily considered a monopoly: the public school system. Some economists (Milton Friedman, for example) point out that the public school monopoly contains all the undesirable features of an industrial monopoly, i.e., a no-choice situation, high costs, lack of innovation, and so forth. Not only do consumers have no alternative, they *must* also "consume" the "product" whether they want to or not. Not to do so means prison or detention under the compulsory-attendance laws. To make things more difficult, a child often cannot get out of going to school even if he or she knows the required material since most states will not allow students to take high school equivalency tests until they are sixteen. A few states require them to be twenty-one. Would less compulsion and more choice make for a better system? Many educators and economists think that some alternative system is worth a try.

Friedman, for one, has suggested a *voucher* system where parents would be allowed to choose the kind of schooling they would like for their children.[8] It would be something like the GI Bill for veterans. (No one, for example, tells a student on the GI Bill that he must go to a military academy. The student can go to any accredited school.) Under Friedman's system, you might choose to use your educational vouchers for a public school, a private school, or even an apprenticeship. "Voluntary organizations—ranging from vegetarians to Boy Scouts to the YMCA—could set up schools and try to attract customers." Indeed, the voucher system is an interesting proposal; but whether it would bring about a new age in American education or create new kinds of problems, we won't know until we try it in some form or another.

Oligopolies

We have not yet mentioned the most prevalent type of industrial structure in the American economy. It's not competition, and it's not monopoly. Economists call this type of industry an *oligopoly*, an industry dominated by a few firms. Think of almost everything we buy—automobiles, steel, aluminum, processed food, appliances, gasoline, etc. The companies that dominate each of these industries can often be counted on one hand.

Other major characteristics of an oligopoly-type industry include:

- Emphasis on nonprice competition (advertising, product differentiation, styling, service, etc.)
- Price leadership by the largest firm (U.S. Steel, for example)
- Great difficulty for outsiders to enter
- Limited choice for buyers between a few suppliers

Look carefully at the pyramid (see Figure 2–1) to see how oligopoly fits between competition and monopoly in respect to market concentration. The oligopoly industries are quite concentrated. Indeed, they are closer to the monopoly end of the spectrum than to pure competition.

One of the major features of the oligopoly is *entry barriers*. What if you decided to start a rival company in the automobile industry. What difficulties would you encounter? For one thing, you would need millions and millions of dollars just to build one assembly plant, and even if you built it, you would still be left with a massive marketing problem. You would have to convince a large number of dealerships to handle your product. Even if you did that, why would anyone go out of his way to buy your car? They probably wouldn't, at least until you had established a name for yourself. This might take years and additional millions for advertising—and this still would not include the high cost of financing annual model changeovers. Indeed, potential investors would probably consider your undertaking doomed to failure. Even large corporations (which might have the financial capital

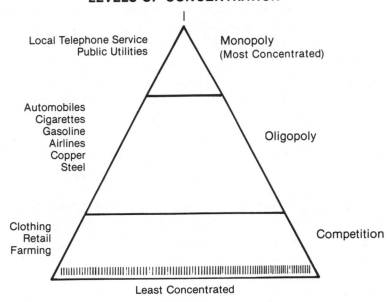

LEVELS OF CONCENTRATION

Local Telephone Service
Public Utilities

Monopoly
(Most Concentrated)

Automobiles
Cigarettes
Gasoline
Airlines
Copper
Steel

Oligopoly

Clothing
Retail
Farming

Competition

Least Concentrated

Figure 2-1

available) would hesitate to plunge into such a hazardous venture. The economic barriers are simply too great.

Well, what has happened to our model of the American economy? We began by saying that it was a market economy, competitive and regulated by supply and demand. Though these concepts are still operational to some degree, we are nevertheless forced to modify some of our traditional viewpoints:

"But aren't we now saying that most of our economy is dominated by oligopolists?"

"Yes."

"And didn't you say that it's very difficult for a newcomer to invade oligopoly territory because there are so many economic barriers?"

"Yes."

"Then, whatever happened to the so-called free enterprise ideal?"

"Well, to be truthful with you, it really hasn't existed for a long time, except in farming, local retail and services, and some small-scale manufacturing. I'm sorry but that's the way it is."

Chapter 3

SUPPLY AND DEMAND

You can hardly open up a magazine or newspaper without hearing someone refer to the idea of supply and demand: "high food prices result from greater demand than supply" . . . "the scarcity of new housing boils down to the supply and demand for money" . . . "the world energy situation can only be understood through supply and demand." I even heard a man say "economics is really nothing more than understanding supply and demand." An exaggeration? Yes, but not by much. So what does it all mean?

The Demand Curve

Let's begin with demand. To demand something means much more than just having a desire for a product; it implies that you have a need for that product *and* the money to buy it. As an example, your effective demand for a hamburger will be made evident only when you actually go out and buy one. Thus, economists are interested in how many hamburgers people buy at different prices. By observing the quantity of goods bought at a variety of prices, we can work out what is called the *demand curve*.

Suppose, for example, that the price of sweet corn is $5 a bushel. Let's say that people buy 5 bushels at that price. Then, if we lower the price to $4, we note that they will buy 10 bushels, and so forth. As we lower the price, observe how much more corn people will buy:

P($)	$5	$4	$3	$2	$1
Q(bu)	5	10	20	30	40

This information, in turn, can easily be graphed (see Figure 3–1).

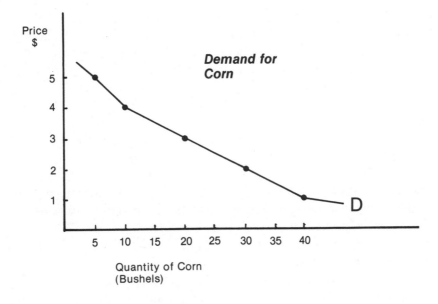

Figure 3-1

The lower the price, the greater the quantity that is demanded. Makes sense, doesn't it? For example, when your local grocery store lowers the price on certain vegetables, more of those vegetables will usually be sold. Behind this simple economic law, however, is some fairly complicated reasoning; let's look at what's involved.

One reason is that regular buyers of corn (as an example, the Smith family) now find that their *real incomes* have gone up slightly. Their money income has remained unchanged (i.e., the Smith's take home pay of $250 per week stays the same), but the lower price has increased their purchasing power, i.e., their real income. Lower corn prices mean that the Smith family can buy more of all goods, including corn, with their $250 weekly salary. It's as if the Smiths were given a small income raise when they walked into the grocery store and saw that corn was marked down from 50¢ a pound to 12¢. Their greater real income probably means that they will purchase more of the other items they like too, such as canned tuna; but for now we are just interested in the fact that they bought more corn. We will call this the *income effect*.

The second reason for buying more when the price goes down is that we gain more total satisfaction if we buy a quantity of a low-priced good over a high-priced substitute. For example, tuna and hamburger are substitute goods: they both provide protein for family meals. If last week they were the same price but this week tuna is much cheaper, we gain in total satisfaction if we substitute the cheaper tuna for the higher-priced hamburger. This is called the *substitution effect.*

Both effects—the income effect and the substitution effect—contribute to an economic law; i.e., as you lower price, quantity demanded increases. Sometimes economists refer to this law as the *law of downward-sloping demand* because the demand curve does indeed slope downward, demonstrating the inverse relationship between price and quantity.

Shifting Demand

Let's now look at the demand curve from the eyes of a business-person. We learned that the curve itself is a useful tool that shows at a glance how much will be sold at differing prices, but business-people would like to go one step further. They would like to see the demand curve for their product shift to the right, which means that even more of a product can be sold at the same price. Look, for example, at Figure 3–2 and note that for any given price the new expanded demand curve shows greater quantities demanded.

Surely this is good for businesses—more goods sold at a given price. The question concerning us now is what causes the demand curve to shift? It is not a change in price because when the price of a good changes we simply move up or down along a stationary demand curve. (See Figure 3–1.)

But what about advertising? Yes. It is commonly acknowledged that the purpose of advertising is to shift the demand curve to the right and to expand the market by increasing the number of customers for your product. Indeed, anything that brings about a broader base of potential customers will shift the curve. For example, when the United States recognized the People's Republic of China and trade between the two countries was legalized, a new market for U.S. products, ranging from aspirin to computers, suddenly opened.

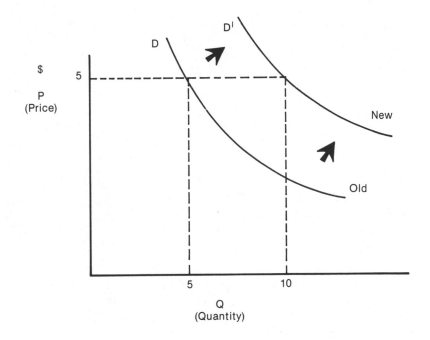

Figure 3-2

What else will shift the demand curve? Let's return to our example of canned corn. Suppose that canned peas are a substitute for canned corn. What would happen if the price of corn remained constant at 50¢ per can, but the price of peas suddenly went up from 50¢ to $2 per can? The demand for corn would increase! On the other hand, if green beans (another substitute for corn) went down in price from 50¢ to 25¢, the demand for corn would decrease. The businessperson, therefore, will be watching very carefully for what happens to the price of substitute goods because this can greatly influence the demand for his product. In summary then, the higher the price of a substitute good, the greater the shift in demand for the product that remains low in price.

If the two products are complementary, however, it can work the other way around. Gasoline and cars are complementary. The demand for cars thus tends to go down (i.e., shift to the left) if the price of gasoline goes up. Businesses, therefore, must keep a wary eye on what is happening to the prices of those goods that "go with" their products.

Changes in tastes and fashion also cause demand curves to move forward or backward. Also, a new use for an old product will shift the demand to the right. A leftward shift will usually occur when our incomes go down; when incomes increase, demand shifts forward. There can be exceptions, however. A poor family, for example, whose diet consists mainly of potatoes, may experience an increase in income and *reduce* its demand for potatoes. Under these conditions, potatoes are considered an *inferior good*. Most goods, however, are what we call *normal goods*, and an increase in income brings about an increase in demand.

In a free and decentralized market, a demand curve is never stationary for very long; it gets battered around like a ship in a stormy sea. An environment of rapidly changing incomes, tastes, and prices of substitute or related goods makes it all but impossible to accurately predict the curve's behavior. In the more controlled markets of oligopolistic industries, the power of advertising causes demand curves to be more manageable and predictable than they would be in a pure-market situation.

The Supply Curve

Let's now turn our attention to the *supply curve*. A supply curve shows how much suppliers would like to provide at different prices. For example, you might ask Farmer Brown, "How much would you want to supply to the market if the price of corn were $5 a bushel?" Perhaps he would reply, "At $5 a bushel, I'd supply 35 bushels." Next you might ask him what he would produce at $4 per bushel, and so on. Let's say he gives you the follow ing information:

P($)	$5	$4	$3	$2	$1
Q(bu)	35	30	20	12	0

Based on this information, the supply curve can be graphed as shown in Figure 3–3.

Farmer Brown's supply curve is therefore sloping upward. This means the higher the price, the more he wants to supply, and the lower the price, the less he's willing to supply. In fact, at the price of $1 per bushel, he does not want to supply any corn at all! Other

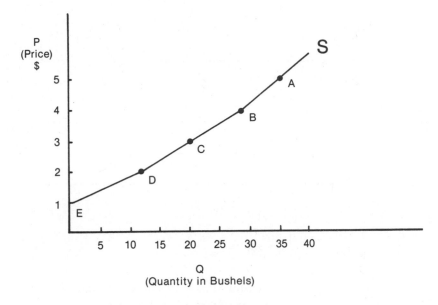

Figure 3-3

farmers will probably respond in much the same way. Instead of staying on an individual level with 35 bushels for $5, we might ask our supply question (in theory) to all the farmers. For example, we may find out that 35 million bushels will be supplied at $5, 30 million at $4, and so on. The curve will have the same original shape regardless of the quantities involved.

Remember how the demand curve in Figure 3–2 shifted back and forth? The supply curve can shift too, as shown in Figure 3–4. A rightward shift in the supply curve means that at a given price, a larger quantity will be supplied. This increase in supply might take place if more suppliers move into the market. If businesses move out of the industry, the supply curve often shifts to the left.

Perhaps the major cause for an increase in supply is technological advancement. Good examples include Henry Ford's introduction of the automobile assembly line and the development of new and improved hybrid corn seeds. Shifting the supply curve to the right through technology has resulted in lower prices and the creation of mass-consumption markets. On a piece of scratch paper try drawing a simple market curve with stationary demand (downward sloping)

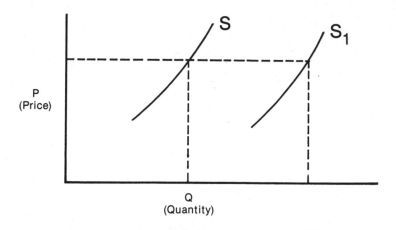

Figure 3-4

and stationary supply (upward sloping); then shift the supply curve to the right and see what happens to the price.

What else can cause a shift in the supply curve? If the costs of production (for example, labor costs) go up, the supply curve will shift backward (i.e., to the left). In addition, certain industries, such as farming, must always contend with supply changes caused by the weather; extremes in weather conditions can have a great impact on food commodity supply and, hence, on food prices. So it goes—the supply curve, as with demand, is buffeted about by unpredictable forces.

Market Equilibrium

Now we're ready to go one important step farther. We have enough information to combine the supply and demand curves to form a single market. Carefully examine Figure 3–5, which was created by putting our old corn supply and demand curves together on the same graph.

In Figure 3–5 we have a visual representation of what demanders will buy at different prices and of what suppliers will sell at different prices. Note that there is *only one price* where quantity supplied will be equal to quantity demanded. This is called the *equilibrium price*, and according to the graph that price will be $3 per bushel. At $3, suppliers will want to offer 20 units of corn, and de-

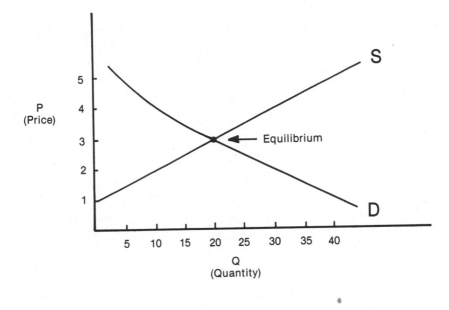

Figure 3-5

manders will buy the same quantity. No other price offers that mutual satisfaction.

What happens now if the price of corn is something other than the equilibrium price? To answer this question, imagine a large warehouse: on one side we find corn suppliers and on the other we have corn demanders. In the middle is the auctioneer, who does not yet have a clue as to the true equilibrium price. Just to get things started, the auctioneer shouts out in a hearty voice, "Five dollars!" Can you see what will happen at a price of $5? According to our curves, the suppliers will want to sell 35 bushels, while the demanders will only buy 5 bushels. Something is wrong: the price is too high. A surplus of corn is piling up in the suppliers' corner, while the demanders sit tight. The oversupply begins to glut the warehouse. The auctioneer realizes his mistake and has no alternative but to lower the price.

Now, however, he goes to the other extreme. He yells out "Two dollars!" What happens then? The glut quickly disappears as the quantity of low-priced corn is frantically bought up by eager demanders. After the dust settles we find many frustrated demand-

ers wanting large amounts (30 bushels) of $2 corn, but suppliers are unwilling to provide more than 12 bushels at that price. Again, there is something wrong! The frustrated demanders start to put pressure on the auctioneer to raise the price again. After more trial and error, we finally arrive at the final price (the equilibrium price) of $3.

In our example we had an unimpeded market where the price had complete freedom to move to equilibrium. However, in the real world prices may not be so free. Suppose that the corn farmers (who are only a small fraction of the total voters) got together and formed a political lobbying group called CORN (Corn growers Organization to Raise Net Profit). They quickly obtain hundreds of thousands of dollars that they spend on dinners and other favors for legislators. In addition, they find money left over to finance the reelection of "friendly" candidates. When legislation comes up regarding a support price for corn (often called a *price floor*), the lobby is hard at work to get a favorable vote. After considering the bill, the legislators pass it with votes to spare. CORN is able to report back to its members that from now on the government will support corn prices.

What exactly does this mean? A *support price* means that the government will guarantee the farmers a price *above* the equilibrium. In other words, the free-market forces will be inoperative while the support price is in effect. Let's look at this situation in a graph (see Figure 3–6).

In Figure 3–6, we see exactly what effect this interference will have. If the support price is $5, we will have 35 units supplied but only 5 units demanded. Clearly, the difference between these two amounts will be a surplus that the government will be compelled to buy up at $5 per bushel—indeed a profitable deal for CORN! Their members can produce more corn than they would have at the equilibrium output and receive a higher price for it. Their market is stabilized, and their prices are guaranteed.

It's a bad deal for most everyone else, however. As consumers and taxpayers you and I will pay more for corn ($5) and get less (only 5 units), while we also pay more in taxes to provide government subsidies to the corn growers. In addition, we will be paying even more taxes to finance the storage of this government surplus. There are many similar examples in American industry (especially

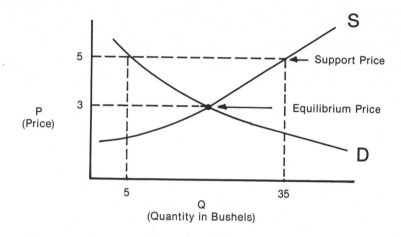

Figure 3-6

in agriculture) where the taxpayers' money artificially raises prices and thus impedes free-market forces. This happens because when it comes to legislative support, special interest groups speak with a "shout," while the consumer (and taxpayer) with no special lobbyists speak in a "whisper."

Now let's reverse the situation. What if the government establishes a lower price than equilibrium? The government would in effect be saying, "You cannot legally charge more than $2 for a bushel of corn." This $2 price would be called a *price ceiling.* What happens in the market? Like our warehouse example earlier, the lower price will generate greater quantity demanded than supplied. The frustrated demanders want to bid up the price, yet now the government won't allow these prices to rise. A permanent *shortage* is therefore created. What then is the rationale for a price ceiling?

Sometimes the government will impose price ceilings on certain key items in an attempt to slow down inflation. But just as our example predicts, sooner or later we will begin to experience shortages. In time of war, however, shortages already exist, and the purpose of a ceiling is to prevent prices from "going through the roof." If it is a necessary item (food, gasoline, fuel oil, etc.), a price ceiling may not be enough. Often, so-called *black markets* are created in which the price is illegally bid up. (Never underestimate the power of the market!) When black markets do develop, one potential solution is to allocate scarce commodities with ration tickets or stamps. Rationing, however, needs an expensive bureaucratic support system, and even then black markets sometimes develop in ration tickets or stamps! No matter how you handle it, shortages usually turn out to be a political nightmare.

Assuming now that government price interference has been abolished, recall that prices *still* may change due to shifts in supply and demand. For example, as shown in Figure 3–7, after a period of wartime economic austerity, a rapid increase in the supply (S_1) can come about when new suppliers come into the market or when the industry experiences some rapid technological advancement. If either of these things takes place, the equilibrium price will eventually fall as a result of competition, and emergency measures to handle the shortages will not be necessary.

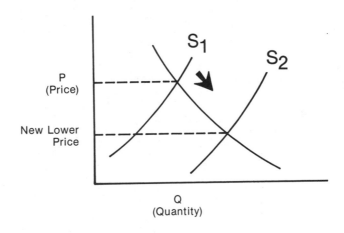

Figure 3-7

On the other hand, if the supply curve (S) shifts to the left, prices will rise. For example, this is what happens if bad weather reduces the supply of corn. If demand is stable, price must increase.

Remember, too, that demand isn't always stable either. Demand curves can move backward or forward for the following reasons:

- Changing incomes
- A change in the price of a substitute or complementary good
- A change in taste
- Advertising
- A change in the number of buyers

What will happen to the equilibrium price if there is an increase in demand? By drawing it out in Figure 3–8 we can see.

You might find it interesting to examine the commodities page in the business section of your daily newspaper. See how rapidly the prices of corn, wheat, soybeans, and other commodities can change on a daily basis because of shifts in supply and demand.

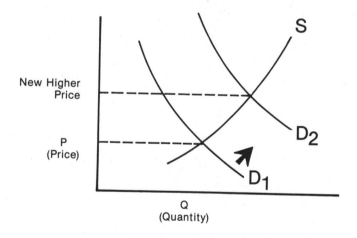

Figure 3-8

Price Elasticity

Another important idea associated with demand is *price elasticity*. Let's consider a practical example relating to a friend of mine who owns a pizza restaurant in Arizona. He charges $5 for a top-quality small pizza. It wasn't long ago that he was asking people whether or not he should raise the price to $6. Of course nobody knew for sure, but some did know enough to ask him the following: "How

many fewer pizzas would you sell if you raised the price by $1?"
What they really wanted was an estimate of his price elasticity. It
would be nice if he could increase his price that much without
losing any customers, but he might find that he will lose most of
them. Two possible demand curves for small pizzas are shown in
Figure 3–9.

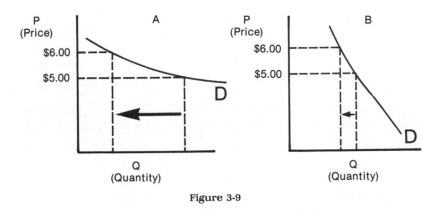

Figure 3-9

Although both curve A and curve B are downward sloping
(remember our law of downward-sloping demand?), curve A is
much flatter than B. To put it another way, curve B is much steeper
than A. If A reflected the demand curve for small pizzas, would it
be wise to raise the price? Probably not. Economists would say that
this curve is very *elastic*; i.e., the quantity demanded is very
responsive to a change in price. Even with a small change in price,
we see quantity demanded as shown in graph A zooms down to
less than half of what it was. Most businesses raising their price
would rather have a demand curve like B, because they can raise
their prices a great deal without losing much quantity demanded.
We call this kind of curve an *inelastic demand curve*; i.e., the quantity demanded is not very responsive to a price change.

What kind of products have inelastic demand curves? One
example is table salt. If salt is now 30¢ a box but doubles in price,
people will still demand about the same amount. However, if we
double the mortgage interest rate from 10 to 20 percent, we will
find a drastic reduction in the number of homes demanded. New
housing would thus be an example of an elastic good; i.e., it is quite
responsive to a price change.

Let's examine a few other examples. Gasoline and toy balloons are inelastic. You could raise prices a substantial percentage on both these items and still not have a great reduction in demand. Can you see a pattern that might allow you to predict elasticity? Why are some goods sensitive to a change in price while others are not? Some general principles for determining inelastic demand might include the following:

- It's a necessary good (gasoline, heating oil, prescription drugs, telephones).
- It's a small part of one's budget (toy balloons, coke, paper clips).
- There are few substitutes (insulin, light bulbs, diamond rings).

Note that salt meets all these criteria. No economic good, however, is inelastic at all prices. If we walked into the grocery store and discovered that the price of salt was not 30¢ a box but $10 a box, quantity demand would certainly be affected! In this case, you would probably learn to eat your food with less salt, and your favorite restaurant would sell you small salt packets instead of putting a salt shaker on the table.

Let's get back to my friend and his pizzas. The relative elasticity of demand for the pizzas will depend mainly on how many substitutes—both direct and indirect—are available. A *direct substitute* would be a Pizza Hut restaurant down the street, whereas an *indirect substitute* might be cooking at home. If my friend happens to be a monopolist and people regard eating pizzas out as a "necessity," then a price rise more than likely will benefit his business.

Is there any way that he can affect the elasticity of demand for his pizzas? He can if he can convince people that he has a truly unique, superior, and "necessary" product. Note the words, "if he can convince people"; he does not necessarily have to have a better or different product.

Advertisements for Bayer aspirin, for example, have convinced people that their product is truly different. Most druggists say that "aspirin is aspirin," but by convincing headache sufferers that Bayer is superior, the company has successfully made its demand curve more inelastic than it otherwise would have been. Their advertising has also resulted in a greater demand for their product; hence, they are also able to charge a significantly higher price than most of their competitors.

Our theory has still not enabled my friend to determine whether the demand for his pizzas is elastic or inelastic. The only way to know for sure is to actually raise the price and see what happens to sales (*total revenue*). We can say with some accuracy that if you increase your price and total revenue goes up, the demand between these two prices is inelastic. If you increase price and the total revenue is reduced, the demand is elastic. Let's call this the *businessperson's definition of elasticity*.

Note that the demand in Figure 3–10A is inelastic. It should be apparent that the low-price total revenue (price times quantity) is quite small. To tell for sure, simply estimate the area of the total-revenue rectangle at the lower price. Now compare it with the large area of total revenue at the higher price, which has been shaded in. By raising the price in the inelastic example, total revenue is increased. This is, of course, what my friend wanted when he raised his price. Note what would have happened if demand had been elastic. In diagram B we see that the increase in price reduces the quantity demanded so much that total revenue goes down.

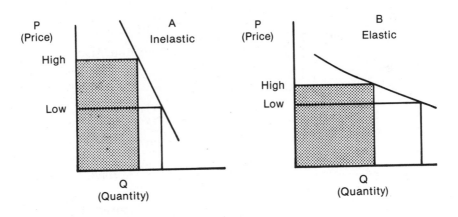

Figure 3-10

A final point to remember: if you are a businessperson, it might be in your best interest to lower prices, particularly if your demand curve is elastic. A lower price on an elastic demand curve will generate so much more business that total revenue will go up. In addition, we often find that an expanded scale of operation will lower unit costs of production. After World War I Henry Ford combined these two ideas (elastic demand for cars and economies of scale) and reaped a personal fortune of over a billion dollars. It pays to know about elasticity!

Let's now take a moment to review what we have learned about this subject. Elasticity is basically a measure of how much the quantity demanded responds to a change in price. An elastic curve is very responsive; an inelastic curve is not very responsive.

Elasticity can be determined by observing what happens to total revenue (or total sales) when you change your price. If, when we raise the price, total revenue goes up, we have inelastic demand (see Figure 3–11). If total revenue goes down, we have elastic demand. (Note: If you find yourself confused about what happens to total revenue when the price is changed, simply sketch an exaggerated demand curve, either very flat or very steep, and see what happens to revenue when the price goes up or down.)

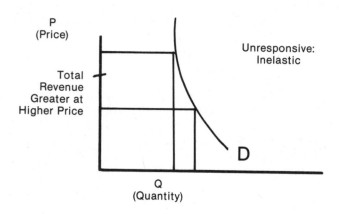

Figure 3-11

So far, so good, but we have not yet learned how to determine the precise degree of elasticity. As an example, we have two products—salt and gasoline—with inelastic demand. Which one is more inelastic?

Or Let's suppose that the President of the United States deter-mines that gasoline supplies may be threatened and it would therefore be wise to reduce the nation's consumption by 15 per-cent. There are, of course, different ways to handle this situation. First, he might ask American drivers to reduce consumption vol-untarily. If this doesn't work, he could establish a gasoline rationing system. We know, however, that this kind of rationing invites black market counterfeiting and requires an expensive bureaucracy to make it work. The third and probably quickest way to reduce consumption would be to raise the price to the con-sumer via an increase in the gas tax. But how much would the total price have to go up in order to reduce the quantity demanded by 15 percent? Would a 15 percent increase in price do the trick, or 30 percent, or perhaps even 75 percent? This ques-tion leads us to our third and most exact definition of elasticity, *the economist's definition.*

To measure the precise value of elasticity we divide the per-cent change in price into the percent change in quantity demanded:

$$E_p(\text{coefficient of elasticity}) = \frac{\text{Percent change in quantity demanded}}{\text{Percent change in price}}$$

If this ratio is greater than one, it is elastic, and if the ratio is less than one, we call it inelastic. For example, if we find out that the gasoline price must go up by 30 percent before we get a 15 per-cent reduction in gas consumption, then the exact elasticity would be:

$$\frac{15\%}{30\%} = .50$$

Since the ratio is less than 1, it's inelastic. If the President had known beforehand that the coefficient of elasticity for gasoline was .50, he would have known exactly how much gasoline prices would have to increase before consumption would decrease by the desired amount.

As another example let's assume the demand for my friend's

pizzas is very elastic. He goes ahead and raises his price by 20 percent but finds that the quantity demanded goes down by 80 percent (he miscalculated!). Under these conditions, what would be the elasticity of demand? Using the above formula, the answer would be:

$$\frac{80\%}{20\%} = 4.0$$

The ratio is greater than 1, so the demand is elastic. In the real world, you may never know the exact elasticity. It may change over time, or it may be one value in a low price range and a totally different value in a higher price range. Still, the most successful businesspeople seem to have an uncanny instinct for elasticities and how they affect sales and profits.

Now what about you? What products do you buy? How elastic or inelastic are they to you? If the price of your favorite newspaper or magazine were raised considerably, would you still buy it? Would you buy your favorite hamburger or pizza if the cost went up 20 percent? These are the kinds of interesting economic questions we can all ask ourselves.

In summary, we have come a long way in understanding the workings of a market. We have discovered how supply and demand operate and how the natural forces of the market drive prices toward equilibrium. We also saw what happens when these natural forces are impeded by price supports and price ceilings. We know that the supply and demand curves shift in response to outside economic forces. Finally, we explored the mystery of price elasticity and have found out how such information can be of value to consumers, businesspeople, and government.

Thus we know quite a bit about single markets, but what about the vast interconnections between these single markets and the overall economy? What about the massive amounts of money, goods, and resources flowing in and out of millions of interrelated markets of households and businesses? How does all this fit together to form an economic system? We will soon see.

Chapter 4

BUSINESSES AND HOUSEHOLDS

We are now ready to take a new perspective on our economy. In this chapter we will enlarge our "economic vision" to include not only the single supply-demand markets discussed earlier, but also the major economic institutions of businesses and households that give life to these individual markets. Instead of using an economic "microscope" to focus on a particular market, we now need a pair of economic "binoculars" to help us see the broad outlines of our large and complex economy.

Let's begin with an analogy. The operation of our economy is something like the operation of your automobile. The performance of both depends upon two vital flows. On the one hand, gasoline (which is its primary operating "resource") flows from the gas tank through the carburetor into the cylinders where, upon combustion it produces power to run the car. On the other hand, you have the circulating flow of lubricating oil that travels around and around to various parts, reducing friction in the bearings, pistons, etc. Take away either one of these two flows and your automobile will soon stop functioning.

Economic Flows

Our economic system also depends on two vital flows. The first is *money*, which some economists consider a kind of "lubricating agent" because it makes economic exchange simpler and smoother. Money flows through resource markets (land, labor, capital) into the pocketbooks of householders, then back to the markets for goods and services, bubbling up into the hands of businesses—a continuous circulatory stream that never ends unless the economic system breaks down. The other flow is of *real things*—actual goods and services, land, labor, and capital. They also flow through the markets, pushed on by monetary impulses responding to supply and demand (eventually becoming used up or consumed). It's a fascinating system. Let's look at a graphical representation of this in what is commonly called the *circular flow diagram* (see Figure 4–1).

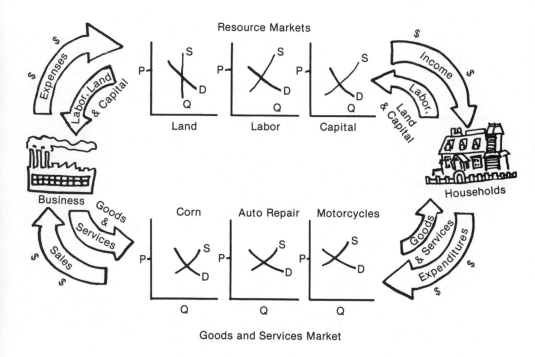

Figure 4-1

The clockwise flow is money. Starting, for example, in the upper left corner, we find dollars flowing out of businesses (expenses) into the resource markets. It is there that these dollars are translated into the demand for land, labor, and capital.

When the resources are sold to the business sector, the so called expense dollars are suddenly translated into *incomes* for the households. These dollars then flow out of the households into the markets for goods and services. We look at these same dollars and now call them *expenditures*. Demand then stimulates supply in the product markets. As payment is made for corn, auto repairs, or motorcycles, the dollars become *sales* for businesses, providing them with working capital to start another round of productive flow. The cycle thus begins all over.

It sounds like a simple, foolproof system, doesn't it? The chance of a breakdown does exist, however. There is no absolute guarantee that the money supply or the amount of total spending will be correct. For example, if the money supply is too low, the economy will slow down because of insufficient currency to make basic transactions. On the other hand, if there is too much money, we will find ourselves in an inflationary situation where there are "too many dollars chasing after too few goods." Similar problems can arise when there is also too much or too little spending.

Whose responsibility is it to regulate these flows? The responsibility lies primarily with the government sector. Along with the business and household sectors, government also plays an important role in the operation of our economic system. (We will have much more to say about this sector in Chapter 5.) For now, however, let's take a close look at the business sector. How do we define a business? How are businesses organized? How effectively do they operate in a capitalist setting?

The Business Sector

There are approximately 15 million businesses in the United States. The majority of them are small retail or service businesses and other single-proprietor operations including farming. Operating these small enterprises often means overworking Mom and Pop to keep the business going. To make things worse, they frequently end in bankruptcy. (Three out of five new businesses fail before the third year of operation!) Let's now play a little game. Assume that you have carefully considered the odds, and you have decided to plunge into a new business. You might try to write, publish, and market your own book for example, or perhaps you would like to manufacture wood burning stoves or run a candy store. A repair service would also be a possibility. For our purposes here, though, let's assume you go into manufacturing.

The first question, of course, is "What are you going to make?" You don't wish to compete with a large oligopolistic industry because of the many economic barriers (see Chapter 2). You will obviously want a new product for which there is a need; you also want one that can be manufactured by one or two people—a tough problem.

One day you read in the *Wall Street Journal* that sales of cat food have quadrupled in the last decade. You begin to think, "Yes, about half my friends have cats, and you know, their cats always want to be let in or out. Why couldn't I make an entrance/exit device to let cats enter and leave at their own pleasure? It would have to be designed so that heat is not let out, and it would have to be easy to install. . . ." You convince yourself that you can make a go of it. You then work hard for six months on a prototype, and by the end of the year you have your cat loving friends trying out your new invention—KITTYOUT.

Now you need to think about the business end of your operation. You have several options. You may decide to set up what is called a *single proprietorship.* The proprietorship is perhaps the most simple business organization. It can be started up with a minimum of red tape—no charters or extensive reports needed. "A good deal," you say to yourself—until you find out some of the disadvantages. Should you want to expand your small operation, you might find that no one wants to give you a loan. You try the local banks; they smile pleasantly and say, "We're sorry." The Small Business Administration (an agency of the federal government) also lends a kindly ear but tells you that the enterprise is as yet unproven. "Please come back," they say, "when sales and earnings are more stable."

You also can face the disadvantage of *unlimited liability*, which means that if things go badly, your creditors can sue you not only for your business assets but also for your personal assets. Your child's educational fund could be liquidated as a result of a bad business decision!

Yet, you decide business is going OK for now, and your major worry at present is finding the financial capital to expand. You begin thinking of alternatives, and one comes to mind: a partner. You invite a friend (or relative) to join you and form a *partnership* in order to provide additional financial capital as well as a helping hand. There is now, however, more red tape. A partnership is a legal entity, and if your partner leaves you (or dies), you usually have to start all over. Plus, you are still faced with the problem of unlimited liability. Nevertheless, we'll assume that you and your partner are not worried much about the liability problem; sales are now excellent, and you are becoming intoxicated with visions of unlimited profits. Expansion is the only thing on your mind. You ask yourselves, "How shall we expand?"

You might, for example, take the route of *vertical expansion*. Perhaps you have been purchasing sheet-metal supplies from a local sheet-metal shop, and you now decide to buy him out. Thus, by expanding vertically you are taking over another stage of production.

Or, instead of taking over early stages of manufacturing, you might go to the other extreme of marketing the product, i.e., setting up your own shops to sell KITTYOUT. Until now you were selling them to a regional distributor, who, in turn, sold them to established retail shops. (In the larger economy, the oil industry is a good example of this. They often own or control almost all stages of production: oil wells; pipelines; refineries; and, of course, distribution through local service stations.)

Another option is *horizontal expansion*. This means doing more and more of the same operation. You might buy out the competition, or you might set up another small-scale factory in another location. Either way, your expansion activities would concentrate on the assembly stage.

Another choice open to you is expansion by *diversification* —to bring out several products. They may be related to your original product, or they may be totally different. For example, you might decide to manufacture an improved cat or dog house, or even a DOGGYOUT (using the same design and engineering principles utilized in your successful KITTYOUT).

Many large American corporations prefer to have such wide diversification that there is often little or no relationship between the products. Such a business that expands through buying up unrelated businesses is called a *conglomerate*. For example, International Telephone & Telegraph (IT&T) is usually considered a manufacturer of telephone equipment. One may be surprised, therefore, to discover that in the early 1980s IT&T owned a large number of companies in widely different areas including coal mining (Carbon Industries), oil (Eason Oil), insurance (Hartford Fire), hotels (Sheraton), and bakery products (Twinkies and Wonder Bread). Even the lawn-care products you use may be of IT&T origin (Scott & Sons) or the seeds you used to plant your last garden (W. Atlee Burpee). If you need a loan to help finance the purchase of an IT&T product or service, they have a number of separate credit subsidiaries to help you out (Kellogg Credit, Thorp Finance, etc.). Pick many of the largest U.S. corporations and you will find a similar pattern.

Why do the giants absorb these small unrelated businesses? Some economists say such behavior is sometimes a personal "power trip" or an exercise in empire building. Another answer is that conglomerates can efficiently spread their overhead this way. A small company might not have sufficient working capital to afford a business economist, a market researcher, or an advertising division, but the large parent company can afford these important marketing aids and can give assistance when needed. Diversification is also a kind of insurance policy against a sudden shift in demand away from a single-product line such as hula hoops or cigarettes.

There can, however, be a darker side to the diversification merger trend. These giant conglomerates often operate with a kind of cold detachment. They can play with the fates of factories, businesses, and employees with the calculated ruthlessness of a chess player sacrificing pawns in order to save the king. Economist Ernest Mandel captures this feeling of absentee ownership in his provocative article, "Where is America Going?":

> They retain ultimate power—the power to open or to close the plant, to shut it in one town and relaunch it 2,000 miles away, to suppress by one stroke of their pens 20,000 jobs and 50 skills acquired at the price of long human efforts.[9]

But we've gotten a little ahead of ourselves! Our KITTYOUT business is still only a partnership—not a large conglomerate. The major question facing our enterprising partnership is still, "How can we best grow?"

At this stage of development the answer to our question is probably to form a *corporation*. Among the major advantages of a corporate form of ownership are the new opportunities that are available for obtaining financial capital. A corporation, for example, can sell equity (or ownership) stock as well as float corporate bonds. In addition, obtaining a loan from established financial institutions (i.e., banks, credit unions, etc.) is often easier for corporations than for unproven single proprietorships or partnerships. *Limited liability* is another advantage of the corporate form; the debts of the corporation are "limited" by law to extend only to the corporate assets—not to the assets of the owners (as in a proprietorship or partnership). There are even tax advantages. The maximum tax rate on profits for most corporations is often lower than that for the other two types of businesses.

Our partners, therefore, hire a lawyer to draw up a charter, and various friends and relatives buy into the little company. Thus, KITTYOUT, INC. (Incorporated), joins the ranks of the more than 2 million corporations that exist in the United States. To be sure, our little company is not yet in the big time; it probably never will be. As discussed in Chapter 2, it is extremely difficult to become a major competitor in an oligopolistic industry.

To get an idea of just how big some of these giant companies are, imagine a list of the 2 million or so corporations, with the larger companies up at the top and the smaller on the bottom. If we were to tally up the assets of the 200 largest corporations at the very peak of our chart, we would discover that this small group of companies (less than one tenth of 1 percent) owns *over half* of all manufacturing assets in the country! These corporations indeed dominate the mainstream of American business.

In our example of KITTYOUT we looked at the different forms of business enterprises and noted some of their advantages and disadvantages. However, we have not yet examined the inner workings of a business. How do businesses combine resources to produce goods and services? What rules, if any, do they follow for best results?

Diminishing Returns

One law of economics that businesses must be aware of when they combine resources is the *law of diminishing returns*. What exactly is this law all about? I think it's best to explain it with an illustration.

A few years ago I helped a neighbor farmer (we'll call him Chester Olson) bring in his hay. Chester has just one tractor, one hay baler, and one hay wagon; we call these his *fixed inputs*. His *variable input* is labor. He can choose to work by himself or with any number of hired hands. Chester told me that if he works by himself, he can bring in only 2 loads of hay per working day. He brings in so few loads because he has to bale the hay, pick it up off the ground, stack it on the wagon, unload it from the wagon into the barn, and then climb up into the hot, sticky mow and stack it neatly—a big job for one man!

If I help Chester, the total output per day goes from 2 to 5. My additional contribution (sometimes called *marginal physical product* [MPP]) was 3 full loads of hay above and beyond what Chester could do by himself. Because a second person (myself) increased per worker output, we can say that we were in a stage of *increasing returns*. If we add a third person (Steve), we find that total output goes up only 1 additional load to make 6 total loads. With Steve added to the production force, total output goes up but at a *diminishing rate*.

Beginning with Steve (our third person) we have reached *the point of diminishing returns*. Why did they begin with Steve? Is he lazy? No, he isn't. If Chester or I had been that third person, the same thing would have happened. The reason we find diminishing returns with Steve is that we had a fixed set of machinery to work with. If there was additional equipment, perhaps just one more hay wagon, that third person might give us a lot more loads. When we speak of diminishing returns, we therefore must assume that *all inputs except one are fixed*.

How will the knowledge of diminishing returns help Chester make decisions concerning the number of people to hire? Can we automatically assume that Chester shouldn't hire that third person? If Chester is a good businessman, he should take a careful look at how much extra money the third person's extra load of hay will bring and compare it with the cost of hiring him. To illustrate, if the value of the additional load is $50 and he has to pay Steve only $20, then it would be profitable to hire him despite diminishing returns. The general rule is to keep hiring people as long as the value of the additional hay (the value of the MPP) is greater than the extra wages Chester must pay to get that hay.

Chester really has it quite easy. Outside of keeping his old baler running, all he has to worry about are diminishing returns, the price of hay, and the cost of hiring an extra hand. Imagine, however, the complex decisions that must be made when we produce something as complicated as an automobile. How would you go about finding the ideal mix of resources to produce a car?

Perhaps the best way to build a car might be to simply give an engineer the following proposal: "Here is my design, tell me how to build it." A good engineer, however, should come back with more than one solution. He might say, "Here is one way to build your car that is almost completely mechanized, but here is another method that is more labor intensive (uses more human labor)." He may go on to tell you many other different ways to build approximately the same car. The bumpers might be made of plastic or steel, the engine block of cast iron or aluminum. In fact, he may give you an entire book describing the different possible techniques that will meet your design specifications. How do you choose?

The answer, of course, is that for any given product, you *should choose the lowest-cost technique.* If you don't, your rivals may, and then you might find yourself out of business. It should be emphasized that in choosing the lowest-cost technique, the economy will gain in efficiency. Returning to the idea of supply and demand, we want ideally to conserve the most scarce resources and to use the most abundant ones. If a resource is scarce, its supply will be low, and if it is in demand, the resource will command a high price. In trying to minimize your production costs, you will attempt to avoid using that scarce resource. Abundant resources will command low prices in the market place. You will find yourself choosing these lower cost, more plentiful resources more and more often. It's a simple idea when you think, for example, of how much more low

cost plastic is being used in the place of relatively high priced steel. Consumers, in turn, benefit by relatively lower cost products.

In summary, low cost equals efficiency. This constant drive to lower cost is indeed one of the most remarkable and beneficial characteristics of a capitalist economic system. Ironically, it is one of the most destructive aspects of our economic system as well. Why is this so?

Pollution

The drive to operate businesses at the lowest cost possible has also contributed to our massive pollution problem. Take, for example, Gary, Indiana. If you have ever driven past the steel factory complex in Gary, you probably had to close your window. The air is unbearably dirty. Why do the steel companies pollute the air? Do they want to increase the death rate and incidence of lung disease? Obviously not. They pollute the air and water for a simple reason: it's cheaper to pollute than not to pollute.

Of course in almost every such case there is a technology available that will reduce pollution to reasonably low levels. However, if they can get away with it, why shouldn't producers attempt to push the clean up costs onto society (i.e., make them *social costs*) instead of paying these themselves? Thus, in a strange way our capitalist system tends to reward polluters: the more pollution you can get away with, the lower your costs are, and hence the greater are your profits. In a few incidents, where short-run profit making is pushed to an illogical extreme, the attitude and actions of a company are difficult to believe:

> "Profit-ability" was the 1970 slogan for Union Camp, a company whose paper-bag plant helps make the Savannah River one of the foulest sewers in the nation. The executive vice-president of the company, answering Nader's Raiders' charge that his firm was dangerously depleting groundwater supplies, replied, "I had my lawyers in Virginia research that, and they told us that we could suck the state of Virginia out through a hole in the ground, and there was nothing anyone could do about it." Union Camp's director of air and water protection noted for the benefit of The New York Times that "it probably won't hurt mankind a whole hell of a lot in the long run if the whooping crane doesn't quite make it . . ."[10]

Fortunately, most businesses don't operate with such total disregard for the environment. Nonetheless, the short-run pressures to keep costs down continue to create problems in a capitalist economy. In fact, this is what we might now call the *first tragic flaw of capitalism*; i.e., in the great efficiency drive to lower the costs of production (which is generally beneficial to consumers), we have simultaneously provided an irresistible temptation to pollute. What can be done about this problem?

In theory, the economic remedy is quite simple: force producers to pay *all* costs of production. *Neighborhood effects*, where the pollution costs are passed on to society at large, should not be allowed. Perhaps the easiest way to enforce this rule is to impose a pollution tax. The government would be saying in effect, "Until now you have behaved as if the air and water were a free resource—a free trash can that never fills up—but from now on, you will have to pay dearly for using that trash can by paying a pollution tax. In fact, we will make the tax so high that you might well consider buying your own garbage cans and collecting your pollutants yourself."

A more direct approach to the pollution problem is to state maximum levels of pollution (as the government has done with automobiles). Yet there are drawbacks to the various methods of pollution control, as you probably know if you have recently purchased a car. Prices will rise, and, in some cases, short-run economic "efficiency" will be sacrificed.

Still, why shouldn't producers, and ultimately the consumers of steel or paper (or any product from a high-pollution industry), assume the full costs of production—even the pollution clean-up costs? If we are truly concerned about minimizing poisons in our environment (including not only the visible pollution but also the invisible poisons—DDT, radioactive materials, methyl mercury, etc.), then we perhaps ought to act now, not for ourselves so much as for future generations. Paying the extra price in the short run may turn out to be a good investment in the long run.

The Household Sector

The other major sector in our economy is the household. If the business sector organizes resources and supplies goods and services, what economic role does the household sector play?

Households are in a pivotal position in our economy: On the one hand, they supply resources to businesses (land, labor, capital, management), and on the other hand, they are the consumers. They are the more than 80 million household units that purchase approximately two-thirds of our total economic output each year. In what form do households receive their income? Three quarters of all income flowing to resource suppliers is in the form of wages and salaries. Corporate profits represent about 10 percent of the total, and income from rents, interest, and proprietorships combine to make up the remaining 15 percent.

Once the money's in our pocketbooks, what do we do with it? Americans spend about 80 percent of their income, and income taxes take approximately 15 percent. The remaining amount, about 5 percent, is saved (Americans are not known to be great savers!). On the average households spend about 45 percent of their money on services (household operations, health, transportation, education, recreation, restaurant services, etc.), 40 percent on nondurable goods (food, clothing, gasoline, etc.), and only about 15 percent on durable goods (anything with a useful life of over a year). Columnist George Will vividly reminds us that there has been a dramatic shift away from durable goods, which, over the years, has brought about a fundamental change in American industry:

> . . . golden arches, not blast furnaces, are becoming the symbols of American enterprise. Today McDonald's has more employees than U.S. Steel. This "once great industrial giant" used to make big locomotives, big Buicks. Now it makes Big Macs.[11]

Why then are services today such a large part of the average family budget? Part of the answer is that it takes more and more repair and maintenance services (and more skilled individuals) to match the quantity and complexity of today's durable goods and components of modern housing and transportation. More important perhaps is the great increase *in the cost* of professional services (medical, dental, educational, legal, etc.). The prices of durable goods, on the other hand, have been rising relatively modestly—some product prices have even gone down in the past couple of decades (radios, TVs, computers, pocket calculators). Service costs, in turn, have skyrocketed mainly because of relatively low *productivity*. Let's look at this idea a little closer.

Productivity is how economist's measure the output gained for an hour of input; for example, a 60-word-per-minute typist is twice as productive as a 30-word-per-minute typist. Let's assume that a decade ago a factory employed 50 people and turned out 100 radios a day. By utilizing labor-saving technology, that same factory today might produce 500 radios with only 10 people, thus demonstrating a dramatic increase in productivity. But why did the factory mechanize? They were forced to do so in order to offset the higher and higher costs of labor. In addition, they were able to mechanize without great difficulty, because it is relatively easy to adapt technology to an assembly line operation. Such mechanization thus helps to keep product prices lower than they would have been without it.

Let's now take the example of Joe the barber. Poor Joe provides an important service to people, but he finds it very difficult to increase his productivity. There he stands with scissors, clippers, and comb, as his father did twenty-five years before him, but Joe feels he must increase his prices to match inflation and higher wages throughout the economy. Households must therefore pay proportionately more for haircuts, medical and dental care, education, government operation, and other services as long as wages continue to rise in an economic environment of relatively low productivity change.[12] Some economists feel that without substantial increases in the productivity within our major industries (services, manufacturing, agriculture, etc.), it will be very difficult to eliminate inflation. (There are, of course, other factors that contribute to inflation. These will be examined in detail in Chapters 8 and 9.)

Another observation can be made about households. Look around you. You will note with some interest (or perhaps some resentment) that some households receive very large incomes whereas others receive very small ones. Why are some wages high and others low? To answer this we must refer again to the system of supply and demand.

We need both supply and demand working for us in order to reap high wages. This means that the supply of people with your particular skill must be low while the demand stays high. High salaries for doctors, for example, are not so much a matter of great skill or life saving capability as they are a result of a low supply of doctors and a high demand for their services. If we could imagine for a moment that there were millions and millions of gifted doctors in the United States, their average wage might conceivably fall below that of an automobile mechanic. In fact, back in the 1930s the American Medical Association fought hard to keep the supply of medical practitioners low, realizing that an oversuppply might depress wages. The United States continues to have a shortage of medical personnel partly because of those restrictive policies. Many other types of professionals have also restricted entry into their occupation with licensing and certification requirements.[13]

In summary, if we are only looking at the financial benefit of the household, the lesson should be clear: "Seek ye an occupation with few practitioners in a market of high demand, and woe unto him who by accident or design finds himself in a market of low demand and a large supply of skilled applicants." What is your occupation or planned occupation? How will supply and demand affect the market for you?

The discussion of incomes resulting from the supply-demand situation in the resource markets leads us to our final, and perhaps most significant, observation about households in a capitalist society. Recall from Chapter 1 the basic economic question, "How does the economic system distribute the available output?" We are now able to answer that question. Output goes to those individuals and families who have sufficient incomes from the resource market to generate demand in the goods and services markets. If you cannot compete (for one reason or another) for a decent income, you will not have the "dollar votes" in the product markets. Supply, therefore, will be forthcoming only if there is effective demand (i.e., *purchasing power*).

A major problem arises, of course, when economic needs and demand are not even remotely in balance. For example, a family might have a critical need for nutritious food; they may even be starving. Yet if they cannot generate effective demand (because of a lack of income), no supply will be forthcoming to these individuals. An exaggerated (but real) example of this occurred during the 1930s when farmers plowed under perfectly nutritious food while people went hungry; there was insufficient income and therefore not enough demand. It's the same situation today among our poverty groups and also in the less developed countries of the world.

On the other hand, we might find (even during a depression) a wealthy family feeding their dogs steak every day, because the income is there, the effective demand is there, and thus the economic system responds. We therefore now have a *second tragic flaw of capitalism*, i.e., its tendency to be cold and unresponsive in the absence of effective demand—no matter what the basic need may be. What is to be done about these flaws? How does our basically capitalistic system resolve these conflicts?

We deal with them primarily through government action. Government then is the third major sector in our economy. In a sense government takes over where private enterprise capitalism fails. Government is a large sector and exerts tremendous influence in economic affairs. It's time we took a closer look at its function and operation.

Chapter 5

GOVERNMENT

Why Government?

I once met a man who stated quite emphatically that society would be better off with no government whatsoever, except for police protection and national defense. "Government is basically evil," he said, "it's not only very costly, but every government action subtracts from individual freedom." He concluded that everything the government is doing now could be accomplished more efficiently by an unregulated free enterprise market system.

He's partly right—at least his implication about government costs was correct. We have witnessed a virtual explosion of taxes and government activity in the past few decades. For example, between 1950 and 1980, per capita income rose a hefty 600 percent (inflated value), but total per capita taxes increased over 900 percent! Looking at it slightly differently, total federal, state, and local expenditures in 1950 were 27 percent of the gross national product (GNP), while at the beginning of the 1980s they had jumped to approximately 35 percent! Thus we must again ask, "Why government? What is it doing for us?"

Of course, we have already begun to build a good case for government activity, starting with the circular flow chart in the previous chapter. To review, we might ask, "Without government who would provide for (and regulate) the money supply?" We have seen that money is essential to the operation of our complex economy, and that the amount of money in circulation must be carefully adjusted to changing economic conditions. Recall, too, our discussion of capitalism's tragic flaws. We might ask how our present private enterprise system, without government intervention, would halt pollution. How do we prevent businesses from using our air and water as "free garbage cans" in their drive to lower costs of production? Self-regulation has not worked very well, nor will it work as long as pollution-prone industries feel pressured to minimize costs and maximize profits. There seems to be only one realistic solution to this problem: the government must step in to force producers to pay the full costs of production, including pollution control.

We must also note that in many cases the pollution problem cannot be solved on the local level alone. There are two reasons for this. First, the neighborhood effects of polluted water (or air) often extends beyond the confines of a specific locality. A river does not recognize municipal or state boundaries. If some company pollutes the Mississippi River in Minneapolis, it will affect not only the residents in Moline, Illinois, but also people farther down river in St. Louis, Missouri, and New Orleans, Louisiana.

Second, national pollution laws are necessary to prevent polluters from shutting down in a state with strict controls and moving on to a more lenient state. Local governments would hesitate to stop polluters if it meant throwing people out of work. The question then arises, "What about international pollution? Shouldn't there be worldwide laws (and provisions for enforcement) to prevent the pollution of the oceans and global air currents?" If we apply the logic of neighborhood effects on a global scale, we must conclude that in certain cases, international laws will become necessary. The market system, on its own, simply can't do the job.

According to some observers, the question we should be asking is not so much do we need controls, but rather, will we be able to control worldwide pollution in time? Indeed, there is already growing evidence that the oceans are becoming less habitable for marine life. Industrial pollution, garbage, and invisible poisons have been detected in almost every major ocean zone. In addition some scientists, such as Stanford biologist, Dr. Paul Ehrlich, predict the eventual extinction of a wide variety of life forms if present pollution trends continue.[14] We therefore have a growing awareness that the problem of worldwide pollution cannot be solved by the market system on its own. Government action is needed.

The other basic flaw in capitalism is its inability to meet fundamental human needs in the absence of effective demand. There are many families and individuals in our society who, for one reason or another, do not earn sufficient incomes to purchase the minimum necessities of life. Some are too old, others are disabled, many are children. There are also unskilled mothers who can't find work, and men whose skills are no longer in demand. We must ask, "What do we do with these people—the economic failures and rejects?" In his critique of "Reaganomics" (i.e., large cuts in social programs and tax reductions for upper-income groups), historian Arthur Schlesinger, Jr., argued that our government's sensitivity to people in need has helped maintain capitalism's amazing continuity:

> Capitalism has survived because of a continuing and remarkably successful effort to humanize the industrial order, to cushion the operations of the economic system, to combine pecuniary opportunity with social cohesion. It has survived because of a long campaign mounted by liberals, to reduce the suffering—and thereby the resentment and rebelliousness—of those to whom the accidents of birth deny an equal chance.[15]

And even if social stability were not the major issue, few of us would want fellow Americans to starve.

Income redistribution comes in all kinds of packages: welfare, public health, Medicare, etc. Although there is general agreement that the government should play *some* role in *income redistribution*, there is much argument over *how much* public subsidy should be available for the poor. Indeed, there are few subjects in economics that generate such heated and bitter debate. Some have suggested that income be redistributed in the form of government jobs or even a guaranteed minimum income. Should this subsidy level be at a bare survival level, or should there be enough money to provide a family with a moderate standard of living? This subject will be studied further in the next chapter.

We also need government to help maintain competition. Even the most bitter foe of government intervention can appreciate the value of federal and state antitrust legislation. Capitalism left on its own has often produced an increasing concentration of economic power, as large and powerful firms eliminated rivals by means fair or foul. For proof, we have only to look at the pre-antitrust days of the late nineteenth century. It was an age when gigantic trusts monopolized manufacture and commerce with little regard for the interests of the consumer. It may seem a little ironic that we need strong *public* intervention to guarantee the survival of our *private* competitive capitalistic system, but such intervention is indeed necessary.

Without government, who would provide *public goods?* Public goods are essential to the welfare of society, yet they are either too cumbersome or too unprofitable for private industry to supply to consumers. A road is a good example. I doubt very much if you would ever consider building a highway. Even if you could afford it, why would you personally make such a large investment when a lot of other people would also be using the road—and at your expense? We wouldn't even expect General Motors or Ford to build the millions of miles of necessary roads, nor would we expect doctors to finance hospitals or campers and naturalists to totally subsidize national, state, and local parks.

What about libraries, police protection, public TV, and elementary education? These are all public goods, and if everyone is to enjoy them, we need to generate their "demand" through a system of taxation and public expenditure. Without a social commitment to financing public goods, these "necessities of a civilized society" would be available only to the relatively wealthy.

Without government who would enforce the "rules of the game"? Who would make sure that everyone plays fairly? Someone must define the legal responsibilities of business operations, someone must enforce contracts and spell out property rights. Someone must keep an eye out for misleading advertising, for foods and drugs that might impair the public health, and for unsafe products that could kill or maim thousands of consumers. We can be sure that this "someone" will probably not step forward from the ranks of private enterprise. We know that some businesses left on their own will engage in deceitful advertising or sell baby cribs in which hundreds of infants could strangle themselves or manufacture toys that are dangerous for children. In these cases and many others, we can't expect consumers to always know how to protect themselves.

But how far do we go? Where is that thin line between government as "big brother" and government as legitimate protector? We know, for example, that some people slip and fracture their skulls in their bathtubs each year. Should we require all persons to wear safety helmets when they step into the tub? Of course not. But what about requiring children and adults to wear helmets when they ride bicycles or motorcycles? Just how much regulated safety is too much? To what degree should we pursue a philosophy of individual responsibility and "let the consumer beware"? Taking this issue one step farther, when does excessive government protection tend to *destroy* consumers' initiatives to defend themselves?

We ought to also take a look at the *cost* of consumer protection. For example, would it be wise to require Detroit to build an automobile bumper to withstand a crash of fifty miles per hour? This is a good idea in theory, but how much more would this "super" bumper cost the consumer? Just where do we draw the line?

Unfortunately, the study of economics does not always give us hard and fast answers to these questions. Economists, with their tools of analysis, can indeed help determine the economic costs and benefits of different actions and policies. In the end, however, such decisions are usually made by lawmakers and regulatory agencies that attempt to strike a political balance between the interests of businesses, consumers, and taxpayers.[16]

There is a final question we might ask concerning government's role in economic affairs: "What about the business cycle, or, more specifically, what about depressions?" We learned a long, hard lesson during the Great Depression of the 1930s: Capitalism had no self-correcting mechanism to automatically pull the economy out of a severe slump. This fundamental defect might be considered the *third tragic flaw of capitalism.*

We now know that in a depression, or even a recession, the government will be pressured to take initiatives to stimulate additional spending, even if it means a budgetary deficit. Corrective measures are also needed in periods of high inflation. The government thus functions as a kind of economic manipulator who, like the white knight in the fairy tale, attempts to slay the "double-headed dragon" of depression and inflation. It is by no means an easy job, as we shall see in Chapter 8.

Our government "white knight" can have an unpleasant side, however. We know that some government activity is badly planned, expensive, and (at times) downright harmful. We can cite numerous examples of overregulation and needless meddling in affairs that are none of the government's business. We have, for example, seen the effects of a top-heavy and insensitive bureaucracy.

We have also seen certain safety laws enacted that are good in theory but, when the fine print is read, turn out to be unrealistic impediments to the operation of legitimate small businesses. We have seen some bad effects from restrictive zoning and outmoded building codes as well as unnecessary harassment from inspectors, all of which can stifle innovation and initiative. We have seen government-sponsored urban-renewal programs disembowel whole neighborhoods and build public housing monsters in their place. And finally, we have seen how chilling the effects of government intelligence systems can become—an insidious world of phone taps and computer-bank retrieval systems where a sense of privacy is all but destroyed. No, not all government action is good.

But certainly some government is essential in a complex society. If government destroys some freedoms, it enhances others. Although it does so imperfectly at times, government subsidizes education for everyone, creates employment in times of recession, and enforces equal-employment rights. Government also builds clinics and public parks, supports agricultural research, and looks after the environment. It finances countless programs that truly help people who need assistance. Without government intervention, our complex economy would have a difficult time surviving.

The ambivalence of big government—combining both the good and bad (and often not being able to tell the difference)— sometimes creates an identity problem for this benevolent titan. Perhaps no one captured this sense of ambivalence better than did Associated Press writer Saul Pett, when he likened our federal government to:

> "... big, bumbling, generous, naive, inquisitive, acquisitive, intrusive, meddlesome giant ... with a heart of gold and holes in his pockets, an incredible hulk, a '10-ton marshmallow' lumbering along an uncertain road of good intentions somewhere between capitalism and socialism, an implausible giant who fights wars, sends men to the moon, explores the ends of the universe, feeds the hungry, heals the

sick, helps the helpless, a thumping complex of guilt trying mightily to make up for past sins to the satisfaction of nobody . . . a malleable vulnerable colossus pulled every which way by everybody who wants a piece of him, which is everybody."[17]

We thus can recognize the tremendous political pressures on government to intervene in economic affairs. But how does this "colossus" actually operate? For example, how is the public money spent? Exactly where are our government priorities and how does our tax system work? There are so many different taxes and thousands and thousands of areas of public expenditure (federal, state, and local), it's no wonder that the average taxpayer is bewildered. So where do we begin?

Taxes And Expenditures

Let's begin with the broad flows of government finance on the federal level. The largest single source of federal income is the *personal income tax* that many of us dread when the middle of April rolls around. In fact, almost half of all federal revenue comes from this tax. The second largest tax, contributing about one third of all federal tax receipts, is the *payroll tax* (*social security*). The *corporate income tax* comes in a distant third in importance. *Excise taxes* (a tax on a specific item like cigarettes) plus *customs duties* and *estate taxes* make up the remaining part.

Where does the federal government spend our tax money? The largest single area of federal spending is domestic social expenditures—social security, health, education, and manpower training; these categories take up about half of all federal expenditures. The next largest area is for defense and defense related spending. Yet if we add the various categories that are defense-related (such as veterans benefits, interest on the public debt from American wars, international military aid, etc.) to the regular national security costs, we find that expenditures on "past wars and future defense" account for somewhere between one third and two-fifths of the federal budget.[18]

On the state level, we find that on the average the *sales tax* contributes over half of the revenues; and the other half is derived from personal and corporate income taxes plus licenses, permits, and fees. The states spend over a quarter of their revenues on education with public welfare coming in a close second. Highways, health, and public safety follow third in overall importance.

The local tax scene is dramatically different. Local governments derive almost all their revenues from the *property tax*. Education takes almost half of the money; police and fire departments run a distant second. The total amount of federal, state, and local taxes spent on publicly supported education is a very large sum indeed.

It might be interesting to compare your community with mine (Menomonie, Wisconsin). Our residents pay about $40 ($40.66 to be precise) for every $1,000 of assessed valuation of property. In addition to my $40.66, the state gives our city a tax credit of $6.61 for that amount. Of the combined amount ($47.27), 40¢ goes back to the state; $14.86 goes for city government and police and fire protection; $7.36 goes to the county for hospitals, roads, etc.; and the largest portion, $24.65, goes toward education. Now what about *your* local taxes? How much do people in your area pay, and what are your government's spending priorities? You might be surprised at the answers!

Tax Philosophies

What are the basic differences between the taxes we pay? We generally categorize a tax as being either a *benefits-received tax* or an *ability-to-pay tax*. The philosophy of benefits received taxation is the following: "He who pays the tax ought to get the benefits from the expenditure of that tax." Perhaps the best illustration of this is the gasoline tax, specifically earmarked for highway construction and maintenance. Hunting license fees, tuition for state universities, and the airport tax (to pay for antihijacking security) are other examples. In each case the money from the tax is earmarked and funneled back into a direct service for the taxpayer. To many people the benefits received philosophy seem like the fairest possible system. But if this is true, why don't we base all our taxes on this principle?

If we used only the benefits-received principle, there would be some major problems. For example, how would we pay for national defense? Would everyone—rich and poor alike—pay the same dollar amount? That would hardly be practical. How would we finance public schools on a benefits principle? Would we only tax the families with children (and the larger the family, the greater the tax)? How then would we guarantee that everyone received an equal opportunity for a good education? We couldn't. For this reason, and others, we have the ability-to-pay tax, which does not penalize lower income groups and deprive them of the various benefits of government expenditures.

More specifically, the ability-to-pay philosophy says, "He who has more financial resources (income and wealth) should pay more tax." Most economists feel that the best example of this kind of tax is the *progressive income tax*. A progressive tax means that the greater your income, the greater percentage of tax you pay. To see exactly how this works, closely examine your income tax schedules. You will find that the lowest tax bracket is around 11 percent, while the highest is 50 percent. At first glance, the 50 percent figure may seem somewhat excessive, but this rate can often be reduced by a good tax accountant who knows the loopholes.

Tax loopholes are legal methods (and there are many) of reducing a potentially high income tax to lower levels. Unfortunately, these reductions are often made at the expense of those who do not know how to use the tax laws to their advantage. Each dollar, for example, that is not paid because of a legal tax shelter must eventually come out of someone's pocket. In the early 1980s it was noted that the extent of legal tax avoidance meant the loss of progressive tax revenues of over $200 billion dollars! Writer Phillip Stern, in his book *Rape of the Taxpayer*, calls our loophole-filled tax system "welfare to the rich."

What then are these mysterious loopholes, these tax shelters that allow some people to pay little or no tax? One of the most common is the special *capital-gains tax*. Capital gains comes from the increase in value of property. Your property might be common stock (100 shares of General Motors stock, for example), real estate, an old painting, or a race horse. If you purchase your property at a low price, hold it a year or more, and then sell it at a higher price, you have earned capital gains income, representing the difference between your purchase price and your selling price. The loophole comes in when you pay tax on only 40 percent of that income. Most people, of course, do not have the extra cash to buy speculative property or large blocks of common tock. Although proponents of capital gains say this tax break encourages vital investment, it can also be said that it often rewards the grasshopper (speculator) at the expense of the ant (worker).

Another income shelter is the *tax-free municipal bond*, a method of borrowing by municipalities to pay their government costs. Wealthy individuals often purchase these large denomination bonds (which pay slightly lower than normal interest rates) and wind up paying no federal tax on the interest income.

Then there are the *hobby farms*. Hobby farms can provide a favorite tax break for professionals and others with large incomes. They buy a farm, operate it at a loss, and then write off the loss against their regular income. All this hardly seems fair to the average full-time farmer who is forced by the law of economic survival to make a profit. It is easy to see why people often resent the apparent inequities of our tax system.

Finally, there is the issue of *personal exemptions* versus the tax credit. To show how the exemption works, let's compare two families. First, Joe Jones is a lower-middle-income wage earner in a 20 percent bracket. Joe and his wife have one child. Our tax law states that Joe can subtract from his income a certain amount (let's assume $1,000) for each dependent or exemption. Joe's little girl, as one exemption, is therefore going to save Joe $200 in taxes (20 percent of $1,000).

The other family is John Jacob Harrison III, his wife, and son (John Jacob Harrison IV). They are much more wealthy, say, in the 50 percent bracket. Now the government allows John to subtract the same $1,000 for his son, but the value of John's dependent is going to be worth over twice that of Joe's because he is in the higher bracket. John will save a full $500 in taxes (i.e., 50 percent of $1,000). In general, the higher the tax bracket, the more benefit one gets from any exemption or deduction.

Some states have moved to reduce this inequity by giving each family a tax credit for each exemption. The state of Wisconsin, for example, offers the same tax advantage ($20 off your taxes for each dependent) for everyone, rich and poor alike! Certain economists have suggested scrapping the whole progressive tax system, eliminating all exemptions and deductions (except for legitimate business expenses) and taxing everyone a flat rate of somewhere between 15 and 20 percent: no loopholes, no tax shelters, no expensive tax lawyers. The chance of making such a drastic change in our cumbersome and inequitable tax system is probably quite slim; many special interest groups, representing middle and upper income families, would fight hard to keep their specific little piece of the tax-sheltered loopholes. An additional force against meaningful tax reform are the many men and women from the legal profession (including tax lawyers) who are heavily represented on state and federal legislatures. It's often in their professional interest to keep the tax laws pretty much as they are.

Finally, we come to the *regressive tax*. If a purely progressive tax is a good example of ability to pay, the regressive tax is the opposite. With a regressive tax, the poor *pay a higher percentage of their income* (as taxes) than do the wealthy. A good example is the $1 airport head tax. A dollar is obviously a larger percentage of a poor person's income than a rich person's income. Also, tuition can sometimes be considered regressive as can the property tax. For example, a home-owning retired couple may easily find themselves paying a sizable percentage of their relatively small social security income as property tax.

The sales tax might also be considered an example of a regressive tax since poor families usually pay tax on all their income (because it is probably all spent). The wealthy save or invest much of their income and thus have a sizable portion of their income that is not exposed to the sales tax. When looking at total incomes, the poor often wind up paying a higher percentage as sales tax. There are a number of states that have minimized the regressiveness of their sales tax by exempting some necessary items such as food or drugs.

Generally, most economists feel that a pure progressive-type income tax is a fairer way to raise government revenue than a sales tax. Of course any method of taxing away spending power from the public is going to be unpopular. Taxpayer hostility can often be traced to objections to specific public expenditures. The one expenditure that is perhaps the most controversial is welfare. Let's now take a closer look at this issue and the companion problem of poverty in the United States.

Chapter 6

POVERTY

I would like to begin this chapter with a letter written to the editor of a St. Paul, Minnesota, newspaper. It has, as you will note, a somewhat bitter tone to it as the writer describes her intense resentment toward those who are receiving public assistance:

> ". . . according to a newspaper item one AFDC (Aid to Families with Dependent Children) recipient said 'we are people too.' Yes, they 'are people too,' people who are unwilling to go to work to support themselves and their children as long as they are able to steal from the rest of us who have worked hard and long for many years. May I state that my husband and I and thousands of other hard working people 'are people, too' who are being robbed every day of the year by these leeches who can work, but who will not work, as long as the taxpayers of the city of St. Paul are being bled for money to keep these people sitting at home listening to and watching television programs. . . . What about the rest of us who have worked all of our lives and now find ourselves 'short of money' too, because we have to share with these people our hard-earned money. Where do they think we get our money?

It's certainly an honest letter. It's also a powerful letter: they "steal from the rest of us," we are "robbed by these leeches," and "the taxpayers are being bled for money."

But it's also a misleading letter because the writer seems to be blaming all the poor for their own poverty. There are, in fact, more than 30 million men, women, and children (mostly children) who are unable to participate successfully in our competitive capitalist system. For one reason or another they simply do not have adequate incomes to buy the basic necessities of life.

Still, research indicates that most adults want to work and will work given the chance. In fact, nearly two thirds of the male heads of impoverished households do work, counting either full-time or part-time work. One third of the heads of households (either male or female) in poor families have full time jobs, yet they remain poor because wages are simply too low. If, for example, a person worked full time, forty hours a week, fifty-two weeks a year at the federal minimum wage, that person's yearly income would nevertheless fall below the income definition of poverty for an urban family of four!

The author of the opening letter was apparently not aware of the actual statistics of our welfare programs. The federal government reports that on a national average most welfare recipients are children. The second largest category includes the blind, aged, and disabled. Next are the mothers of those children, and last come the able-bodied fathers (less than 1 percent). Of this small percentage on welfare, 80 percent said they wanted to work, and one in three was enrolled in some kind of work training program.

The question of welfare cheating is another controversial issue. Do welfare recipients engage in fraud and deception? "Statistics reported by states indicate that four tenths of 1 percent of welfare cases are referred for prosecution for fraud. The number of cases where fraud is established is even smaller." What about the widespread belief, "once on welfare, always on welfare"? This is another myth. Examining national averages, half of the families on welfare have been on welfare for twenty months or less. Only 6 percent have been receiving welfare for more than ten years. The myths roll on. Are welfare families "living it up"? Probably not—over thirty states pay welfare recipients less than the states' own definition of poverty.[19]

Of course there are the infuriating (but exceptional) cases of families that live "high off the hog": buying color TV sets, expensive new cars, and other items that many hardworking, taxpaying families feel they cannot afford. These are the cases that welfare critics love to hear; they make the headlines and become the grist for spiteful and unverified gossip. Such criticism is generally undeserved. Most poor people don't want to apply for welfare assistance but need to in order to survive. In short, the poor ought to have the understanding of all those who aren't doing as badly—not misconceptions based on prejudice or sentimentality, but a true understanding of the reality of poverty in the United States.

What are these realities? One of the most influential books on this subject is Michael Harrington's *The Other America*. Although Harrington's statistics are dated (the book was published in 1962), his report is to a large degree still true in the 1980s. What specifically does Harrington say?

First of all, he says the poor are *invisible*. They live off the beaten track. We do not notice the pockets of poverty in the U.S., whether the poor live in the hills of Appalachia, or the densely populated ghettos of our great cities. As our superhighways glide over and around America's depressed areas, we are no longer forced to see their angry faces or their substandard living conditions.

He also says the poor are *politically invisible* (unlike the poor of the Great Depression), making them vulnerable to shifts in national sentiment and often powerless to initiate programs or to defend themselves within the political arena.

> . . . the poor are politically invisible . . . The people of the other America do not, by far and large, belong to unions, to fraternal organizations, or to political parties. They are without lobbies of their own; they put forward no legislative program. As a group, they are atomized. They have no face; they have no voice.[20]

Many of the poor also lack internal vitality. They may have tried to rise above their circumstances but have failed for one reason or another. Another attempt leads to another failure, until they are beaten down—until their self-respect and dignity are all but destroyed.

> And nothing to look backward to with pride,
> And nothing to look forward to with hope,
> So now and never any different.
>> (From "The Death of the Hired Man" by Robert Frost)

Poverty Groups

The poor also belong to different subgroups that share the common problem of low income but have their own special diffi-

culties. There are, for example, the aged. Although their poverty
level has come down considerably during the 1970s (due mainly to
inflation-adjusted social security and Medicare), some 15 percent
of this group still fall below the poverty line. Others are caught in
what Harrington calls a *technological cross fire*: technology has

extended their lives (a person sixty-five years old can expect to live seventeen more years!), but it has also made their specific skills superfluous. In a culture where men and women are defined by their skill, occupation, and level of income, the people themselves become superfluous. Few authors have caught this overwhelming sense of uselessness better than French writer Simone de Beauvoir. She writes:

> The sadness of old people is not caused by any particular events or sets of circumstances: it merges with their consuming boredom, with their bitter and humiliating sense of uselessness, and with their loneliness in the midst of a world that has nothing but indifference for them.[21]

Another poverty group is the structurally unemployed. They are people who, even though they have skills and even though the economy may be booming, still find themselves without work. This can happen, for example, when employment opportunities disappear because of a fundamental change in technology or perhaps a major shift in consumer demand. Such structural changes in the economy often leave "pockets of poverty" that can continue for years and years. This group includes the underground coal miners in Kentucky and West Virginia and the iron ore workers in northern Michigan who watched their livelihoods dissolve as giant strip mining machines took over. It includes New England textile workers whose jobs were "exported" to low-paid Italians, Mexicans, and Taiwanese as well as autoworkers and steelworkers whose factories have been permanently closed down as the nation slowly changed from durable goods industries to services and high technology.

Other poverty groups include the migrant workers of the Midwest, the marginal farmers and sharecroppers of the deep South, and the millions living in the black and Spanish-speaking slums of our Northeastern cities. And since Harrington's analysis, we've witnessed a surprisingly large poverty increase in single parent households, 90 percent of which are headed by the mother. The rise in the divorce rate, combined with little or no financial commitment from the fathers (over half of these families, for example, receive no child care support), has created the most significant change in poverty statistics in the last decade.

The reality of poverty is also being born with the "wrong" set of parents, with the "wrong" color skin, or in the "wrong" part of the country—born into a *vicious circle* where the odds—the statistics of deprivation—are weighed against you from birth to death.

Nonwhites, for example, begin with average incomes of only 60 percent that of whites. As for education, over twice as many whites

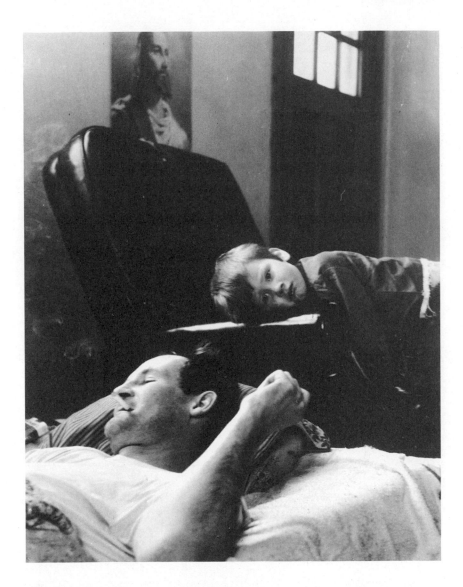

finish high school as nonwhites. All the way down the list, whites enjoy clear-cut advantages in every economic category. One out of every two whites has a *white-collar* occupation, compared with one in three nonwhites. Unemployment is at least double for nonwhites in all age groups, and nonwhite unemployment among young college graduates is more than triple that of whites. When we examine the unemployment statistics for minority teenagers,

we discover that between 40 and 50 percent of all nonwhite teenagers are actively searching for employment but can't find jobs!
Indeed, this may be America's most profound economic tragedy—
that a sizable group of young men and women are not allowed to
become integrated into the mainstream of society with an entry-
level job.

This vicious economic circle can be viewed as a kind of
sickness—with the cure often out of the patient's control. Communities with low incomes, for example, will very likely have substandard schools, staffed either with young and inexperienced
teachers (at the lowest end of the salary scale) or uninspired
teachers who are not good enough to move on (even though they
would like to). Students receive little educational encouragement
and tend to drop out more frequently than middle class students.
Students coming out of poor public schools wind up with the economy's most disagreeable and lowest-paying jobs—or no jobs at all.
These conditions bring in a new generation of low income families,
and the vicious circle begins all over again.

You can start anywhere in the circle and eventually wind up in the same place. There are other factors to consider as well, such as racial and sexual discrimination, mental and physical handicaps, poor health, lack of transportation, crime, and defeatist attitudes. Each additional factor adds a new dimension of difficulty for those trying to break out of the circle. Of course, there have been some successful breakaways by people who beat the system with intelligence, hard work, and considerable good luck. They made it and are now the proud, highly skilled tradesmen, wealthy businessmen, and even bank presidents and professors. But like the welfare myths (the cheaters, the ten children families living it up with color TVs and Cadillacs), these breakaways are the exceptions, the statistical abberations. The truth is that the vicious circle of poverty is just that, and to make any headway against the overwhelming odds one usually needs help.

Government Assistance

But what kind of help? Henry Thoreau once said, "If I knew for a certainty that a man was coming to my house with the conscious design of doing me good, I should run for my life—for fear that I should get some of his good done to me." Most poor people would probably agree with Thoreau's distaste for the "do-gooder," meddlesome approach. The poor often resent the battalions of government researchers and the well intentioned volunteer workers who often irritate more than they help. This is not to say that certain government and private programs have not done some good.

We have to keep in mind, though, that poverty is basically an economic problem; its solution, therefore, must also be economic. In short, the poor need one of two things:

1. Access to decent jobs with adequate pay

or

2. Government subsidized incomes

When we can guarantee everyone in the United States access to a job or a minimum income, we will have come a long way toward removing capitalism's basic flaw of "need versus demand." How far have we gone in this direction? What are the programs that deal with the income problem, and how effective are they?

Our government has chosen to help the poor in two basic ways: *transfer payments* and *goods and services*. Specific programs direct transfer payments to certain qualified families. These programs are aimed at the elderly, blind, and disabled (Supplemental Security Income program) and to children and their mothers (Aid to Families With Dependent Children *AFDC*). Social Security, Unemployment Compensation, and Veterans' Benefits are also considered transfer payments, although they are paid to people in all income groups and not just the poor.

The second form of help our government gives is goods and services in lieu of cash. A prime example of this is the Food Stamp program. Another example is Medical Assistance or Medicaid, where the family is provided with medical care, and the bill is paid by the government. Others are public housing and rent supplement programs. In larger cities, there are also free medical clinics. Whether these types of service programs should be "cashed out," with the government supplying money directly to the family instead of the free services or stamps is a subject of debate. If this were done, the family could then use the cash to compete for food, housing, and medical care in the free market.

To return to transfer payments, let's take an in-depth look at one of our largest income subsidy programs—welfare—and focus in mainly on the AFDC program. We already noted the intense resentment directed toward the beneficiaries of welfare and examined some of the myths surrounding it, discovering that many of our opinions are simply not supported by fact. However, we have yet to analyze this program from the standpoint of its economic effectiveness. Is welfare good or bad? Does it help or hinder the poor? Evaluating the program as a whole, most economists feel that the present day welfare system is less than a complete success. Some feel it is poorly designed, inefficient, and expensive, often doing more harm than good in solving the overall problem of poverty. Let's look at some of the problems.

First, welfare does not always satisfy the basic economic needs of the people. Remember that in over thirty states the amount of maximum welfare paid does not even meet the state's own definition of poverty. The states come up with a figure that reflects a poverty level of living, then pay the welfare family anywhere from 50 to 100 percent of that amount.

Next, the welfare system (like many bureaucracies) is often inefficient. Study the welfare procedures in your city or county or visit your local office and talk to the employees. You will soon realize that great sums of money and manpower are often wasted on red tape, paperwork, "means tests," questionnaires, evaluations, and investigations. A great deal of energy, money, and manpower are consumed by this bureaucratic machine, and as a result valuable resources are not available to the poor themselves.

Welfare can also be dehumanizing. Unsympathetic administrators can be suspicious, demeaning, and condescending to new applicants. Those already on welfare are subjected to inquiries and potential surveillance of their lives. Welfare agencies often reflect the prevailing attitude that to receive public assistance is shameful ("they have only themselves to blame"), thus, many of the poor are too proud to ask for financial help even if they need it.

Finally, our present welfare system has the unintended effect of encouraging the breakup of families. In over twenty states, for example, a woman with children is refused aid if her able-bodied husband is still a part of the family (even though he may be unemployed). Financial pressures frequently translate into personal tensions and animosities that often end up in separation or divorce.

Indeed, one wonders why we have retained such a destructive and inefficient income-subsidy system for so long. We tolerate it partly because welfare does have its advantages. Welfare does allow children to stay with their mothers, and it does add something to the meager incomes of the aged and disabled. In addition, it has paid for health services and nursing care where they were desperately needed. Furthermore, billion-dollar bureaucracies, no matter how inefficient or potentially destructive, have an uncanny knack for survival within the existing political system. Yet there must surely be a better way to deliver financial assistance to the millions of poor Americans without the drawbacks we have outlined here. Some economists feel that, in fact, there is a superior method; it's called the *negative income tax*.

The idea for negative income tax originated with Milton Friedman, a conservative economist and an influential maverick of the economics profession. Friedman has long advocated policies that adhere to a fundamental criterion: the enhancement of personal economic freedom and choice. He generally believes that a decentralized market system will best meet this objective, although it won't necessarily alleviate poverty. Friedman's alternative for our present welfare system, the negative income tax, was first outlined in his book *Capitalism and Freedom*, and since the early sixties it has gained wide respect.

To understand Friedman's idea, let's look at the income situation of three different families—Jones, Smith, and Baker. We will assume that Smith has the largest income of $10,000. Next comes Jones with $8,000 and finally Baker with $5,000.

Smith	Jones	Baker
$10,000	$8,000	$5,000

What amount of federal income tax will each of these three families pay? Let's review the procedure for determining income tax with the Smith family.

Smith will not pay tax on his entire income of $10,000 because everyone is allowed to subtract certain exemptions and deductions from the gross income. Remember that each dependent (including the taxpayer) is worth $1,000. Thus for a family of four, the total exemptions (what can be subtracted from the gross income) will be $4,000 ($1,000 × 4). Taxpayers are also allowed specific deductions. Middle and upper income families often itemize interest, sales and other taxes, medical care costs, business losses, etc. There is also a standard deduction that is usually taken by lower-income families.

To return to the Smith family, we now know that Smith has $4,000 in exemptions. If we assume he has the same amount in his standard deductions, the combined total will be:

Exemptions	$ 4,000
Deductions	4,000
Total	$ 8,000

Thus, instead of paying tax on his full $10,000 income, Smith is allowed to subtract exemptions and deductions worth $8,000. His taxable income will therefore only be $2,000. As the lowest tax rate is around 12%, Smith will pay a net tax of $240 (12% of $2,000).

For simplicity's sake, let's assume that each family in our example has the same dollar value of deductions: Jones and Baker are also allowed $4,000. It should be obvious that if Jones has four exemptions (worth $4,000) and $4,000 in deductions, he will not have to pay any tax at all on his $8,000 income ($8,000 − $8,000 = $0). Baker's income of $5,000 is the lowest of the three. Baker also has exemptions and deductions worth $8,000 and thus will not have to pay any tax either.

The question of equity now arises. There is a large difference between Jones's and Baker's incomes; why does the government treat them the same? Baker has $3,000 of *unused exemptions and deductions* for which he is getting no financial recognition. If we were to institute the negative income tax, Baker would receive some kind of financial credit for his unused exemptions and deductions. The government should therefore give Baker a nega-tive tax (i.e., a *tax rebate*) amounting to some percentage of the $3,000. Friedman suggested rebating 50 percent of any unused exemptions and deductions. Thus the Baker family would receive a check from the government for $1,500 (50 percent of $3,000). This supplementary income added to his regular income gives Baker $6,500 to spend.

Now let's look at Baker's situation if he were to lose his job. What would be the subsidy if there were no income at all? If exemptions and deductions are worth $8,000, the family would get 50 percent of that amount, or $4,000. This figure represents an *income floor*: Every family of four in the United States, even if the earned income was zero, would receive at least this amount. Nega-tive income tax is, in essence, a guaranteed-income plan.

What about incentives? Let's suppose that after Baker lost his job he was offered part-time janitorial work at $3,000 a year. Is it to his financial benefit to take the job? With his $3,000 income he would subtract the same $8,000 in exemptions and deductions and wind up with a subsidy of $2,500 ($3,000 − $8,000 = − $5,000; 50 percent of $5,000 is $2,500) His total income would be $2,500 plus his earned $3,000, or $5,500. Yes, he is better off with the job.

You might argue that a 50 percent rate (i.e., keeping only 50 of each earned dollar) is not enough incentive to go to work. But there is nothing in the basic idea that says the percentage must be 50 percent. The percentage could be determined so that you would keep 90 percent (or 100 percent) of the first $3,000 or $4,000 earned. After this "grace period" the percentage might go back to 50 percent. At any rate, the percentage rates, exemptions, and deduction levels could be experimentally worked out to give enough supplementary income for a respectable standard of living and still not destroy work incentives.

We can now begin to see some of the major advantages of this program. In Friedman's words:

> It is directed specifically at the problem of poverty. It gives help in the form most useful to the individual, namely cash. It is general and could be substituted for the host of special measures now in effect.

Let's review the specific advantages. In comparison with the present-day welfare system, the negative income tax would do the following:

- It would cover all in need.
- It could easily be adjusted to guarantee a decent standard of living for every family.
- It would eliminate the humiliating and dehumanizing aspects of the present system. Income supplements would be an informal matter like receiving a tax refund or social security check. Low-income families, as with everyone else, would be trusted to fill out their federal tax forms honestly.
- It would be a simple system. The bureaucratic paperwork, questionnaires, forms, means tests, etc., would be replaced by a simple income tax statement.
- Social and rehabilitation workers' talents could now be directed toward helping families solve specific problems (jobs, housing, transportation, upgrading nutrition, etc.) instead of wasting their abilities and skills on the red tape involved in money transfer.
- There would be no extra financial advantage that would force a family to break up.
- It could be designed so that it did not discourage work.

There are some disadvantages as well. The negative income tax program would, in the short run, be more expensive than the present system. More people would be covered, and minimal-income levels would probably be higher. Where the money would come from is another matter to consider. If the major tax loopholes were closed, a large amount of tax money could be available. Eventually we may even be able to reduce our vast military budget. Friedman does feel, however, that in the long run the positive work incentive effect (if jobs are available) and eliminating all other subsidy programs (welfare, food stamps, veterans' pensions, and perhaps even social security) would make the cost of negative income tax lower than that of all of our existing supplemental income programs combined.

Yet however we pay for it, we must *first* decide that we really do want to help the poor. We do have the resources, but we seem to lack the public will. A while back I received an advertisement in the mail called "Shop the Other America." In it was a statement that strongly supported the need for a change in our country's attitude:

> Before we can decide how to accomplish the goal of eliminating poverty, or whether we can afford to do the job, we must first decide that we want to do it—that we will no longer expect children to fill hungry bellies with Kool-Aid and candy, to be the prey of rats, to be weakened with tuberculosis, to grow up amid filth and organized vice, to be taught in deteriorating classrooms by teachers who have lost hope, and that we will no longer allow old people to huddle in lonely, heatless rooms, living on pennies, unable to afford needed medicines and services.

We began this chapter with a strong statement from a woman writing to a St. Paul newspaper and ended with another statement that is equally strong in emotion but light years away in ideology and purpose. Reconciling these two honest, but opposite views is the unfinished business of every American.

Chapter 7

MACROECONOMICS

In Chapters 4 and 5 we moved away from the "microscope" approach (supply and demand) and went on to examine the major economic sectors of businesses, households, and government. Now we are ready to take an even broader point of view. This chapter is an introduction to large (macro) economic concepts; it will be as if we were looking at the broad outlines of our economy from some point in outer space using an "economic telescope," allowing us to view the whole picture at once. Economists call this panoramic view of the economy *macroeconomics*.

You probably know quite a bit about macroeconomics already; in fact, you undoubtedly have read about it in the papers, hear about it on the news each evening, and listen to arguments about it every election year. Macroeconomics is the *study of inflation, unemployment, recession, the gross national product (GNP), economic growth, and other broad concepts of an economic system.*

Who uses macroeconomic concepts? Our economic soothsayers use them when they attempt to divine the future. Forecasters ponder charts and tables like veteran handicappers at the race tracks. They pore over income trends, savings and interest rates, consumer attitudes, housing starts, auto sales, birth rates, and other economic indicators, and then they ask such questions as, "Will we have recession or inflation next year (or both)?"; "Will interest rates go up or down?"; "What will happen to productivity?"

Then there are the popular oracles (and sometimes charlatans) of the various investment markets—stocks and bonds, commodities, and gold and silver—who use macroeconomic ideas to help them predict the ups and downs of their respective markets. A fraction of a percent change here can add or subtract thousands of dollars from a client's account.

There are also the economic philosophers who ask some of the larger human questions: "Where is mankind now and where are we going?" "What is the impact of materialism and technology on society today, ten years from now, or even a hundred years from now?" "Futurists" also utilize macroeconomic ideas and indicators.

Finally, our public officials are interested in macroeconomics. They have immediate, urgent concerns. They are like harried physicians constantly checking the pulse of the economy, anxious to learn of strength or weakness, of growth or stagnation. These are the men and women who have directly or indirectly accepted the responsibility for maintaining the economic health of the country. They include not only the President of the United States and his staff but also Congress and the decision makers in the Federal Reserve banking system.

Their economic power stems from controlling the federal budget, the money supply, and interest rates in response to changing economic conditions. A good understanding of macroeconomics is their best tool for intelligent planning and decision making.

Wealth And Gross National Product

Perhaps the best place to start our exploration of this vast area of economic theory and reality is with the idea of wealth—a yardstick by which many countries judge each other. Indeed, the United States is the envy of the world because of its tremendous manmade and natural wealth. If we were to add up the value of all our buildings and structures, our equipment and inventories, our land and other natural resources, we would be worth something over 15 trillion dollars (a trillion equals a thousand billion). This figure, however, does not tell us very much about our *current* economic health. Why? There are two reasons.

First, wealth must be utilized before it can contribute to present-day living standards. Black Africa, for example, has tremendous natural wealth, but this wealth has generally not been put to use, and, consequently, their people remain economically poor.

The second reason is that the value of a nation's resources in the form of wealth does not necessarily tell us anything about current production. Without a continuous flow of new goods and services, a nation will eventually consume its available wealth—like a retired couple who use up their savings and are eventually forced to sell their belongings to purchase food. Our economy, like a growing family, must have a continuous flow of income and real output if it is to maintain present living standards.

What we are looking for is a concept that goes beyond wealth, a concept that will tell us something of the total output that our land, machines, and labor produce year after year. This concept is the *gross national product (GNP)*. Economists define GNP as a measure of the final total value of all goods and services produced in a year's time. Like the amount of wealth, GNP is an enormous figure—almost too large to comprehend. At the beginning of the 1980s, for example, total GNP was approximately 3 trillion dollars per year!

We should pause a moment to consider the difficulties in computing a precise value of GNP. Of course, much of our total output can easily be traced by simply adding up total incomes (as shown on our tax returns, for example). There are, however, many goods and services that do not see the "light of day" and are never officially recorded. An unrecorded "cash" transaction (designed to bypass the Internal Revenue Service) is one example.

Probably a much larger category of unrecorded production takes place (perfectly legally) under the heading of *nonmarket transactions*. We are all a part of this "underground" market in one way or another. For example, each time we do something for ourselves that we *could have paid someone else to do*, our economic activity goes unrecorded in the official GNP statistics. Joe Smith, for example, tunes his car every month, but Joe, of course, doesn't pay himself (and record it on his income tax). Yet if a garage had done the same work, the labor bill might have been around $50. The garage, in turn, would have reported that amount to the government as "services performed," and Joe's tune-up would have become part of our GNP.

Obviously, these do-it-yourself projects, from growing your own food to remodeling your basement, cannot be accurately accounted for in our national income statistics. The nonmarket transaction problem is considerably amplified when we note the billions of dollars of unpaid household services that are performed mainly by women. Then add to this the billions of dollars of unpaid volunteer services. Although our government does attempt to estimate the value of some of these unrecorded transactions, it is impossible to be precise.[22]

Another problem associated with GNP is our strong belief in the dictum that "happiness is a rising GNP." We often assume that when GNP is rising we are all automatically better off. Many economists, however, are now beginning to voice some important concerns about this philosophy.

For example, before we can say we are better off when GNP goes up, we first might look at what is happening to the *population* during the same period of time. If output rises by 1 percent and population goes up 3 percent, the average family will suffer a *decline* of 2 percent in their standard of living. It's a simple principle that is often ignored, especially in the less developed countries where population growth frequently outstrips the rise in GNP.

Another point to consider is the *distribution* of the GNP pie. A rising GNP, for example, may be translated into 25 percent more housing, but if the extra houses are second homes for wealthy families, then we can hardly say that the average citizen is benefiting. Brazil perhaps is a good example of this. This South American country has certainly been a "growth economy," but the fruits of its rising GNP have been mainly concentrated in the modern sector. The majority of poor Brazilians who live in the nonindustrial economy benefit very little, if at all. Our generalization, "happiness is a rising GNP," in this case turns out to be a cruel mockery to the masses who watch income differentials widen as the years go by.

We should also consider the question of *quality*. Does the quality of our GNP change over time? Indeed, it does. Many people would argue that the quality of our merchandise and services has declined over the years. They point to shoddy workmanship, inferior materials, and "planned obsolescence" as proof of deteriorating quality. There may be some truth to this. Industry might reply, however, that the quality of some products has actually improved. Radios and televisions, for example, are cheaper and more reliable now than they were twenty years ago; radial tires are not only safer but will outlast the tire of yesteryear; and the razor blades on the market today (stainless steel, two-track, bonded, etc.) are superior to the old, soft-steel blue blade of grandpa's time.

What is your own opinion about the quality of products and services? On balance, has it gone up or down? Either way, product quality is an important factor to consider when comparing GNP statistics from year to year.

Instead of looking at individual products, we might also examine the general *composition* of the overall GNP. It has been said, for example, that if we all came down with cancer, it would boost the GNP. Hospital revenues and the incomes of doctors, nurses, radiologists, and drug companies would go up—at least temporarily. Yet clearly no one could say that we were "better off."

There are thus economic "bads" as well as "goods." Many economists are beginning to look at GNP growth to try and analyze which expenditures are truly beneficial and which are not. For example, it is generally agreed that health-care costs associated with air and water pollution do not add to our net economic well being, nor do, for example, excessive military expenditures.

British economist Leopold Kohr has identified a whole range of products (and services) that he labels *density commodities*. These goods are purchased by consumers, government agencies, and businesses simply to *offset the impact of living in a high density environment* and among large scale social institutions (schools, businesses, cities, etc.).[23] Density expenditures include the cost of traffic accidents, many legal services, commuting expenses, escapist media, chemical relaxants and stimulants, and the ever more powerful headache remedies ("Life got tougher, so we got stronger," says an Excedrin advertisement). Add to this list those expenditures associated with crime (squad cars, prisons, exotic burglar alarms and foolproof locks, personalized handguns, mace, etc.), and you begin to get an idea of how much our GNP is devoted to these goods. We are forced to purchase density goods, says Dr. Kohr, not because they offer us a net improvement in our standard of living, but because we have evolved a society where such goods are a necessity to offset the negative side effects of modern urban life. Again, the billions and billions of dollars spent on these types of goods may not add much to the net welfare of the population, yet they are all counted as part of our official GNP statistics.

Another related idea is the question of *balance and priorities*. Are we spending too little on civilian public goods such as parks, education, libraries, mass transit, rehabilitation of the cities, and too much on private goods? Economist John Kenneth Galbraith suggests this in his book, *The Affluent Society*:

> The family which takes its mauve and cerise, air conditioned, power-steered, and power-braked automobile out for a tour passes through cities that are badly paved, made hideous by litter, blighted buildings, billboards, and posts for wires that should long since have been put underground. . . They picnic on exquisitely packaged food from a portable icebox by a polluted stream and go on to spend the night at a park which is a menace to public health and morals. Just before dozing off, amid the stench of decaying refuse, they may reflect vaguely on the curious unevenness of their blessings. Is this, indeed, the American genius?
>
> . . . the penultimate Western man stalled in the ultimate traffic jam slowly succumbing to carbon monoxide, will not be cheered to hear from the last survivor that the gross national product went up by a record amount.

Since Galbraith wrote those lines in the 1950s, the arguments over GNP and the quality of life have taken a quantum leap. The battle lines are being drawn. A large group of intelligent and serious individuals contend that economic growth should be halted to preserve the environment and conserve the remaining nonrenewable resources. Zero GNP growth is their goal. In this group would be Herman E. Daly and Paul Ehrlich plus Ehrlich's many followers in the Zero Population Growth (ZPG) movement. Perhaps the extreme side of this position is that of Professor Ezra Mishan of the London School of Economics. Consider, for example, his comment:

> You could very well have stopped growing after the First World War. There was enough technology to make life quite pleasant. Cities weren't overgrown. People weren't too avaricious. You hadn't really ruined the environment as you have now.[24]

Most economists, however, continue to be defenders of growth, agreeing with Adam Smith's historic contention that "the progressive state is in reality the cheerful and the hearty state to all orders of society. The stationary is dull, the declining, melancholy."

One might also pause to consider Irving Kristol's argument that growth is, in fact, a *necessary precondition* to a modern democracy where "the expectations of tomorrow's bigger pie, from which everyone will receive a larger slice . . . prevents people from fighting to the bitter end over the division of today's pie."[25] Defenders of growth also point out that very few families can say that they are satisfied with their current economic status. In addition, they remind us that we still have many low income people in the United States who are likely to be permanently poor in a zero-growth economy. Finally, the pro-growth people point out that it is much easier to deal with pollution in a growing economy. Cleaning up the environment will be expensive, and the additional resources must come from somewhere.[26]

These defenders of growth are greatly disturbed that an increasing number of people want to go back to the "good old days"—those days that the pro-growth people believe were not so good. They ask, "Why can't the environmentalists understand that technology and economic growth conquered nature for the benefit of mankind?"

Author Mel Ellis, a naturalist who has demonstrated a unique sensitivity for both economic and environmental problems, once wrote:

> Man almost literally made the cow, the fat corn kernel, the plump turkey, the beautiful rose. And if he erred in his enthusiasm and polluted his raw materials, his resources, he still made the world enormously better.[27]

I think most environmentalists do understand the benefits of technology, progress, and economic growth, but their attention is directed at different concerns. They are listening to different sounds. Essayist E. B. White once summed up this attitude with the comment, "I would feel more optimistic about a bright future for man if he spent less time proving that he can outwit Nature and more time tasting her sweetness and respecting her seniority."[28]

Their immediate concerns are not with the eradication of poverty or the benefits of high-speed air travel or the advantages of the computer over the abacus. They do not see a thousand acres of timber as so many completed homes; instead they see the grandeur of the forest and its enduring value as a generator of oxygen and a habitat for wildlife, and they work for its preservation. Instead of seeing Appalachian hills as a source of strip-mined coal to heat homes, they ask, "What will be the adverse consequences of strip-mining for the land and its inhabitants?"

> The D-9 bulldozer is the largest built by the Caterpillar Tractor Corporation. It weighs some forty-eight tons and is priced at $108,000. With a blade that weighs five thousand pounds, rising five feet and curved like some monstrous scimitar, it shears away not only soil and trees but a thousand other things—grapevines, briars, ferns, toadstools, wild garlic, plantain, dandelions, moss, a colony of pink lady-slippers, fragmented slate, an ancient plow point, a nest of squeaking field mice— and sends them hurtling down the slope, an avalanche of the organic and the inorganic, the living and the dead. The larger trees that stand in the path of the bulldozer—persimmons, walnuts, mulberries, oaks, and butternuts—meet the same fate. Toppled, they are crushed and buried in the tide of rubble.[29]

Environmentalists, in short, are distressed by the ugliness of overdevelopment. They are angered by worldwide pollution and by the growing lists of endangered species, and they feel that these are the unnecessary consequences of man's selfishness. They are saddened by our blindness—a blindness to things that may be lost forever. Of those who favor "development at any cost," the environmentalists ask, "Why can't you see what uninhibited growth is doing to those things we must preserve for future generations?" The great debate over growth is based on simple, yet profound, differences in values. It will, undoubtedly, remain one of the major public issues for years to come.

Consider one more major challenge to "happiness is a rising GNP." Imagine the following scene: George Franklin was overjoyed when his income was pushed up to $25,000 a year; George had never thought he would make that much money. Yet by the end of the year, the Franklin family felt poorer than ever. Not only had they failed to save any money, but Mrs. Franklin claimed that their standard of living was worse now than it was five years ago. What went wrong?

The answer to this question should be obvious since we are all adversely affected by the same economic malady. The problem, of course, is *inflation*. Not only does inflation distort and diminish your income, my income, and George Franklin's income, but inflation also distorts our GNP statistics.

A simple example can illustrate this point. Let's pretend that the U.S. economy produces only one product, wheat. We will assume a time period of three years and watch what happens to GNP when the wheat price is inflated from $1 to $5 per bushel.

Year	Output (bu of wheat)	Price/bu	GNP (Price × output)
1	3	$1	$ 3
2	5	$4	$20
3	9	$5	$45

Take a look at the GNP column. If someone gave you only the GNP figures ($3, $20, $45), would you say these figures were a good representation of output? Of course not, because they are not giving you the whole story. The GNP figures are, in fact, greatly inflated compared with the increase in actual output of wheat: GNP increased to fifteen times its original value (from $3 to $45), while output went up only three times (from 3 to 9 bushels). In short, if all you saw were these GNP statistics, you would have a very distorted picture of the economic situation. Economists have a name for this "distorted" or inflated GNP; they call it *money GNP*. Using the same idea, we can now see why George Franklin felt a little bewildered when he discovered that his money income did not give him any additional purchasing power. Money income and money GNP are, by themselves, inaccurate indicators of the real economic situation.

Unfortunately, the money GNP is the figure that is commonly quoted by newspapers, public officials, writers, and teachers. The 3 trillion dollar figure mentioned earlier was, in fact, money GNP. Is there any way of getting a more accurate picture of our GNP? What we need is a realistic value for GNP in which we remove the impact of inflated prices.

To adjust for inflation, we must compare each year's output with the wheat price of a single *base year*. Choose any of the three years for your base, then apply this base year price to all the other years. For example, let's choose year 1 as our base. We then multiply the base year price ($1/bu) times the actual output of the other two years. The result is *real GNP*, which, as you can see below in Table 7-b, gives us a much more accurate picture of each year's production than did money GNP.

Year	Output (bu)	Real GNP	
1	3	$3	
2	5	$5	Year 1 = Base Year
3	9	$9	

Of course the United States does not produce one product but millions and millions of goods and services. How do we adjust for inflation when there are so many different prices to consider? The same principle applies, i.e., we use base-year prices to compare output of all the other years. The only difference is that now we must average the price changes of many goods instead of just one. This average price level can easily be summarized in one statistic called the *price index* (or *GNP price deflator*). The price index for the base year is always equal to 100 (no matter which year we choose), and any change in price will be reflected by a percentage change in the index.

For example, if we use 1972 as the base year (price index = 100), and we find that between 1972 and 1980 prices went up 77 percent, then the price index for 1980 would be 177. Knowing that the index was 177, we could then convert the output of 1980 into "1972 dollars." This would give us the real GNP for 1980.

Suppose, therefore, you hear someone bragging that the U.S. GNP in 1980 was an impressive 2,627 billion dollars. You now know that this person is giving you the inflated figure of money GNP. So how do you calculate real GNP for 1980? You would simply divide the price index for 1980 (177) into the money GNP ($2,627 billion) and then multiply your answer by 100. On a piece of scrap paper you thus make the following computation:

$$\text{Real GNP} = \frac{\$2,627 \text{ billion}}{177} \times 100 = \$1,484 \text{ billion}$$

Now you know the value of real GNP (1972 prices) for the year 1980. The $1,484 billion figure is thus considerably less than the inflationary $2,627 billion figure that was originally quoted. Unfortunately, the distinction between real and money GNP is rarely made, and the public therefore is often misled.

We are now prepared for what might be called "The Shortest Economic History Course Ever," as we sum up fifty years of U.S. economic history—in less than a page!

Year	Money GNP ($bil)	Price Index 1972 = 100)	Real GNP ($bil)
1930	90.7	31.8	285
1935	72.5	27.9	260
1940	100.0	29.0	344
1945	212.3	37.9	560
1950	286.2	53.6	534
1955	399.3	60.8	657
1960	506.0	68.7	737
1965	688.1	74.4	925
1970	982.4	91.4	1075
1975	1528.8	125.6	1217
1980	2627.0	177.0	1484

(1972 = Base year)
Source: BEA Department of Commerce

Do you notice any interesting trends in these figures? If you read them carefully, you will notice three major economic events in this fifty-year history.

The first significant event is the deflation (a drop in prices) and the great depression of the 1930s. It was an insecure decade for Americans with high unemployment, a severe drought, and widespread poverty.

The second period of interest is the great upsurge of real economic growth from the early 1940s to the late 1960s. In an accounting sense, this thirty-year period was a phenomenal age of American prosperity. The decade of the 1960s alone averaged nearly 4½ percent *real* growth per year! By the middle of this decade political writer Theodore White would write in his book, *The Making of the President* (1964):

> There was no doubt that John F. Kennedy and his economists had brought about the first fundamental change in American economic policy since Franklin D. Roosevelt—and the nation glowed with a boom that was one of the world's wonders. The boom terrified Europeans, angered the underdeveloped in the world, baffled the Russians.

Yet only five years later, after our long Vietnam war, the glow of economic boom and prosperity turned into a bonfire of inflation, the third major event of this period. During the 1970s overall prices in the United States rose some 94 percent—a greater percentage increase than in any other comparable period!

Thus it is inflation and, at times, high unemployment that mar much of our economic history—and continue to plague us into the 1980s as well. It is these two extremes of economic sickness that we will now examine in more detail as we continue our exploration of macroeconomics.

Chapter 8

UNEMPLOYMENT AND INFLATION

What do you think would happen if everyone in the United States woke up one morning and decided that from now on they would spend only one-half the amount of money that they had been spending? A very unlikely situation, yet suppose it really happened. What would be the total economic effect of this group decision?

The effect would be very large indeed. To see the impact of this large spending cutback, let us pull out our economic microscope once again and focus in on one small retail store—Joe's Super Sport Shop of Plum City, Washington. Joe's business will, in effect, become a microcosm of what will be felt by businesses all across the country. What will happen first?

Joe will immediately begin to notice that fewer customers are coming in. Before long, he may let go one of his part-time clerks. But for Joe himself, so far, so good. He is not yet facing any major problems. As time goes on, however, he begins to notice something very disturbing: his inventory is piling up. As Joe walks into the back storage room, he stumbles over a large box of unsold baseball mitts that he had ordered earlier according to his usual needs. Things are a little more serious now.

Most likely, Joe will try to get rid of his excess mitts by putting them on sale. Even more important (to the economy), though, he will probably send a message to the baseball mitt distributor in Seattle to hold off on any more shipments.

The bad news is channeled up to Ajax Mitt Manufacturers, Inc., of Blackstone, Maine. Ajax, in fact, is getting the same bad news

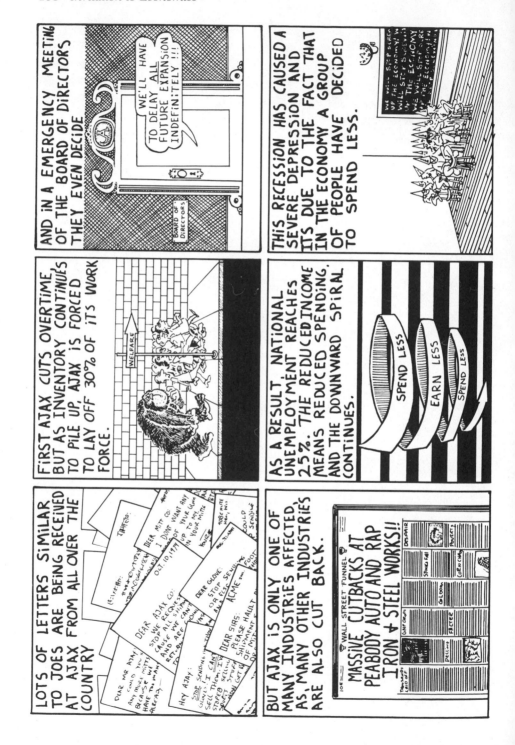

from all its distributors around the country. At first the Ajax company cuts overtime, but they soon realize that in order to avoid a pileup of inventory, they must lay off 30 percent of their work force. The directors meet in emergency session to discuss the new plant that is scheduled for ground-breaking ceremonies next week. They decide to halt indefinitely all expansion plans.

Of course, similar actions are being taken by other industries throughout the nation. Major layoffs take place in the auto, steel, and housing industries, and orders for new plants and equipment are reduced to a fraction of last year's level. National unemployment soon rises to 25 percent.

With many people on a reduced income (or no income), spending falls to lower levels, and the downward spiral continues to drag the economy down even further. What is the result of this seemingly simple decision to curtail spending? It has brought us a devastating depression! It's as simple as that. Thus, the major cause of recession, depression, high unemployment, etc., is that *somewhere in the economy enough individuals or groups of people decide (for any number of reasons) to spend less.* These people do not necessarily have to be consumers; they can be some other major spender in our economy such as businesses or government. Economists summarize the three major categories of spending as:

- Consumption expenditure (C)
- Business investment (I)
- Government expenditures (G)

Thus we can now say that any large reduction in C, I, or G spending will set forces into motion that can lead to a recession or possibly a depression.

Returning once again to our example, let's assume we are now going through the stage called *recession*. What is a recession, and how does it differ from a depression?

Recession Vs. Depression

Economists say we are in a recession when the economy experiences at least a half year of declining real GNP. By this definition, our economy has experienced eight recessions since World War II: 1949, 1954, 1958, 1960, 1970, 1974, 1980, and 1982. In terms of unemployment, the most severe of our recent recessions was in

1982 when, for a number of months, over 10 percent of the labor force was out of work. The mildest recession was in 1970, with only 5 percent unemployment.

If a recession is a bad cold, a depression is pneumonia. In effect, a depression is a severe and prolonged recession. The great depression of the 1930s, for example, lasted a full decade with unemployment rates ranging from 12 to 25 percent (1933). In no year during the decade of 1931 to 1941 did the national jobless rate drop below the 10 percent figure!

Depressions have a touch of economic insanity. During the 1930s, there were idle machines and idle men and women who *could* have been producing goods and services the nation desperately needed, but the unemployed people sat idle, and their machines rusted—and nobody knew what to do about it.

There was a comparable tragedy in the countryside as well. In one part of the nation, fruit and grain ripened and livestock fattened in our great fertile valleys, but the farmers destroyed the livestock, burned the grain, and let the ripened fruit rot while people went hungry because many had little or no income and therefore no purchasing power. Writer Caroline Bird, in her fine book *The Invisible Scar*, retells a number of anecdotes that illustrate some of the sadness and suffering during those years. Here are a couple of examples:

> Minors tried to plant vegetables, but they were often so hungry that they ate them before they were ripe. On her first trip to the mountains, Eleanor Roosevelt saw a little boy trying to hide his pet rabbit. "He thinks we are not going to eat it," his sister told her, "but we are." (pages 26-27)
>
> A year after his defeat by Roosevelt, Hoover—who had repeated so many times that no one was starving—went on a fishing trip with cartoonist "Ding" Darling in the Rocky Mountains. One morning a local man came into their camp, found Hoover awake, and led him to a shack where one child lay dead and seven others were in the last stages of starvation. Hoover took the children to a hospital, made a few phone calls, and raised a fund of $3,030 for them. (page 39)

In addition, disastrous weather conditions in some parts of the country added to the general economic suffering. In the Midwest wheat belt there were desperate, bankrupt farmers who choked on dust from the worst drought that anyone could remember.

There seemed to be some malicious and sinister force in the air that paralyzed economic activity and turned topsy turvey the economic laws that had always worked for our benefit—a force that almost broke our spirit:

> The women studied the men's faces secretly, for the corn could go, as long as something else remained. The children stood nearby, drawing figures in the dust with bare toes, and the children sent exploring senses out to see whether men and women would break. The children peeked at the faces of the men and women, then drew careful lines in the dust with their toes. Horses came to the watering troughs and nuzzled the water to clear the surface dust. After a while the faces of the watching men lost their bemused perplexity and became hard and angry and resistant . . . Then the women knew that they were safe and that there was no break. Then they asked, What'll we do? And the man replied, I don't know . . . But it was all right . . .
>
> (From *The Grapes of Wrath* by John Steinbeck)

We now know something of what that sinister force was. It was caused by a large reduction in spending in all major sectors of the economy set off by the great stock market crash of 1929.[30] This inability of pure capitalism to regulate itself—that is, its inability to avoid the ups and downs of a business cycle is, as we noted before, capitalism's third tragic flaw. We will soon see how this problem is dealt with in a modern economy. First, however, let's go back to the example at the beginning of the chapter.

Remember we had first decided to spend less, then quickly found ourselves in a recession, and then later dropped into a deep depression. Let's now assume that after this unhappy time people, businesses, and government decide to begin spending again. What will be the new scene at Joe's Super Sport Shop?

Joe's business immediately picks up, forcing him to rehire his part-time help. He no longer trips over surplus boxes or baseball mitts. In fact, when Margie Miller comes in to buy her autographed Lou Gehrig Little League baseball mitt, Joe discovers that he is all sold out. He quickly dials his distributor in Seattle, who at that very moment is writing purchase orders to the Ajax Mitt Co. Ajax immediately rehires laid-off workers as the plant gears up for full-capacity production. Finally, the directors of Ajax, Inc., meet and approve the ground breaking for not one but two new Midwest plants.

Happy times have returned. Things are humming along in all of the economy's major industries. Everyone appears satisfied as more and more expenditures flow through the system, buying up greater and greater amounts of goods and services. Notice too that once there is upward motion in the economy, everything tends to reinforce the trend—greater spending generates more employment, more income, and more investment spending. Each of these new spending dollars in turn generates another round of spending and enlarged incomes. The pace accelerates—perhaps too fast. At some point the total demand begins straining the available supply as resources become fully employed. The result is the beginning of *inflation* as a large number of dollars "chase" after a limited supply of output.

At first, of course, there is not much to worry about. A few prices pop up here and there as inventories are depleted; product shortages are a little more frequent than before. Yet if demand expands too fast, the existing plant capacity will soon become over-loaded as we reach full utilization of our labor force and industrial capacity. Businesses will be under pressure to expand to meet the demand, yet there simply won't be enough resources. As they attempt to buy existing raw materials and to attract skilled labor, businesses find they have to pay more and more. Labor unions will be quick to take advantage of the "seller's market" for labor, and before long wages are pushed up. Businesses don't mind too much since they can usually pass their increased costs on to the consumer in the form of higher prices. Inflation that results from higher costs is often referred to as *cost-push inflation*. Higher labor costs, however, mean fatter pay-checks. This extra demand pulls prices up again (too many dollars chasing after too few goods), and we experience another round of demand-pull inflation.

These two factors (excess demand, higher costs) pull and push the economy again and again, as if bending a wire back and forth. The heated-up economy soon reaches a breaking point. This hyperinflation can be as devastating to an economy as a depression; both are extremes that can and must be avoided. We will look at more details of these two problems in a moment, but first, let's summarize we have learned thus far.

The diagram in Figure 8–1 looks something like the supply and-demand graph in Chapter 3. Here, however, the up-and-down axis represents the overall price level. Any upward movement on the price scale can be directly translated into inflation. The bottom axis represents output and employment. If output is high, we know employment will also be high; if output is low, employment will be low as well. Since both values are directly related, we will simply call the bottom axis "Employment and Output." We might give our diagram the following title: "What More Spending Does to Prices, Employment, and Output."

Let's begin at point A—in the midst of the depression. Note the relatively low price level combined with a small GNP and high unemployment. As we begin to spend more, we move along the solid line to the right. Each additional dollar spent means greater employment and output *without* any inflation penalty. This remains true all the way through Phase I, until we reach point B. After B any additional spending not only brings greater output but also some degree of inflation. We call this Phase II or the *trade-off* area. In other words, if we want higher levels of output and employment, we must accept a trade-off in the form of higher prices. Once we reach C, however, what happens? If we spend beyond point C, we gain nothing in output and employment (because the economy is operating at maximum output), but we completely lose out because of hyperinflation.

We might generalize and say that to operate in either Phase I or III is a great mistake since we can gain employment (without any

What More Spending Does to Prices, Employment and Output

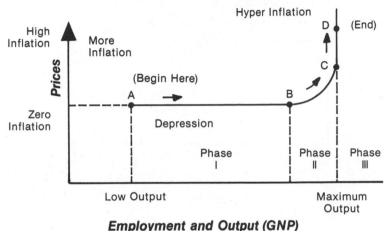

Figure 8-1

inflation penalty) in Phase I, but Phase III represents nothing more than sustained inflation (with no employment advantage). No, the logical place to operate (if we are in control of things) is in the trade-off area. Let's magnify this section of our graph (see Figure 8–2) to see precisely how it operates.

The reality of trade-off is actually a variation of the old saying, "you can't have your cake and eat it too"; i.e., we can't have full employment and zero inflation at the same time. Trade off thus forces us to choose which objective we value most—high employment or low inflation. For example, if we operate in the Stage 1 area of trade-off, we are choosing a low-inflation, high unemployment situation. On the other hand, if we choose an area near Stage 3, we are opting for full employment with high inflation. It often boils down to a very difficult political decision. Have you ever heard the statement, "If we are ever going to solve this inflation problem, we've got to have a recession"? This is the sort of hard choice the trade-off dilemma forces us to make. How then do we choose? Can we tell which of these problems—inflation or

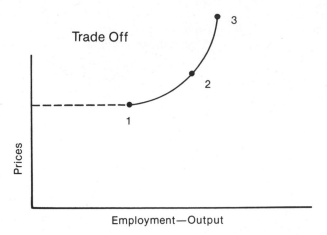

Figure 8-2

unemployment—is going to give us more trouble? Economists can't say for sure since each of these problems affects us differently. Let's therefore take a closer look at the specific economic impact of both these economic maladies.

Inflation

First, consider inflation. Exactly why is inflation bad? Most people have jobs during high inflationary periods, and inflation by itself does not normally reduce output. The problem with inflation is that *it distorts the economy*; it redistributes large portions of the economic pie away from some people and places that income into the hands of others—often unfairly or free of charge.

Indeed, some groups do fairly well during inflationary times. Anyone on a *flexible income*, for example, will usually do all right. Labor unions with bargaining clout (and inflation based escalator clauses in their contracts) tend to benefit. So can large corporations. Since demand is usually high, these businesses are often able to raise their prices in response to higher labor and raw material costs. The *speculator* who purchases property, gold, etc., at bargain prices and then sits back to "let inflation do its work" also benefits from inflation. Finally, those who *borrow* large amounts of money often find themselves in good shape during this period because they will be able to pay back their loans in easy-to-come-by inflated dollars.

It shouldn't be difficult to see which groups are the hardest hit by inflation. *Fixed-income* families suffer the most, particularly those who are retired and living on set pensions or other retirement incomes. There are many other fixed-income groups: the millions of marginal workers in low paying industries with no unions, retail clerks, hotel and restaurant workers, and others who work at or below the minimum wage.

With borrowers gaining because of inflation, lenders often lose out, as do savers who are forced to sit back and watch (with great bitterness) their saved-up purchasing power evaporate under the heat of rising prices. The so-called virtues of a nation—hard work and thriftiness—become cruel hoaxes, and the vices of speculation and excessive borrowing are rewarded. Inflation thus becomes an insidious disease that saps economic incentives, a disease that renders people unsure of the present economic reality and fearful of what the future will bring.

Unemployment

Now let's look at the other side of the trade-off dilemma— unemployment. To be unemployed means more than "just not having a job." By definition, a person is unemployed if he is actively seeking employment (by registering at employment offices, etc.) but cannot find work.

Surprisingly, not all unemployment is undesirable or harmful to the economy. Economists say there is about 4 percent *frictional unemployment*; those in this category are looking for work for the first time or are voluntarily changing jobs. They are indeed actively seeking work, but their situation is not terribly serious. In fact, without some frictional unemployment our economy would lose a measure of efficiency that is brought about by labor mobility. Since there is no way to reduce this kind of unemployment (nor would we want to), we can say that our economy is "fully employed" when we are at or near this 4 percent level. Or putting it slightly different, when 96 percent of the labor force is employed, we could say our economy is operating at full capacity.

Much more unemployment than that, however, spells trouble. For every additional 1 percent, we can say that about 1 million additional workers have lost their jobs. Thus, a 6 percent unemployment rate implies that something over 2 million people (above the frictional level) are out of work.

When recession strikes, we usually find another category of unemployed, i.e., a sizable group of *discouraged workers* who never appear in the national statistics. They've simply given up hope of finding work. We don't know who all these discouraged unemployed are, but they include, among others, married, college educated women who would like a good job but can find nothing available where they live and lack the mobility to move to where the jobs are. There are middle-aged men and women who are fired, phased out, or laid off (indefinitely). These individuals may have worked for years, but now they find out that no one wants to hire them. There are also many Americans from minority groups who have simply given up trying to find jobs because of racial discrimination. These are just a few examples of the disappointed dropouts who exist in an economic limbo.

Then there are also the *structurally unemployed*. We already know (from Chapter 5) something about this group. They are workers whose skills have become obsolete or whose jobs disappeared when the factory or mining operation shut down. They are workers whose problems cannot be readily solved by more spending and greater economic expansion. They therefore need retraining for new skills and often need assistance to relocate to areas where jobs are available.

Finally, we come to *Keynesian unemployment,* named after British economist John M. Keynes. This kind of unemployment results from a lack of spending and the resulting business cycle downturn as described at the beginning of the chapter. It was Keynes who first devised the theory that such unemployment can be significantly reduced by instituting government programs designed to stimulate additional spending. This was indeed a revolutionary idea since few economists before Keynes had ever dreamed of manipulating an economic system.

Sure, Western economies had always experienced the business cycle (wide swings from unemployment to inflation and back), but the nineteenth and early twentieth century economists (often called the *classical economists*) felt that an economy would automatically correct itself. It had to they thought, because when output is produced by businesses, there must be an equivalent amount of income generated by that production. As French economist Jean Baptiste Say (1767-1832) said in his famous "Say's Law," "Supply creates its own demand."

So what did the classical economists say would happen if we suddenly experienced a significant downturn in the business cycle resulting in high unemployment? They reasoned that the unsold output would eventually force prices down. Low prices would in turn stimulate demand, and soon businesses would be rehiring the workers that had been laid off. What happened, though, if some people didn't get their jobs back?

The classical economists had a logical answer for this too. The lower wage would force cost-conscious businessmen to hire workers at lower wages. The wage rate might drop considerably, but eventually everyone would be back at work, or so the reasoning went. The classical economists thought the worst thing that could happen to this neat, self-correcting system was to allow government to interfere. In short, the bywords of the classical age might have been "stay cool and everything will take care of itself."

But then the Great Depression arrived. Something was terribly wrong. Unemployment went from bad to worse—and it *stayed* that way year after year. Prices dropped, as did wages and interest rates. But there were no consumer spending sprees, and businesses didn't invest or rehire the unemployed—even at the lower wage rates. Farmers found prices so low that at times they didn't bother to haul their crops to market. Incomes in turn were so depressed that few consumers had sufficient purchasing power to buy up what was available. The nation was running out of patience: You don't "stay cool" for five years or more when you are out of work. What we needed was a new theory that worked. The time was ripe for the genius of J. M. Keynes. Let's now examine his theory in greater detail.

Keynes And The Great Depression

To fully understand Keynes's ideas, we must develop a new model of our economy. It will be something like our old demand model, but now we have to take into consideration the markets for *all* goods and services. When we talk about total supply, we mean the real GNP. As for the total demand, we are speaking of the sum of all

types of spending—consumption, business investment, and government spending.

What would the total supply curve look like in our new model?
Recall that our supply curve in Chapter 3 was a description of how
much of one product suppliers wanted to provide at different
prices. We now want that same information with respect to total
supply, but this time we are dealing with the variables of spending
and output instead of price and quantity.

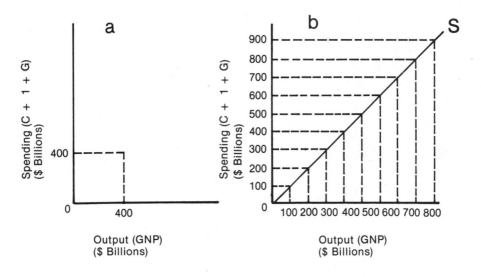

Figure 8-3

Thus we ask the suppliers (all businesses): "If the expected
amount of spending were $400 billion dollars, how much output
(GNP) would you want to supply?" It should be obvious that if
spending were at a level of $400 billion, businesses would theoreti-
cally want to supply the *same* amount of GNP, i.e., $400 billion (see
Figure 8–3a). To put it differently, suppliers would only produce
$400 billion of GNP if they could be sure that it would be bought
up.

All the other points on our total supply curve (see Figure 8-3b)
are thus quite easy to locate. For example, if there were $800 bil-
lion worth of spending (C + I + G), then businesses would want to
supply $800 billion worth of GNP output. In general, any amount

of spending will be matched with an equivalent amount of GNP supply. Each dot on the curve is therefore in a straight line equally distant from both the output and spending axes. Our supply curve (which doesn't really curve) thus begins in the lower left corner and shoots straight up to the right on an angle of 45 degrees.

Now let's look at total demand. To draw our demand curve, we must answer the following question: "How do spenders react to changes in their income?" Let's look at an example. Suppose your individual income this year was $5,000, but next year it was reduced to $2,000? What would happen to your spending pattern for next year? Most people faced with this situation would probably spend more than the $2,000 income at least in the short run. We will say you spend $4,000 even though your income is lower. (For a while, therefore, you will be borrowing money.) This point in Figure 8–4 is in the lower left corner, representing $4,000 spending but only $2,000 income. Let's now move up the income scale: Your income is now $8,000, and you find that you are

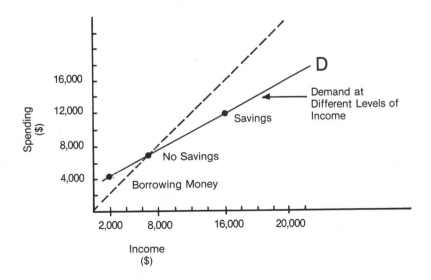

Demand Curve for an Individual

Figure 8-4

spending all of it. We will label this point on our demand curve "no savings." Finally, at a $16,000 income you are able to save some since you're spending only $12,000.

But what about the overall economy? Will the total demand—that is, C + I + G—have a shape similar to the demand curve in Figure 8–4? Yes. It is reasonable to assume that at low income levels we tend to spend more (at least in the short run) than our income, and as our incomes leap upward, the tendency is to save. Community spending patterns would thus be similar to patterns of individual families. Let's see now what "total supply" and "total demand" look like together (see Figure 8–5).

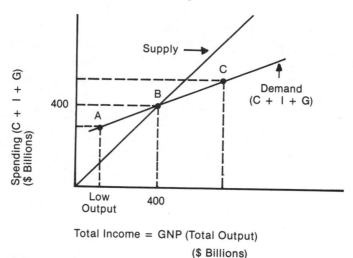

Figure 8-5

Note in Figure 8–5 that we have added GNP (total output) to the horizontal axis along with total income. The reader may wonder how we can equate both concepts. Are they the same?

Yes, because for every dollar's worth of output there will also be a dollar's worth of income generated. Thus, if we added up the incomes from all economic activity (wages, rents, profits, and interest), the total would be equivalent to the final value of our goods and services (GNP). Take, for example, the chair you are presently sitting in. Isn't its final price a "summary" of all the different incomes that went into producing and distributing the chair? Thus, by definition, total incomes = GNP = total output.

Returning to our diagram of total supply and demand (see Figure 8–5), we see that there is an equilibrium level, point B, of income where aggregate supply crosses aggregate demand (just as in Chapter 3 we had an equilibrium for the supply and demand for corn). To prove that B must be the equilibrium, let's see what would happen if we were not at this point. What will take place at point A for example?

At point A, we find that the spending level (C + I + G) is *greater* than the amount of output produced. There can be no equilibrium under these conditions because if spending is greater than output, businesses must crank up their factories to meet the surplus demand (remember that businesses want to supply whatever is demanded). Thus at A, forces are set into motion that push output to higher levels (i.e., toward B).

The economy can't remain at point C for very long either. Here, the amount of spending is *less* than the amount of output. This situation forces producers to cut back output—GNP will go down, and soon we will return to the equilibrium point. B is the only point on our graph where production exactly matches the level of spending; hence, it is the only point of continuous stability.

We are now in a position to understand John M. Keynes's great discovery. He saw that an economic system might be in a *stable equilibrium at a depression level of GNP*; i.e., graphically, if supply crossed through demand at a low level of national income, the country might sit there for years and years. Classical economists talked endlessly about falling wages and falling prices in the 1930s, but these same self-regulating mechanisms never pulled us out of the worst depression in U.S. history. What was needed was a new economic policy.

Fiscal Policy

What was Keynes's prescription? If we closely study the total supply-demand graph, we should be able to see what ought to be done. What is needed is to somehow "lift up" the total demand curve to an ideal point where supply crosses demand at a full employment level of GNP. Let's see how this would look on our supply-demand graph (see Figure 8–6).

Politicians, facing unhappy citizens without jobs, are not interested in some obscure theory; they need policies that can be translated into direct action. Keynes's basic prescription for lifting the

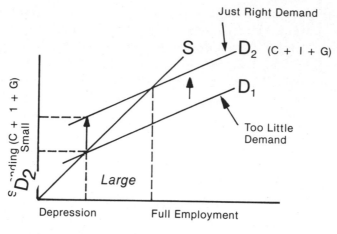

Figure 8-6

total demand curve was to have the government stimulate demand by *injecting new spending* into the economy. It can do this in two ways:

1. Increase government spending G (without altering taxes)
2. Decrease taxes (without altering government spending), thus increasing C, consumption spending

Either or both of these two *fiscal* (budgetary) policies will shift the total demand upward as can be seen in Figure 8–6.

Now look closely at the diagram in Figure 8–6. Do you notice anything unusual? A careful examination of the upward shift in demand shows that a relatively *small* increase in spending results in a *large* increase in output and incomes. For example, a $10 billion increase in government spending might result in a $20 billion (or more) increase in GNP. In short, any extra dollars spent are supercharged dollars! Economists call this the *multiplier effect*. Why are these new spending dollars multiplied? Let's look at an illustration. If, for example, the government cuts my taxes by $5, my own income will have gone up by that amount. I may spend all or part of that $5. Let's say I save $1 and spend the rest. My $4 expenditure suddenly becomes extra income for someone else, perhaps the plumber who fixed my leaky bathroom sink. The plumber, in turn, will save a little and spend the remainder, and so will the next person and the next. Now if $5 of extra spending has a super-charged effect, so will an extra $5 billion or $50 billion. Of course, this effect can work in reverse too; i.e., a $5 billion reduction in spending will obviously reduce GNP by much more than the original $5 billion.

Although the strategy to cure a recession can be rather simply stated—increase government spending and reduce taxes—the administration of these policies is another story. Any time you adjust expenditures and taxes you are tampering with the federal budget. What would the impact on our federal budget be if we lowered taxes and simultaneously increased government expenditures? We would obviously have a *deficit*, and budgetary deficits are usually considered "bad economics." Indeed in the 1930s, "spending your way into prosperity" seemed rather odd to some and even dangerous to others. The federal budget simply had to be balanced.

A serious and unfortunate occurrence, the economic disaster of the 1930s, might therefore have been avoided with a little budgetary manipulation. Even as recently as the Kennedy administration, members of congress were not totally receptive to the idea of stimulating the economy with a tax cut. However, when the Kennedy tax bill was passed in 1964 the sluggish economy steamed ahead with such speed that the taxes collected on higher incomes eventually paid back the deficit that had been incurred by the original tax cut!

It was, in fact, the spending for the Vietnam War *and* expensive social programs (of the late 1960s) plus the huge upsurge in OPEC oil prices (of the mid-1970s) that spoiled what might have been an age of real economic growth with only moderate inflation. Instead, the decade of the 1970s brought Americans a new age of high inflation.

So what would J. M. Keynes have said about inflation? What fiscal policies would now be in order? To answer this, let's take a look at the inflation problem on our total-supply-and-demand graph (see Figure 8–7). Obviously, the problem is now *too much demand*. The economy is producing maximum output, but the spending level is even greater than the available GNP. It's a classic example of demand-pull inflation where "too many dollars are chasing after too few goods." Looking at the chart, we see that the demand line is intersecting with supply far above the ideal and should come down to a noninflationary equilibrium. Although we may not be able to achieve zero inflation and full employment at the same time, there is no reason why we can't try for a balance of moderate inflation and near full employment (see point A).

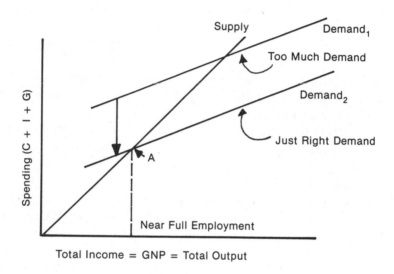

Figure 8-7

The correct antiinflationary prescription to pull demand down would therefore be to raise taxes, lower government spending, and generally work toward a budgetary *surplus*. Indeed, this solution seems relatively simple. So why is it so difficult to administer an antiinflationary economic policy?

To come to grips with the problem of inflation, we must understand the mysteries of the political process, since fiscal policy is ultimately decided by the President and Congress. Let's return for a moment to Keynes's prescriptions for combating unemployment. Although at one time there were some qualms about budgetary deficits, the remedies themselves—cutting taxes and increasing spending—can be almost "enjoyable" for a politician. Everyone likes a hefty tax cut, and the special interest groups—from the Army to the Peace Corps, from the poverty worker to the peanut farmer— thrive on additional spending programs. The cure for a recession then is a kind of "happy problem," because every politician from the President on down stands to gain in popularity with each new tax cut; with each new subsidized program; and, of course, with each additional worker put back on the job.

Inflation is something else, however. The economist's recommendations to increase taxes and cut back vested interest programs can be political suicide. In fact, a number of economists have concluded that the Keynesian remedies for inflation are simply inoperable because of these political realities.

Thus, up to the 1970s we could say that the Keynesian revolution in economic policy gave us a good measure of economic security. Indeed our record has been pretty good in avoiding serious economic downturns since the 1930s. Most economists felt then that unless there were new and unknown factors looming in the near future (war, global drought, etc.), we would probably never live through a great depression again—thanks in large part to J. M. Keynes!

But then the 1970s arrived with an energy crunch and unacceptable rates of inflation. Suddenly Keynesian policies did not seem to be working. Not only was there political paralysis in dealing with inflation (including the failure of price-wage controls), but we were also moving toward a new era of inflation and recession combined. By the mid-1970s we were hearing the ominous word *stagflation* (stagnation + inflation) more and more, and by 1975 it was apparent that for the first time in our history, we would have inflation rates of over 8 percent combined with a bonafide recession! Some economists were advocating contractive fiscal policies to combat inflation, and others wanted just the opposite; i.e., large tax cuts to help put people back to work. In short, there were no longer any simple Keynesian remedies.

Thus, the stage was set in the early 1980s for a new approach to emerge—*supply-side economics*. Supply-side theory revolves around two key ideas that are intimately intertwined: economic incentives and economic growth. More specifically, the assumption was made that what our stagflated economy needed was not more spending stimulus but *greater incentives to improve the supply of goods and services.*

The government (under the Reagan administration) chose to encourage these incentives by reducing overall tax rates. The centerpiece supply-side legislation in 1981 was large, across-the-board, individual tax-rate cuts, which were designed to stimulate work effort and generate greater savings. It was hoped that this tax cut would translate into more investment spending, and the additional investment plus work incentive would, in turn, enhance the nation's productivity (output/worker). Improved productivity might then moderate inflation and promote growth. Finally, the resulting growth would (according to the theory) generate such a large increase in the nation's income that the additional tax revenues would eventually pay back the short-term loss of revenue caused by the lower tax rates. If everything worked as intended, we would have a balanced budget and higher growth and productivity, but without any inflationary penalty.

Supply-side recommendations also included more generous tax credits for business investment and reducing the web of government regulation that often frustrated business activity while adding to costs. The supply-side theorists claimed that far too much attention had been paid to stimulating the demand side, to enforcing cumbersome regulations, and to evolving a tax system that discouraged saving and work effort, thus leaving the supply-side of the equation to languish with low productivity and high inflation.

Actually, supply-side economics is not an entirely new idea. We already noted Jean Baptiste Say's emphasis on supply, which he was certain would, sooner or later, "create its own demand." Also, economic philosophers David Hume (1711-1776) and Charles Montesquieu (1689-1775) warned their eighteenth-century readers that excessive tax rates would cause a diminishing work effort. In fact, no one perhaps better described the central thesis of supply-side economics better than Montesquieu, when he wrote:

> Nature is just to all mankind; she repays them for their labors; she renders them industrious because she attaches the greatest recompense to the greatest works. But if an arbitrary power snatches away the rewards of nature, one will learn distaste for work, and inactivity will appear to be the only good.[31]

Supply-side economics is thus one idea competing for attention. Recall too that there is another group of economists who look upon the future as a period of dwindling world resources and are thus skeptical about the possibility of continued economic expansion. Their ideas, in contrast to those of supply side, revolve around the question of how to rearrange the economic system so that we can be reasonably well off without the necessity for continual exponential economic growth.

At any rate, new theories eventually supersede the old. Creative and innovative ideas, combined with specific policies to deal with changing economic conditions, are continuously needed. Hence, we will always be looking for economic philosophers like an Adam Smith or a John M. Keynes—this time, however, matching wits with our own troubled times.

Chapter 9

MONEY

Choose fifty of your friends, acquaintances, or relatives and imagine that you are all shipwrecked on a large, lovely island in the middle of the South Pacific. At first, it is an idyllic life as everyone lounges on the sunny beach waiting for the rescue ship to sail into view, but after a few days you begin to realize the seriousness of your predicament. With grim faces, everyone gathers on the beach to map out some kind of survival oriented plan.

A government is elected and soon the necessary specialized tasks are taken up by different individuals. Since Joe Jones is a carpenter, he volunteers to build thatched huts for all the families. Smith and Baker are assigned to make fishing boats and nets. Chester Olson will gather wild foods for the community larder.

Time passes. The island economy becomes more specialized and complex. Before too long, however, major problems arise as the group experiences bottlenecks in their transactions. Individuals become frustrated when they attempt to get their thatched roofs mended or to obtain food for the evening meal. What's wrong?

The problem is that our little economy has become so complex that it needs a monetary system to keep it running smoothly. The islanders are currently using *barter* for each and every exchange. This works fine on a limited scale, but add a few more skills and a few more people and the community begins to encounter some major problems.

As an example, suppose that your specific skill is mending clothing. One day you decide you would like some of Chester's fine wild foods, and you propose to trade your service for part of Chester's

1ST DAY

DEAR JOURNAL:
    THERE ARE FIFTY OF US NOW STRANDED ON THIS ISLAND DUE TO OUR SHIPWRECK. WEATHER'S SUNNY & RESCUE BOAT IS DUE SOON.   FOUND A POLAROID CAMERA.

2ND DAY

WE ELECTED A GOVERNMENT TODAY, AND ASSIGNED TASKS TO EVERYONE. JOE WILL BE BUILDING HUTS, SMITH & BAKER WILL BE MAKING FISHING BOATS & NETS, AND CHESTER WILL BE HUNTING FOR WILD FOODS.

stores. Unfortunately, Chester tells you he doesn't need any of his clothing mended; so what do you do? In a moneyless economy, you would have to find a third party who not only needed clothing repaired but also had a service that Chester wanted. If you couldn't find that third person, you would be out of luck.

Thus, everyone on the island begins to see the need to develop some kind of monetary supply to facilitate exchange. Money that is effectively doing its job functions as a universally accepted *medium of exchange*. It also acts as a *standard of value*. As such, the money supply has a single monetary unit (for example, a dollar) that is a common denominator for all economic goods and services. (It's really amazing, for example, that we can compare a dollar's worth of hamburger with a billion dollar nuclear reactor—both with the same unit of currency!). Finally, money can be used as a *store of value*. It can be saved or spent, hoarded or invested. It's a marvelous tool, and, without a doubt, one of mankind's most useful inventions.

The islanders thus elect a banker (John Jacob Harrison III) and give him the responsibility of devising a monetary system for the island. Since John has never thought much about the characteristics of money, he forms a banking committee to discuss the issue. "Let's first list the different attributes that our new money system should have," says John as the committee sits down for a meeting. Baker then makes the first point. "Whatever we use for money must be fairly *durable* and something that can be *easily transferred* from person to person." Everyone nods in agreement.

Then after a moment's silence, Joe Jones suddenly says, "There must be a basic unit (like the dollar) that can be *divided* into smaller units as well as *multiplied* into larger units, right?" The group feels that although this is a sound point in theory, it is impractical on the island because of the limited supply of materials suitable for money.

Chester, sitting off by himself, is thinking very hard about something. He suddenly stands up and says, "Hold on, hold on. The most important thing about money is its *limited supply*—too much of the stuff will make it worthless." Everyone is impressed by Chester's insight. John (the banker) says, "You're absolutely right, Chester, but you haven't gone far enough." There is a hushed silence as John formulates his thoughts and then says, "Yes, our money

15TH DAY

JOHN JACOB HARRISON III'S REPORT
1. MONEY MUST BE DURABLE, EASILY TRANS-
FERED, DIVISIBLE, HAVE LIMITED SUPPLY,
AND BE EASILY DUPLICATED ONLY BY THE
ISLAND BANK.

13TH DAY

PROBLEMS!, EXAMPLE - JONES THE CARPENTER
WANTED SOME FOOD BUT CHESTER REFUSED
TO TRADE !! — WE NEED A MONETARY
SYSTEM - SOME MEDIUM OF EXCHANGE.
JONN JACOB HARRISON IS STUDYING THIS.

supply must be limited, but we must also be able to *expand* the amount of money in the economy as the economy itself expands. We have a problem here because whatever we use for money must be easy for us (the authorized bankers) to duplicate, but very difficult or impossible for any unauthorized person to reproduce. We therefore need to be quite careful of what we choose to use as money."

Baker thinks that buttons could be used. "The banking committee would need authorization to remove all the buttons from the islander's clothing. . . ." But before Baker can say another word, he is told to sit down and think of something else. Someone now suggests "shoelaces." It is argued that the laces could be cut up into different denominations. Other suggestions include everything from braided hair to pieces of paper with the banking committee's signatures. Jones remembers reading somewhere that cigarettes had been used successfully for money in the prisoner-of-war camps during World War II. The committee votes on the various suggestions and decides to try the idea of signed pieces of paper.

The last question the islanders have to face is how the committee is going to make this currency valuable. What, in fact, makes *any* currency valuable? Shifting now from our desert island illustration to the U.S. economy, we might therefore ask, "What makes our own dollar valuable?"

The U.S. Dollar

Many people are under the misconception that the dollar's value is maintained by "backing it up" with a precious metal such as gold or silver. They may be surprised to discover, however, that the last vestige of gold backing (25 percent) was removed by Congress in 1967 in order to release gold reserves for international monetary obligations.

The answer really boils down to an intangible quality that revolves around *trust*. Money is valuable because we have faith that each one of us will accept it as a legitimate medium of exchange. If all of a sudden everyone thought that money had no value, then, indeed, it would have no value. Fortunately, there is no reason for people to abandon faith in their dollars—unless, of course, the government doesn't do its job. An example of this

16TH DAY

STILL MONEY PROBLEMS – WHAT TO USE!
THE SUGGESTIONS SO FAR ARE BUTTONS,
BRAIDED HAIR, CIGARETTES, AND NOTES
FROM THE BANKING COMMITTEE.

LOTS OF ARGUMENT

17TH DAY

TODAY WE'VE FINALLY AGREED ON
ISSUING BANK COMMITTEE NOTES!!
THEY WILL BE OUR OFFICIAL MONETARY
UNITS – EACH ONE WILL CONTAIN
THE SIGNATURES OF EACH MEMBER OF
OUR BANKING COMMITTEE.

would be the event in which the government issued too much money. In this case, money becomes *too* plentiful, and there would be a relative shortage of things to buy. We would then experience inflation. Under extreme conditions of hyperinflation, the population might well lose faith in the government's currency and return to bartering or develop black market currencies.

On the other hand, if there is not enough money to go around, normal economic transactions would be stifled, which can also be dangerous for the economy. We need to have just the right balance between output and money in order for our dollars to remain valuable.

There was a time, however, when our citizens did not accept the legitimacy of the federal currency. The man who became our first President spoke with great fervor on this subject.

> George Washington . . . denounced those who refused to accept at full value the bills of the Continental Congress as "pests to society and the greatest enemies we have to the happiness of America. I would to God that some one of the more atrocious in each state was hung in gibbets upon a gallows five times as high as the one prepared by Haman."[32]

Faith and trust do not come automatically. They are earned by careful monetary regulation and controls. How then is the U.S. money supply controlled? A good question, yet it is one that most Americans could probably not answer correctly.

It is generally thought that our money supply is controlled simply by turning on and off the printing presses. If we want more money, the government just prints it up. This notion is only partly true since our money supply (i.e., immediately spendable assets) is more than just *currency* (bills and coins); it is also in the form of *demand deposits* or checking accounts. In fact, currently there is considerably more money in demand deposit form than in total currency. Thus, in order to control the money supply, we must be able to regulate these demand deposit dollars as well as paper currency. How is this done?

Think of the billions of dollars in checking accounts throughout the United States. Surely much of this money must be derived from a variety of credit forms such as mortgages, installment credit, and business credit. It would be reasonable to assume then that if the government could in some way *manipulate credit conditions*, it would have some control over the money supply. Easy credit conditions usually mean more loans; more loans, in turn, mean more dollars flowing through the economy.

Thus, if the government can control credit conditions, it will not only affect the money supply, but, perhaps more importantly, it will also be able to influence the total amount of spending. This means that whoever is in charge of the money supply (through manipulating credit) can have as much power over the economic system as those who control the federal budget. We already know that the President and Congress decide on the budget, but who is responsible for regulating credit conditions and the money supply?

The Federal Reserve System

The money supply is determined and regulated in large part by our central banking system, the Federal Reserve (often called the "Fed"). In fact, if we were to pinpoint where the major decisions are made on money matters, we would zero in on the seven-man Board of Governors of the Federal Reserve System in Washington, D.C. From there we would move down to the twelve regional Federal Reserve Banks situated in major cities around the country. Take a moment now to look at a dollar bill and see from which Federal Reserve Bank it is issued (the source is written around the large letter to the left of Washington's face). Your dollar was probably issued by a Federal Reserve Bank nearby. The three bills I looked at in my wallet came from Minneapolis (I), St. Louis (H), and Chicago (G).

Monetary control then flows from the twelve regional reserve banks down to the commercial banks that "belong" to the Federal Reserve System. These commercial banks (often called *member banks*) hold stock in the Federal Reserve System and are required to follow certain policies that the Fed establishes. Perhaps you know of a "First National" bank in your area; you can be sure that it is one of these member banks. However, not all banks belong to the Fed. Of all the U.S. banks, only about one third are members of the system. Yet those that do belong are the "workhorses" of the banking industry handling some 70 percent of all U.S. bank deposits.

The profit philosophy of a typical commercial bank is simple: "Borrow money cheap, lend it dear." The difference between the

rate of interest paid out for savings, checking, and other deposi-
tors' accounts and the rate of interest charged for mortgage and
installment loans is the primary source of banking profits. Thus,
the commercial bank's major responsibility is to take in the
deposits from those who want to save and, in turn, to lend out that
money to those who want to borrow. The commercial bank is what
economists call a *financial intermediary*, the middleman between
savers and investors.

If the function of commercial banks is to hold deposits and to
make loans, what then is the function of the regional Federal
Reserve bank? The regional banks are a kind of "banker's bank."
They hold deposits and make loans to member banks. The deposits
are called *reserves* (hence the name Federal Reserve), and the loans
are called *discounts*. The regional reserve banks also function as
clearing houses for the millions and millions of checks that are
sent around the country, and they also supervise the member
banks in their region. Finally, the twelve regional reserve banks
supply their districts with federal reserve notes (dollar bills) and
other currency.

However, the real power within the Federal Reserve System—
the power to influence credit and spending and ultimately unemployment and inflation—rests with the powerful Board of Governors and its various committees. How then do they go about their
job of influencing the money supply, and what mysterious tools
does this small band of government bankers have at its command?

We learned earlier in this chapter that the key to influencing
the money supply is the control of credit. Therefore, if the Fed
makes it difficult for the commercial banking system to give out
loans, this should cause a slowing in the growth of the money
supply. If loans are easy to obtain, the money supply will grow
faster than before. What is needed then is a way to influence the
loan decision of every bank officer in the country. To see how this
is accomplished, we must first understand the concept of bank
reserves.

Every bank that belongs to the Federal Reserve System must
agree to set aside a certain percentage of its deposits in the form of
reserves. For example, the Fed guidelines might say that your local
bank must set aside at least 12 percent of its checking accounts
(*demand deposits*) and 4 percent of its savings accounts (*time*

deposits) as reserves. We call these percentages *reserve ratios*. Let's look at an example to see how this works.

Suppose that our Plum City bank with a total of $1,000 in its checking accounts decides to join the Federal Reserve System. If the reserve ratio for checking accounts is 12 percent, then our bank must set aside a reserve of $120. After thinking about this situation, the Plum City First National Bank directors might decide that if they want to make any loans, they better have some *excess reserves* above and beyond the required $120. Do you see why?

The reason is the following: If any of the Plum City bank's customers borrow money and then cash their loan checks at another bank, Plum City would lose reserves and the other bank would gain them. To explain, assume that our bank (with only $120 in reserves) just loaned Sam Smith $500. This money, of course, immediately goes into Sam's checking account. Suppose that he then takes the full $500 and spends it all out of state while vacationing in Florida. If Sam spends his money this way, there won't be sufficient funds to transfer to the Florida bank (remember that all payments between banks involve a transfer of reserves). Therefore, in order to *safely* loan Sam $500, the Plum City bank would be wise to have at least $500 in excess reserves to cover the loan.

In summary, a bank's capacity to lend out money will depend primarily on the size of its excess reserves. If there are generally large amounts of excess reserves in banks throughout the country, we will usually find *easy* money conditions, and if banks around the country are holding few excess reserves, we can then expect *tight* money conditions. We should also note here that if there are "new" dollars loaned out and therefore "new" money created, other banks will receive this additional money. They can, in turn, use this money (after putting away a fraction as required reserves) for further expansion of the money supply—something like the multiplier effect of the last chapter. Naturally, this monetary multiplier works in reverse if there is a net reduction in loans.

Monetary Policy

The obvious question we must now ask is: "Since the key to controlling credit conditions and the money supply lies in controlling excess reserves, exactly how does the Federal Reserve influence the amount of excess reserves in the overall banking system?"

One way is simply to raise or lower the reserve ratio. To use an exaggerated example, what would happen if the Fed increased the reserve ratio for checking accounts from 12 to 20 percent? Suddenly the excess reserve position (and the potential to make loans) would be diminished by billions and billions of dollars. On the other hand, if the Fed lowered the reserve ratio, the banks would have an automatic expansion of excess reserves and an easing up of credit conditions. Power over the reserve ratio is thus translated into power over the money supply.

Another monetary tool used to manipulate excess reserves is the buying and selling of government securities. U.S. commercial banks are presently holding billions of dollars worth of government obligations—bonds, notes, and other securities. The banks purchase these because they frequently offer attractive interest rates. In order to *reduce* excess reserves, all the Fed has to do is *sell* more securities to the member banks. This reduction comes about because member banks pay for the securities by taking the money out of their reserve accounts. The immediate lowering of these reserves thus reduces the potential loaning capacity of the commercial bank, meaning tighter money conditions throughout the economy.

What if the Fed should decide to *buy* securities from member banks? Everything that occurred above will be reversed. The money from the Fed will enlarge the reserve accounts of the banks so that more "potential" money will be available for regular loans. Buying back securities from the member banks may, therefore, result in more loans; an increased growth in the money supply; and, hopefully, more spending.

The specific group that decides whether to buy or sell securities is the *Open Market Committee*. It should be noted that these open-market operations are used more frequently than changing the reserve ratio. When the Fed changes the reserve ratio—particularly upward—it causes great hardships for banks who are "all loaned up," that is, have already lent out their maximum amount of money. The flexibility and ease of open-market operations make it the number one monetary tool of the Federal Reserve.

Our last major monetary control is called the *discount rate*. Do you remember from our earlier discussion that one of the Fed's services to member banks is a borrowing privilege? The loans that are made to member banks are called discounts, and the interest rate on these loans is, of course, the *discount rate*. By raising the discount rate, the Fed will discourage borrowing by member banks. Those banks who reduce the amount of money they borrow from the Fed will themselves have less money to lend out to their own customers. On the other hand, lowering the discount rate will encourage member bank borrowing, and these banks will then have more excess reserves to meet the local demand for mortgages, installment loans, and so on. Lowering the discount rates might also *indirectly* influence other interest rates throughout the economy. For example, after hearing that the discount rate has gone down, most member banks would be inclined to "return the favor" by lowering the interest rates of their own loans. These three controls—reserve ratio, open market operations, and discount rates—are thus the monetary tools by which the Fed not only regulates the money supply but also contributes to the stabilization of the economy.

Let's now summarize what we learned about monetary policies and apply it to what we already know of supply and demand. First, inflation. If our country were facing severe inflation, the probable course of action taken by the Fed would be one, two, or all of the following, as shown in Figure 9–1:

1. To raise the reserve ratios
2. To raise the discount rate
3. To sell government securities

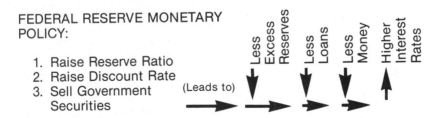

Figure 9-1

If money became very scarce, the overall interest rates might go sky high as they did in 1970, 1974, and the early 1980s. The combined impact of high interest rates and tight money conditions would probably discourage business investment spending (and also interest-rate-sensitive durables such as autos and housing). This sequence of events as graphed in Figure 9–1, ultimately leads to a reduction in investment spending and is thus the basis of the Fed's antiinflationary monetary policies. We have come full circle; our economic controls for influencing spending are now complete.

Recall our old diagram of total supply and demand from the previous chapter. There we described the Keynesian fiscal policies that could raise or lower consumption spending (C) through changes in taxes and government spending (G). The total demand curve might rise or fall, depending on whether we were facing inflation or recession.

Now we know that monetary policies also have a profound impact on the third component of total spending: investment (I). Monetary policies that combat inflation would therefore have the following effect on our total-supply-demand diagram (see Figure 9–2).

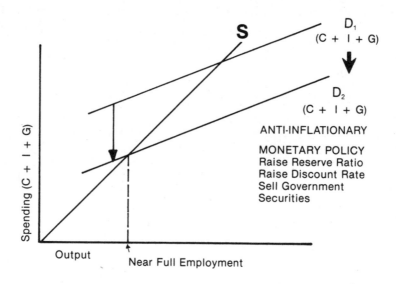

Figure 9-2

For recession, the appropriate monetary policies for easing credit conditions should be:

1. To lower the reserve ratio
2. To buy government securities
3. To lower the discount rate

In theory then, excess reserves would first increase. Then, as the money supply grew, credit would be easier to obtain. More money in the system would eventually drive interest rates down. Easier money plus low interest rates would then encourage investment spending, which would help lift up the total-demand curve.

How closely do these theories match reality? Economists are quick to point out that they are much more effective in combating inflation than recession. During an inflationary period, the monetary screws can be tightened until money and credit are actually squeezed off. In 1970 and 1981, we experienced some of the harmful side effects of ultratight money, e.g., a "depression" in the housing industry when mortgage rates were driven to unreasonable levels.

On the other hand, if we lower interest rates and make credit easily available, we cannot force more investment. For example, our depression years saw very low interest rates, yet the other negative factors, such as stock market slump, low incomes, loss of confidence, and general pessimism, far outweighed the expansionary effects of easy money.

In conclusion, whatever limitations the Federal Reserve System faces, today or in the future, it will nonetheless continue to be a critical economic institution, hopefully helping us to maintain a stable economy, a healthy commercial banking system, and, finally, a trustworthy monetary base in which we can go about our private economic affairs with a feeling of confidence.

Part II
MICROECONOMICS

Chapter 10

WHAT IS MICROECONOMICS?

From the big concepts such as money and banking, or unemployment and inflation, we now return to that world that was encompassed by our "economic microscope," i.e., the world of microeconomics.

This time, however, we will be delving into much greater detail and analysis than we ever dared before. What then is microeconomics all about, and equally important, just how does one *begin* to think about the complexities of this fascinating area of economics?

Design

I like to think of microeconomics as a problem in design. What we will be studying in the next ten chapters is how you, I, the grocer down the street, and even the large corporation—the "bits and pieces" of our economy—design our lives and our organizations to meet certain economic objectives. Microeconomics is like a game with certain rules, constraints, and ultimate objectives. Consumers, for example, are constrained by their limited income. Businesses must work within the confines of their production costs, their competition, and their demand. Both groups must obey the rules of the marketplace.

But what about the goals or objectives of our players? In microeconomics, the key objective is relatively uncomplicated—maximization. Therefore when we as consumers, businesses, or workers put on our respective "economic hats," we want to maximize the following economic goals:

- The consumer attempts to get the largest amount of utility (satisfaction) from his limited income.

- The worker wants to maximize income while maintaining or enlarging leisure time.

- The business tries to maximize profits within the constraints of costs, demand, and competition.

It is perhaps not surprising that economists have been criticized for making and promoting the assumption of "economic man as maximizer." Indeed there may be some justification. The word, *maximization*, itself carries the connotation of operating with a kind of brutal efficiency while pursuing profits or enlarging one's income base at any cost. As mentioned in Chapter 2, there are people who feel that many of our social and economic ills originate from this maximization principle. Some of these problems might include the following: worker exploitation, environmental pollution, wars, and the disappearance of craftsmanship to name a few.

Sometimes we see attempts to develop alternatives to income maximization in an effort to promote greater worker satisfaction. New experiments are tried all the time. I am intrigued, for example, by a little magazine called *Briarpatch Review, a Journal of Right Livelihood and Simple Living* that has suggested an alternative to profit maximization in small businesses:

> If you take "making a lot of money" off the list of reasons for being in business you can pretty easily replace it with "fun," since you then have time to enjoy yourself by interacting with others.[33]

Or consider E. F. Schumacher's provocative book *Small is Beautiful* in which he describes a number of reasons, other than income maximization, why people work. The purposes of work, Schumacher explains in his chapter "Buddhist Economics," should be the following:

> . . . to give a man a chance to utilize and develop his faculties; to enable him to overcome his ego centeredness by joining with other people in a common task; and to bring forth the goods and services needed for a becoming existence.
>
> . . . To organize work in such a manner that it becomes meaningless, boring, stultifying, or nerve-racking for the worker would be little short of criminal; it would indicate a greater concern with goods than with people . . .[34]

Of course, the philosophy of "making work meaningful" is certainly not a new one. As Schumacher points out, these traditions can be traced back to various sources, including Buddhism and, more recently, the writings of Thoreau, Tolstoi, and Gandhi.

Microeconomics can also lead to the tendency to see human beings and organizations in purely quantitative terms—i.e., the more the profits, income, utility, etc., the better. Economists would agree that there is some truth to this allegation as well.

Perhaps economists do promote the idea of maximization to an unnecessary degree. Yet I believe most of them recognize that monetary maximization is really but *part* of our total existence. Any business or individual who becomes totally obsessed with narrow economic goals would indeed become a kind of monster and would have to be restrained. On the other hand, persons or businesses that totally disregard economic objectives will undoubtedly find their level of economic comfort, and perhaps their survival, threatened. It is true, therefore, that for the most part workers, consumers, and businesses do *tend toward* maximization goals. Economists' observations of microeconomic activity can thus help us to understand both ourselves and our organizations in that their theories frequently *do* reflect the way the "bits and pieces" of our economic system actually behave.

We could also look at this maximization process as symbolic of *any* activity or decision-making process that involves finite resources and freedom of choice . This returns us to the introductory statement concerning microeconomics as a process of designing our lives to achieve objectives while simultaneously recognizing certain constraints. I think if we look at microeconomics in this light, we may well discover important insights into human behavior.

Micro vs. Macro

Now let's take another look at the twin concepts of micro and macro and find out just how they relate to each other. Metaphorically, the relationship is quite simple, as we see in Ho-o's famous haiku:

A seedling shoulders up some crumbs of ground:
The fields are suddenly green for miles around![35]

In other words, the macro view is nothing more than the sum total of the micro details.

In economics, we can easily show the difference between micro and macro with graphs. Earlier (Chapter 8) you confronted the Keynesian model of total supply and demand. This graph is redrawn in Figure 10–1.

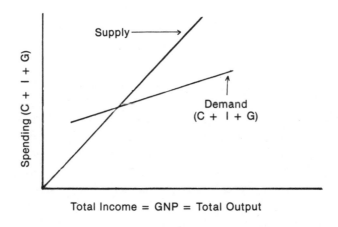

Figure 10-1

Figure 10–1 represents the world of macroeconomics—that area of economics dealing with the broad economic concepts such as gross national product (GNP), unemployment, growth, and inflation. We also saw (Chapter 3) the simple supply-and-demand graph that is depicted in Figure 10–2.

This single market is a good example of the smaller world of microeconomics, summarizing in a few simple lines a mass of information about the behavior of consumers (demand curve) and producers (supply curve). Is there any way to relate on one diagram our macro world of GNP and the micro world of individual markets? Yes! It can be done with our old acquaintance, the circular-flow diagram from Chapter 4 redrawn in Figure 10–3.

Notice in the flow picture that households and businesses deal with each other through the resource markets (on top) and the goods and services markets (on the bottom). As the various markets deliver resources and churn out final products, we begin to get a feel for the "piece-by-piece" make-up of our GNP. (Recall that

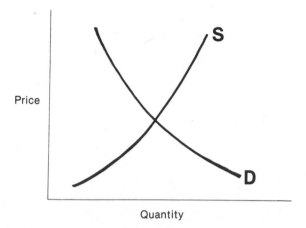

Figure 10-2

GNP, the key macroeconomic concept, is nothing more than the summation of all productive efforts that take place in the individual businesses.)

The economists who study the larger flows (macroeconomics) are mainly interested in the health of the whole system and thus spend much of their time devising policies that will hopefully move our economy toward full-employment, economic growth, and stable prices (see Chapters 8 and 9). On the other hand, those who study microeconomics spend most of their time analyzing the origin, the make-up, and the efficiency of individual markets and other economic processes.

Thus in our study of microeconomics, we will analyze such things as where the supply curve comes from or why a demand curve has its unique shape. You already learned, for example, that an individual's demand curve for say corn or hamburgers is downward sloping. The curve is "showing" us that when we reduce the price, more quantity is demanded. This, of course, is a logical idea, but we have yet to actually *prove* that this negative relationship between price and quantity must always be the case. Establishing such proof is one of our tasks in microeconomics.

Microeconomics can answer other questions as well. For example, why does your demand curve for hamburgers look

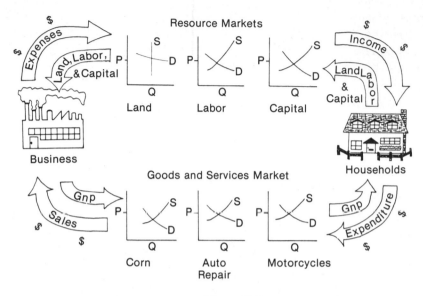

Figure 10-3

different from mine? Why are some people more sensitive to a price change than others? There are many subtleties in back of that simple looking demand curve, subtleties that challenge us to look deeper and deeper into an individual's economic behavior.

We must engage in a certain amount of economic and psychological research if we want to get at the fundamentals of microeconomics. We will, for example, have to take a close look at the consumer's income, preferences, and the prices of related goods before we can see what lies in back of "Joe Smith's" demand for hamburgers or any other product. Of course, once we understand Joe Smith's demand, we will be able to do the same thing for you or me or anyone else. This is what "micro" is all about.

Finally, in microeconomics we will carefully examine the supply curve. We will no longer be satisfied in saying, "It's logical that if corn prices go up, Farmer Brown will want to supply more corn." We must now dig deeper. To understand Farmer Brown's supply behavior, we have to study his costs of production and his revenues, which will help us set up procedures to determine how he maximizes profits at different prices. As you see, it can get pretty involved!

It should be worth the effort, though. By the middle of our micro analysis, we will have built our first competitive market model, and by the end we will have explored in more detail the models of oligopoly and monopoly and differentiated competition. But first things first: Let's now take a careful look at demand, its origins and its fundamental nature.

Chapter 11

BACKGROUND TO DEMAND

Consider the source of our economic behavior. What exactly motivates us to engage in economic activity? In large part, the answer to this question lies in the word, *consumption*, i.e., to use goods and services in order to survive and then to enjoy a standard of living commensurate with both our expectations and our dreams. For some, a small amount of consumption will do, but most of us want to have more of the good things that our economic system can provide.

Utility

From this basic assumption of human behavior, we can infer that any level of consumption brings with it a certain amount of satisfaction—or as economists say, *utility*. Utility can be a difficult thing to measure precisely. It is also difficult to make comparisons of utility between people. Thus, your utility from consuming an automobile or a banana is probably going to be different from mine or from anyone else's. Indeed, there might well be some surprises if we could actually measure utility between people. Depriving you of your fourth Cadillac, for example, might result in a greater loss of satisfaction for you than I would feel if I were to lose my one Ford. Even though you have four Cadillacs, the loss of that one might send you into a state of depression because all of your neighbors might have five or six. Nevertheless, we can say some important things about utility as long as we confine our discussion to one individual. For example, Mary Smith might tell us that she "seems" to be getting about 5 units of utility from eating a hamburger and around 2 units from consuming a banana. To determine if she is accurate about her utility estimates, we will give her 70¢ and offer her the opportunity to buy fractions of hamburgers or bananas. If we then price a full hamburger at 50¢ and a banana at 20¢ and observe that Mary spends her 70¢ for one hamburger and one banana, we could then assume that her rough utility ratio of 5 to 2 is correct.

Let's now make another utility observation, but this time we will stick to the consumption of one product such as the Cadillacs you owned in the earlier example. Even though we can't determine how much utility your fourth Cadillac gave you compared with my one Ford, we can nevertheless say that you probably received more utility from your *first* Cadillac compared with the fourth. Or to take a more realistic example, Mary's third hamburger (in the short run) will probably give her less satisfaction than her second, and her second less than her first.

But since I know more about my own utility levels than yours or Mary Smith's, I will turn to a more detailed illustration of this principle, using my own utility preferences. Thus, after considerable thought and experimentation, I come up with the following utility chart:

HAMBURGERS	MARGINAL UTILITY (MUh)
1	7
2	3
3	1
4	0

From these figures we see that my first hamburger gives me 7 units of utility. The second provides 3 additional units, and by the time I eat my third, my *additional utility* is only 1 unit. Economists call this additional utility (which is assigned to the consumption of a specific unit) *marginal utility* (MU). Obviously, I'm starting to get pretty full after two hamburgers, and after my third hamburger, I am completely full since the fourth is giving me no MU whatsoever. If somebody gave me that fourth hamburger free, I'd leave it on my plate. What, I wonder, would your utility chart look like for hamburgers? You might want to estimate one just for fun.

The Law Of Diminishing Utility

Can we make any generalization about this utility pattern? Apparently, the more one consumes of a given product, the less the MU. This principle would probably be true no matter whom we were talking about or what product we were examining. Economists have called this universal principle the *law of diminishing marginal utility*.

You can apply this principle to many types of human experience. Diminishing MU is worth remembering if you happen to be on a diet since that tenth spoonful of ice cream (or the fourth cookie) will undoubtedly give you less satisfaction than the first. It may also help explain why marriages sometimes go sour or why those once "exciting" jobs eventually become boring.

Sometimes it's helpful to visualize economic relationships such as this. Using the MU data given above, I can graph my diminishing MU curve as shown in Figure 11–1.

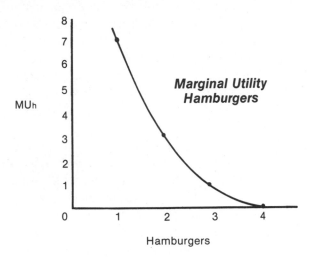

Figure 11-1

Keep in mind that this graph is my MU curve for hamburgers; your curve, or someone else's, would probably look somewhat different. Spend a moment sketching different possibilities, such as the MU curve for a "Wimpy" who can lovingly eat a dozen hamburgers before he gets full. What about a vegetarian? What about your curve, what would it look like?

Now we can begin to make some interesting observations about how a consumer might behave if given a choice between two products. How, for example, would the law of diminishing marginal utility help me find out how to maximize my satisfactions given a limited income?

To see how this is done, let's add a new product to my hamburger example—milkshakes. Let's assume that my milkshake marginal-utility chart looks something like this:

MILKSHAKES	MARGINAL UTILITY (MUm)
1	12
2	3
3	½

To be realistic, we must now add an income constraint. Let's assume, therefore, that I am given, say, $4 per day. To simplify, the price of a milkshake is $1, and the price of a hamburger is $1 as well. With all this information, how do I go about maximizing my total utility; i.e, how do I spend my limited income so that I might enjoy the highest possible level of total satisfaction?

The best method of maximizing my utility would be for me to use what economists call the *marginal decision approach*. Marginal decision making means undertaking a separate decision for each dollar at my disposal; thus, I would take my first dollar and ask the question: "Where will this dollar give me the greatest utility?"

If you compare the chart for milkshakes with that for hamburgers, you can easily see that I ought to spend my first dollar on a milkshake. That first milkshake will give me 12 units of utility, but that same dollar had I spent it on a hamburger would only give me 7 units of utility. My marginal decision-making approach now leads me to the next question: "How can I best spend my second dollar?" Then, "How can I best spend my third dollar, and after that, my fourth dollar?" A summary of my decisions can be seen in the following chart:

	Milkshakes (MUm)		Hamburgers (MUh)		
1st dollar	← 1	12 units	1	7 units →	2nd dollar
3rd dollar	← 2	3 units	2	3 units →	4th dollar
	3	½ unit	3	1 unit	
			4	0 units	

Thus, my second dollar would be spent on a hamburger while the third dollar would be a toss-up since both products would give me the same MU (3 units) per dollar. (In the example above, I chose a milkshake for my third dollar.) My last dollar would, in a sense, "balance things out" so that when all the income had been spent, the MU per dollar's worth of each product (i.e., 3 units per $1) would be equal. If you could obtain more utility from spending your last dollar on another product (french fries, for example), you would obviously want to spend the dollar on that other product.

Now if we had precise information concerning all the products we consumed (and therefore knew the MU of each) and also spent our money exactly as we wished (even for fractions of hamburgers or milkshakes), we would then attain the highest possible satisfaction if the MU per dollar's worth (i.e., the MU divided by the product price *MU/p*) of product A would be equal to that of B, which would equal that of C, and so forth. When these ratios are equal (as in the following chart), the consumer has, in a sense, "solved" his maximization problem; i.e., he has spent his limited income so that he gains the maximum amount of utility.

$$\frac{MU_A}{P_A} = \frac{MU_B}{P_B} = \frac{MU_C}{P_C} = \frac{MU_D}{P_D}$$

A = Hamburgers
B = Milkshakes
C = French Fries
D = Other Things

So far, so good, but there are still people who are bothered by our inability to measure utility precisely, as we tried to do in the preceding example. Fortunately, we do have another method by which we can solve the problem of consumer efficiency without having to give actual utility values. It is called *the indifference curve system*. Let's take a look.

Indifference Curves

First some background. Recall our earlier comment that economists have a little bit of "the psychologist" in them as well as a little of "the newspaper reporter." Economists could conceivably be running around with pencils and pads asking people questions relating to their incomes, consumption habits, work preferences, values, and so on. Answers to these questions in turn give the researcher insight into how consumers will behave under various economic conditions. At some point our economist-psychologist-reporter might eventually be able to discover some generalized principles (such as the law of diminishing marginal utility) that might become the basis of an important economic theory. The indifference-curve system is one of these techniques which allows us to ask some simple questions so that we can then derive some interesting generalizations and conclusions. Let's look at an example.

Pretend that you are the economic researcher and you ask me the following question: "If I gave you 1 milkshake and 3 hamburgers, you would derive a certain amount of utility from that combination, right?" I answer, "OK," and you then go on: "Let's call that amount of utility your "total utility level Y." Now if I reduce the number of hamburgers to 2, how many additional milkshakes would you need to keep yourself at total utility level Y?"

Suppose I answer, "I will need an extra 1/4 milkshake to make up for the lost hamburger. This means I will be totally indifferent about consuming a combination of either 3 hamburgers and 1 milkshake or 2 hamburgers and 1¼ milkshakes."

As a final question, you might ask me how many milkshakes I would need if I consumed only 1 hamburger yet wished to stay at total utility level Y. Let's say that I would need 2 full shakes to be indifferent to the other combinations. The following chart shows the results of your research:

"I am indifferent to"

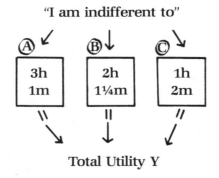

Total Utility Y

Thus, with any of the combinations in A, B, or C, I would be equally well off. That is, I would be "indifferent" about consuming at any of these points because my total utility stays the same in each case. Let's now graph these "points" of indifference using hamburgers on one scale and milkshakes on the other (see Figure 11–2). Once we connect our three points representing combinations A, B, and C, we have a smooth curve showing all the points of indifference. If, for example, you ask me, "Would you prefer to consume at A, B, C, or somewhere in between?," I would have to answer by saying, "I'm indifferent; all points give me equal satisfaction."

My indifference curve in Figure 11–2 might be described as having a "bow-like" shape. Economists say that it is "convex to the origin" with the origin always in the lower left-hand corner. You may wonder why my indifference curve (or anybody else's for that matter) has this general shape. Why isn't it a straight line or in the

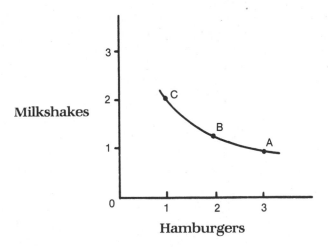

Figure 11-2

shape of a "dome"? The answer to this question lies in under-standing our law of diminishing marginal utility. Let's see how this works.

Look closely again at combination A in Figure 11–2; it repre-sents 3 hamburgers and 1 milkshake. If I happen to be consuming at point A, I am obviously "full" of hamburgers; recall that this third hamburger added very little to my overall satisfaction. Since this third hamburger is not that important to me, I am willing to "trade it off" (substitute) for just a quarter of a milkshake if I move to combination B. Also keep in mind that at point A milkshakes are dear to me since I'm only consuming one of them. Because each fraction of a shake is giving me great satisfaction, I'm unwilling to readily trade it off. Now let's look at combination C. Here, ham-burgers suddenly become much dearer to me while milkshakes are well into diminishing utility. Thus at C, I am willing to forego more milkshakes if I want more hamburgers. It is this subtle change in my desire to substitute milkshakes for hamburgers that gives this indifference line its unique shape.

In terms of geometry, we could say that the slope at point C is greater (i.e., steeper) than it is at point A. Economists call the slope at any given point on an indifference curve *the marginal rate of sub-stitution* (MRS). Thus, the MRS represents the number of milk-shakes that must be substituted to get an additional hamburger. As we gain more hamburgers, the MRS (and the slope) falls as we become less and less willing to substitute milkshakes for an additional hamburger. This falling slope can be seen in Figure 11–3.

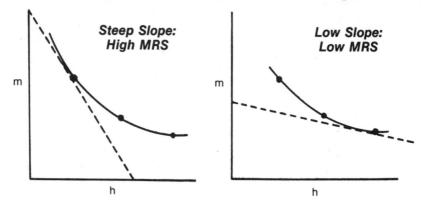

Figure 11-3

Having followed the discussion so far, you ought to have a general understanding of the indifference curve, remembering that your curve might be entirely different from someone else's. If, for example, you happened to "love" milkshakes while you were "so-so" about hamburgers, your indifference curve would be much flatter than mine, implying that it would take many hamburgers for you to trade off even a fraction of your milkshake. This curve might look something like the one in Figure 11–4.

Indifference Map

Needless to say, we could draw thousands of different indifference curves, each reflecting the unique consumption preferences of different individuals. And even for the same person we could show many *different levels* of utility. Remember that up to this point we have only discussed a single indifference curve that represented a total amount of utility at the "y" level. But there is also a curve somewhere below the "y" level that would represent a lower total level of satisfaction—let's call it the "x" level—and another curve showing even higher satisfaction than "y" that we might call total utility "z." Of course, we could have drawn many other indifference curves—ones above and below and between the three curves

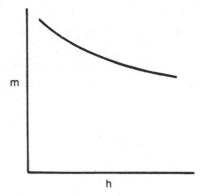

Figure 11-4

shown. These different levels of utility, represented by a series of indifference curves, are called an *indifference map*. My indifference map for milkshakes and hamburgers is shown in Figure 11-5.

One important advantage of using an indifference map over our earlier approach is that we now no longer need to assign actual utility values to the consumption of different products. For example, we really do not know how many *units of utility* are involved on the x curve, but we can still say with some certainty that x indifference

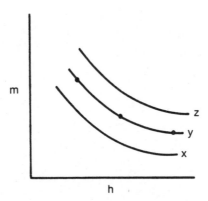

Figure 11-5

curve is lower than y. Thus, with all things equal, *one would rather consume on the higher curve.* The highest level of satisfaction in this illustration would thus be indifference curve z.

Now if products were free, we surely wouldn't hesitate to move up to the highest indifference curve possible. Of course, economic goods are not free, and in the real world we all must make painful choices because we all have a limited income. How then do we integrate a limited income into our analysis? We do it with a *budget line.*

The Budget Line

To understand the budget line, let's go back to the example where I was given an income of $4 per day, and both hamburgers and milkshakes were $1 each. If I were to spend all of my daily income on hamburgers (i.e., no milkshakes), I could buy 4. This means that my $4 budget allows me to operate at a level of consumption where I have 4 hamburgers and 0 milkshakes. Let's note this as one point on my budget line. Of course my $4 could also buy 2 hamburgers and 2 milkshakes or 3 hamburgers and 1 milkshake. These combinations, in turn, all represent other possibilities of consumption given my $4 income. In plotting these possibilities, I have, in effect, a budget line that shows every combination of hamburgers and milkshakes that can be purchased for $4. Figure 11–6 summarizes these data.

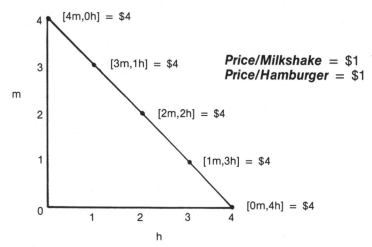

Figure 11-6

Sometimes it's helpful to see a budget line as a kind of "economic straight jacket"—a visual representation of the cruel world of economic reality. Of course we would all like our budgets to be larger, but they are not; and once we've been allowed just so much money to spend, we have to limit ourselves to the consumption possibilities that lie somewhere on the line.

Even though we are limited by this restricted budget, we nevertheless still have a certain amount of choice in terms of selecting the right "bundle" of goods that will give us the greatest satisfaction. This is but one more way to look at the fundamental economic problem of utility maximization. How do we solve the problem this time? How can we be sure we have made the best choice with our $4 income?

To answer these questions, all we need to do is combine the budget line with the indifference map. The combined system is shown in Figure 11–7.

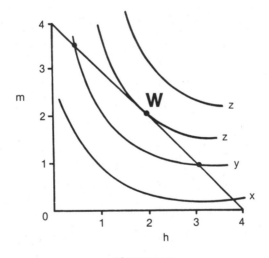

Figure 11-7

The solution can easily be seen on the graph. First note that *it is possible* to consume on indifference curve y. It crosses the $4 budget line in two places. But why should the consumer stop on indifference curve y when it's also possible to climb up to indifference curve z? Notice that there is only one point where the budget line is just tangent to indifference curve z; this point of tangency represents the approximate consumption of 2 hamburgers and 2 milkshakes.

Yet someone might logically ask, "If higher indifference curves represent higher satisfaction, why not go to the highest indifference curve of all, i.e., that of z*?" The answer is, of course, that z* is not consistent with the $4 budget constraint. There is, as you can see, no point on the graph where the highest indifference curve coincides with the budget. The very highest possible level of utility attainable with the $4 budget is the z level shown by that point of tangency, W, in Figure 11–7. Thus we can say that *individuals will maximize their utility by consuming at that point where the indifference curve is tangent to the budget line.*

Total utility will always be maximized at the point of tangency. It does not matter whose indifference map we are looking at, what the dollar income constraint is, or what goods and services we are looking at. This important conclusion will be great assistance to us as we explore the concept of demand in greater depth in the next chapter.

Chapter 12

DEMAND

Our goal in the previous chapter was to develop a simple model of consumer "efficiency" using the indifference curve and the budget line. In Figure 12–1, we see a summary of our efforts. The tangency of the budget line with the indifference curve shows us that point at which the consumer maximizes utility under an income constraint. (Note that we have used the more generalized notations "good x" for hamburgers and "good y" for milkshakes.)

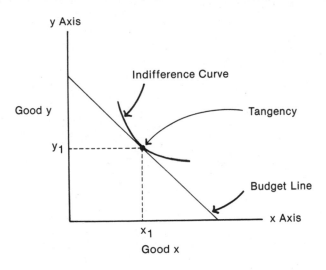

Figure 12-1

This chapter, in turn, will be devoted to using this kind of graphical approach to show a variety of important economic relationships. You'll probably be surprised to see how versatile the indifference curve-budget line system can be for analyzing consumer behavior.

Income Change

For example, let's look at an illustration where we change the income of a typical consumer (Chester Olson) and then see how this change affects his spending patterns.

First, how can we show an *income change* on Chester's indifference-curve graph? Let's assume, for example, that his income increases from $4 per day to $8. Such an income increase can be represented by an *outward shift* in his budget line. Keeping the price of good x at $1 and the price of good y at $1, we see that the new point of reference on the x axis (with the $8 income) will now be 8 units of x. This means that if Chester spent all his income on x, he would be able to buy 8 units. The same is true with good y. In Figure 12–2 we have drawn a comparison between the old and the new budget lines.

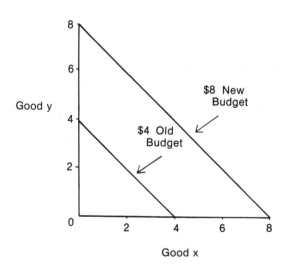

Figure 12-2

Now let's take a variety of income levels and examine the points of tangency with their respective indifference curves. In Figure 12–3a, these points of tangency show us exactly where Chester will maximize his satisfactions at different levels of income. In Figure 12–3b, note that we have connected all the points of tangency with a continuous line. This line is called the *income-consumption* curve. A glance at this curve shows the relative preference between the two goods as Chester's income expands. In Figure 12–3b, it looks as if Chester's preferences are fairly "balanced" between the two products. This may not always be the case, though, as we will soon see.

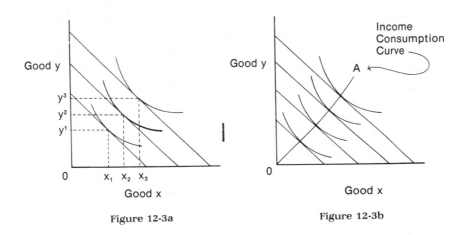

Figure 12-3a   Figure 12-3b

Income Elasticity

Income elasticity generally refers to how spending is altered in response to income changes. For example, our consumption of an *income-elastic* product would generally increase a lot if our income went up. More precisely, it would go up proportionately *more* than the income increase. Mathematically, this would imply that the following ratio would be greater than one:

$$\frac{\% \text{ change in x product}}{\% \text{ change in income}} > 1$$

On the other hand, an *income-inelastic product* would give us a ratio of less than one. What would be an example of such a product?

It is generally thought that food is income inelastic. A simple way to check this out is to, say, *double* someone's income and then see how much that person's expenditure on food increases. If his food demand *does not double* with the doubling of income, then we know that the product is income inelastic.

Returning to Chester, let's therefore double his daily income from $4 to $8 and see what happens. (Note that we are now replacing good x with "food" so that we can observe what happens to his food demand when we raise his income.) In Figure 12–4a we see that Chester is indeed reluctant to double his food expenditures after the doubling of his income. To cross-check our conclusions, we have drawn a $2 budget line to see if food remains an inelastic product at low income levels.

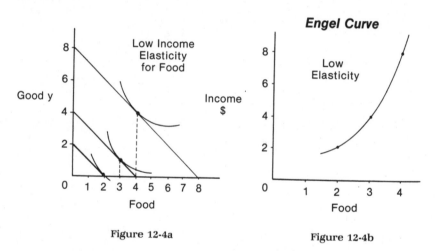

Figure 12-4a   Figure 12-4b

A close examination of Figure 12–4a shows that food is definitely income inelastic throughout the income changes. But how can we be sure? Simply dot down to the x axis (i.e., the "food" axis) and read off how much he purchases at each income level. As you can see, at a $2 income Chester buys 2 units of food, at $4 he buys 3 units, and at $8 he buys 4 units. Although his income has doubled and then doubled again, Chester's food expenditures did not keep pace proportionately.

Sometimes it is useful to graph income levels directly against product consumption as we have done in Figure 12–4b. This relationship between income and consumption is frequently referred to as an Engel curve. The Engel curve, in turn, helps us see the relative income elasticity of a product at a glance. Thus, the Engel curve we have drawn for Chester Olson's food expenditures is a steeply-rising one, implying a low income elasticity. By plugging in the numbers we obtained from Figure 12-4a, we can see that, indeed, it is inelastic.

Food as a general product category may be inelastic, but there may be certain areas of food consumption that are just the opposite. For example, most working-class families enjoy eating out in restaurants but can't do it very often because eating out is often a "luxury" in their budget. Thus, it is quite probable that a doubling of their incomes may well bring about *more* than a doubling of money spent at restaurants. If this is the case, we would then be referring to an *income-elastic* product. Let's see how this situation might look on an indifference curve-budget line system.

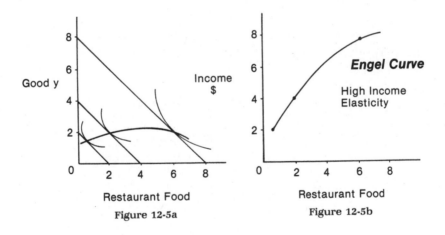

Figure 12-5a

Figure 12-5b

In Figure 12–5 we twice doubled Chester's income (as we did before), but this time we observe that the Olson family has more than doubled its consumption of units of restaurant food. Now carefully examine the Engel curve in Figure 12–5b. By plugging in the consumption data derived from Figure 12–5a, we see that eating out is income-elastic for the Olson family since the percent change in restaurant food consumption is greater than the percent change in income.

The Inferior Good

We have talked a lot about food so far. Perhaps you are getting a little tired of the subject, or, more likely, you may be experiencing a growing hunger for something to eat. But before you take off to the nearest restaurant, let me show one more example. We call it the *inferior good illustration*. First, however, a little background.

Up to this time, we have been discussing products that fall under the general description of *normal goods*. By definition, a normal good is a product or service that you will buy more of when your income increases (or less of when your income falls). There is, however, another category of goods—the *inferior goods*—for which the opposite is true. With inferior goods, as your income *increases*, you tend to buy *less* of them. What are some examples? Potatoes are often cited as an example of an inferior good, as is powdered milk. Note that an inferior good is not necessarily inferior in terms of quality or nutrition (potatoes, for example, are highly nutritious); its inferiority might therefore only be psychological. In this respect, an inferior good might also be called a *poor person's product*; families will tolerate them at low income levels, but as their incomes rise, they discard the inferior in favor of normal goods.

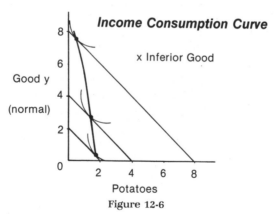

Figure 12-6

How can we show the special relationship between income and consumption of an inferior good? Let's return to Chester Olson's indifference-curve system. This time, though, we'll put the inferior good, potatoes, on the x axis (see Figure 12–6) and a normal good on the y axis. Note how the income-consumption curve for potatoes in Figure 12–6a tends to "bend backward," indicating that fewer and fewer units of potatoes are consumed as income increases.

Finally, it might be useful to see what an inferior good might look like as an Engel curve. The inferior Engel curve looks a little like a downward-sloping demand curve, but in this case, Figure 12–7, it's showing an inverse relationship between income and consumption.

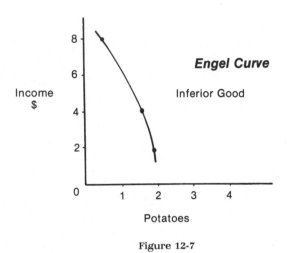

Figure 12-7

Demand

Income changes are certainly interesting microeconomic concepts, but they do not help us get to the heart of the demand curve, which is our major goal for this chapter. What then is the key variable to understanding demand?

To answer this question, it might be helpful to review the fundamental nature of a demand curve. Demand, as you recall from Chapter 3, is the relationship between the *price* of a good and the *quantity purchased* of that good. Can we then derive a demand curve for hamburgers using our friend Chester Olson as an illustration? Fortunately this is not too difficult.

Perhaps the easiest method is to play "economist-reporter" and simply ask Chester how many hamburgers he will buy at different prices. Let's assume he tells us that he would buy 1 hamburger if the price were $2, 2 hamburgers if the price went down to $1, and 4 hamburgers if the price were 50¢. Thus, our "direct-research" method of finding out Chester's hamburger demand gives us the curve shown in Figure 12–8.

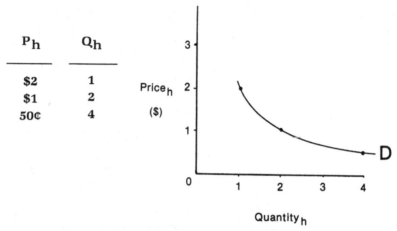

P_h	Q_h
$2	1
$1	2
50¢	4

Figure 12-8

Another method of determining Chester's hamburger demand would be via the indifference curve-budget line system. First, we find out what Chester's indifference map looks like; then all we have to do is *change the price of hamburgers* and observe how these price changes affect his consumption. How then do we show a price change on our indifference curve-budget line graph?

To see how this is done, let's go back to our example of a $4 budget and an original price of $1 for hamburgers. Let's then lower the price to 50¢. Note that Chester's $4 income can now buy a maximum of 8 hamburgers. We can also easily determine where the budget line will intersect the x axis by dividing the income by the price of the hamburgers, i.e., income/P_h. Thus, if hamburgers went up to $2 apiece, Chester could buy a maximum of 2 hamburgers with his $4 income ($4/$2 = 2).

Each time the price of hamburgers changes, the budget line will therefore change its slope. At lower hamburger prices it will generally have a lower slope, and at higher prices for hamburgers the budget line becomes steeper. (We are assuming, of course, that there is no price change with the good y.) We can see the slope changing in Figure 12–9.

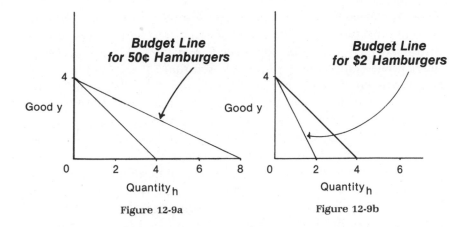

Figure 12-9a

Figure 12-9b

Now all we have to do is trace Chester's indifference-curve map, i.e., draw in those indifference curves that are tangent to the different budget lines. When we connect these points of tangency with a line, we have what is commonly called a *price consumption curve*, as seen in Figure 12–10a.

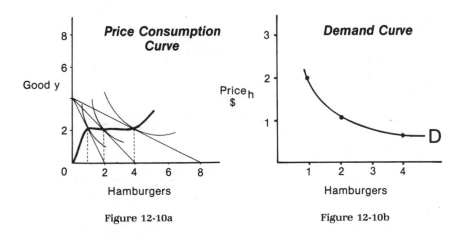

Figure 12-10a

Figure 12-10b

Deriving The Demand Curve

After our long labors, we are now close to that point where we can derive a demand curve from an indifference-curve system. In fact, the last connecting link is really quite simple; perhaps you have already spotted it. All we need to do to find Chester's demand is to read off the number of hamburgers that he will consume at the different prices of hamburgers (see Figure 12-10a). Thus, at the $2 price (the steepest budget line), we see that Chester will demand approximately 1 hamburger. When we lower the price to $1 (the middle budget line), we see that he will demand 2 hamburgers. Last, if we dot down to the hamburger axis from the point of tangency of the lowest sloped line (representing 50¢ hamburgers), we see that Chester will demand 4 hamburgers.

These results, as summarized by the demand curve in Figure 12–10b, are in exact agreement with our experimental method of finding demand via direct research (see Figure 12–8). The different methods of finding Chester's demand are both valid, but the one using the indifference curves took us back to our study of consumption and was built up, in a sense, "from scratch." (Recall that we began our analysis in the previous chapter with the law of diminishing marginal utility.)

Let's now examine a more general situation, using the universal notation of good x instead of hamburgers and "P" for prices. In Figure 12–11a and b, we have drawn a new curve that is a result in a price change of good x from P_4 down to P_1.

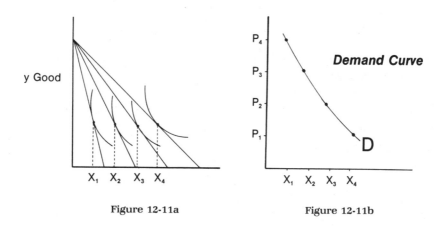

Figure 12-11a   Figure 12-11b

Income And Substitution Effects

In its simplest form, demand is therefore nothing more than the inverse relationship between the price of a good and the quantity demanded. That is, as we reduce the price of good x, we observe that an individual will increase his or her quantity demanded for that product from quantity x_1 to quantity x_2.

What we have yet to fully explain, however, is *why* a person wants more of a given product at the lower price. Recall from Chapter 3 that there were two "effects" that encourage a particular consumer to buy more of a product at the lower price rather than the higher price. One was called the *income effect*, the other was the *substitution effect*. Let's now take another look at these two economic phenomena, beginning with the substitution effect.

Imagine that we have an indifference curve that represents two substitute goods—coffee and tea. Suppose that all of a sudden the price of tea drops to a very low level, but the price of coffee remains relatively high. Tea is now much less expensive than coffee, and its lower price would thus encourage the consumer to purchase more tea. Now he can gain a greater amount of utility by purchasing tea because of its lower price. As a result of the lower tea price, the consumer moves along his indifference curve to a point that favors more tea.

The income effect is a little different. Here the consumer observes a fall in the price of tea and says to himself, "What a pleasant surprise! With the drop in tea prices, I am now a little bit richer; I have more purchasing power (i.e., *real income*) to spend on everything I enjoy." Of course, if tea is a normal good, he or she will spend *some* of the extra real income on tea. Thus, part of the overall increase in tea consumption comes from this income effect.

Interestingly enough, both the income and substitution effects can be shown on our indifference curve. Let's therefore assume that we reduce the price of good x and that there is a total increase in consumption from x_1 to x_2. Our graph shows us exactly how much of the total increase was due to the income effect and how much was due to the substitution effect. Look carefully at Figure 12–12.

Note that in lowering the price of good x there was an increase in quantity demand from x_1 to x_2 or the horizontal distance from point A to point C. Thus, A to C would be representative of the *total change*.

Next note the dotted "phantom" budget line. This line was carefully drawn so that it is (1) tangent to the original indifference curve at point b and (2) parallel to the budget line that represents a

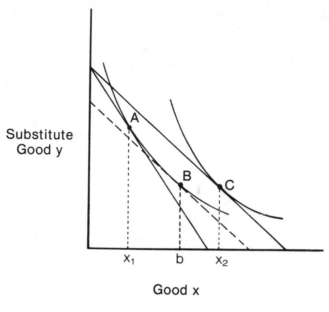

Figure 12-12

low price for x. Perhaps you can now see where the income effect is. It is that increase in x from B to C (or from b to x_2) which was a result of a positive change in real income. Recall that we have always represented income changes (i.e., budget-line changes) by a parallel shift in the budget line (see, for example, Figure 12–2).

The substitution effect is therefore the amount of increase in x that is represented by the horizontal distance between A and B or between x_1 and b. As we discussed earlier, the substitution effect is a result of moving down the original indifference curve, i.e., more of good x and less of the relatively higher priced substitute good y.

To summarize, A to B is the substitution effect, B to C is the income effect, and both effects combined give the total increase from A to C (or from x_1 to x_2).

Well, this pretty much completes our study of demand (Whew!). We have discovered where the demand curve comes from, and we also learned to do some very interesting things with income changes. In addition, we moved a long way toward developing some valuable tools that should make the study of production theory much easier later on.

But before we go on to the next chapter, let us once again look at a simple demand curve—a friendlier curve now—to remind us how far we have come:

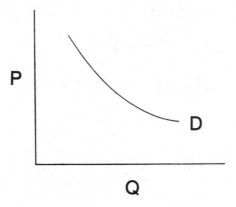

Chapter 13

BACKGROUND TO SUPPLY

The Product-Supply Curve

The simple supply curve should be a familiar image to you—it's a line that moves upward to the right, representing a positive relationship between the price of a product and the quantity of output that producers wish to supply. In other words, the higher the price, the greater the quantity supplied, as shown in Figure 13–1:

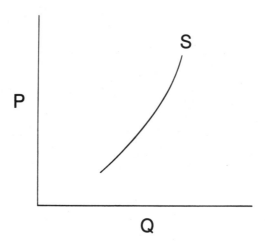

Figure 13-1

But now *why* do you think the supply curve has this particular shape? In our first encounter with supply-and-demand theory, we often hear the common sense explanation, "When a farmer sees an increase in the price of corn, he will logically want to supply more corn to the market. Thus, the higher the price of corn, the more corn . . ."

Although the above statement is probably true, it nevertheless doesn't *prove* much. In order for us to really get at the fundamental nature of a supply curve, we must first understand how a producer maximizes profits. Decisions on profitability will, in turn, take us into the financial regions where profits are determined, i.e., revenues and costs of production. Let's therefore begin our exploration of supply with the subject of *production costs* for it is here that we learn what really goes on "behind the scenes" of an average supplier.

Costs Of Production And Resource Pricing

One interesting thing about product supply is that when we think we have a handle on the right idea, we suddenly discover, "Not quite!" We know that *costs of production* play an important role in understanding profitability, but where do these costs come from? Think about it for a minute. You're probably saying, "Well, costs come from resource markets, i.e., the supply-demand situations for land, labor, and capital. From there we get resource prices, and from these prices we derive costs." But we are still left with a puzzle. In Figure 13-2 we have drawn supply and demand curves for the three major resources—land, labor, and capital. But now we are forced to ask, "*What is the origin of supply and demand for land, labor, and capital?*"

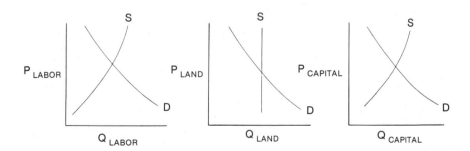

Figure 13-2

Each question raises new ones as we travel backward into the heart of microeconomic theory. It's a process that reminds me a little of Henry Thoreau's attempt to find a "bedrock point of departure" from which he would begin his philosophical search for truth:

> Let us settle ourselves, and work and wedge our feet downward through the mud and slush, . . . till we come to a hard bottom and rocks in place, which we can call reality . . . a place where you might find a wall or a state.
>
> (From *Walden* by Henry David Thoreau)

Can we then find our bedrock concept, a solid principle of production from which we can build our "microeconomic wall"? I believe the concept we are searching for is the famous *law of diminishing returns*, perhaps the most fundamental law in all economics. Exactly how does this law relate to resource markets and costs of production?

Diminishing Returns

Although we have covered diminishing returns before (Chapter 4), let's review the illustration in sufficient detail to see exactly how it relates to costs of production. Recall once again our hay-baling friend Chester Olson. We assumed that Chester had a small farm of say fifty acres with a fixed amount of capital: one tractor, one baler, and one hay wagon. Keep in mind that whenever we discuss diminishing returns, we must leave all resources fixed except one.

We discovered that Chester, working by himself, was capable of bringing in 2 loads of hay per day. Then I join Chester, and my contribution turns out to be an extra 3 loads. Remember that the amount of hay that any one individual adds to the total is called his *marginal physical product* (MPP). Thus Chester's MPP would be 2 loads and mine would be 3 loads. Note that we are now in a situation where the MPP is actually rising: Chester's operation is therefore experiencing *increasing returns*.

It's not difficult to see why we are in the stage of increasing returns. Chester's fixed resources are pretty much designed for two people. Simple efficiencies come about when one person can bale hay while another person can stack it on the wagon. The same two-man efficiency takes place when the hay is unloaded and stacked in the barn. But what happens now when Chester hires a third person? What would the MPP of the third hand be in relation to the other workers?

When Chester hired a third man (Steve), the total daily output went up to 6 loads. Therefore, the extra output (MPP) attributable to Steve is only one load. With the addition of the third worker, MPP is beginning to fall (recall that my MPP was 3 loads). A falling MPP tells us that we have reached *the point of diminishing returns*.

Steve's lower MPP was not because he was a less diligent worker, but because the crew was working with a limited amount of fixed inputs. One more tractor and wagon would have made a major difference in Steve's productivity, but alas, as a condition of diminishing returns, we couldn't change any of our fixed resources.

Incidentally, diminishing returns would also come about if we held labor and land constant and added more capital. Diminishing returns is thus a universal law that operates no matter what variable resource we are looking at.

You may enjoy, as I do, thinking through different kinds of production processes, such as farming, teaching, raising children, operating a restaurant, studying for an exam, or operating a government department, and then trying to imagine at what point diminishing returns is likely to set in. For example, child rearing (like hay baling) is probably most efficient as a "two person" operation. Or to use perhaps a more relevant example for you, in cramming for an exam, you might observe, "I seem to have reached the point of diminishing returns" (meaning that your most recent hour's worth of study brought you a smaller amount of knowledge than the previous hour). Diminishing returns can thus be applied to widely different situations.

Returning again to Chester Olson's farm operation, can we now say that since Steve's low contribution results from diminishing returns, Chester should not hire him? Recall that the answer to this question depends upon the monetary return from Steve's contribution compared with the wage that Chester has to pay him.

Steve's MPP, remember, was only one load of hay. And if that load of hay were worth $50, the worth or value of Steve's MPP would therefore be \$50. We call this amount the *value of the mar-ginal product* (VMP). The VMP of any worker can easily be found by multiplying the MPP by the price of the final product:

$$VMP = MPP \times P_{hay}$$

Once Chester figures out the VMP for *any* worker, all he has to do is compare this amount with the wage paid to that worker. Thus, the general rule for Chester to follow in hiring workers was to *keep hiring people as long as the VMP is greater than the wage.*

This process is somewhat similar to Chester's marginal decision-making process discussed in the last chapter. There Chester (as a consumer) took each dollar, one at a time, and asked where that dollar would give him the greatest utility. Now Chester (as a producer) is still making marginal decisions, but this time he is asking, "Should I hire the first person (i.e., does he contribute to profits by bringing in a larger revenue than his cost)? Should I hire the second person? Should I hire the third?" And so forth. Each person must be a separate marginal decision based upon that person's contribution versus the wage that Chester will have to pay.

Should Chester now hire me? Remember that my MPP was 3 loads. Thus, at \$50 a load, my VMP would be \$150. Assuming now that Chester is paying "the going wage" of \$20 per day, the worth of my output is obviously far greater than the wage. Thus, in regard to my contribution toward the business's profits, Chester's marginal decision would be a resounding "yes." To answer our earlier question relating to Steve (whose VMP was \$50 and wage \$20), we find that with a \$30 marginal profit it is still profitable to hire him despite the fact that we are "into diminishing returns."

What about a fourth person? Let's say that a fourth worker brings in one half a load. Even with such low productivity it is still worth Chester's while to hire him because his VMP (\$25) continues to be greater than the wage (\$20). Chester's margin decision is now a more modest "yes" than before, but it is still a "yes." If the going wage had been \$30, however, there would have been no economic advantage in hiring that fourth person.

Thus, in regard to the profitability of hiring workers, it should be clear that Chester should continue hiring right up to that point where the VMP equals wage. Even if a worker's VMP were \$20.01

and his wage were $20.00, there would still be a small profit involved—and thus Chester should hire that worker. To repeat, Chester *ought to keep hiring until the VMP equals wage*; this then will be the general rule of thumb that, from now on, we will call "Chester's profitability shortcut." This shortcut, in turn, will offer us some insight into the nature of resource markets including the demand for labor. Let's see how this works.

The Demand Curve For Labor

The demand curve for labor is simply a series of points that tells us how many units of labor (i.e., the number of workers) will be purchased (by the producer) at different labor prices (or wage rates). To see how the labor demand curve is related to MPP, let's graph Chester's MPP curve and the related VMP curve using the information we obtained earlier:

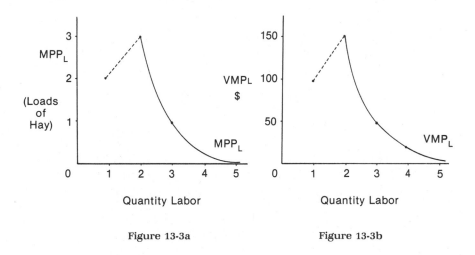

| Figure 13-3a | Figure 13-3b |

Using the information in Figure 13–3, labor demand can be easily worked out. Choose any wage—say $25 per day. How many workers will Chester "demand" if the wage is $25? The best way to answer this question is to go through the marginal-decision making process that we discussed earlier. Should Chester hire the first man (himself)? The answer is "yes," as it is for workers 2, 3, and 4. Our shortcut method gives us the same results; i.e., hire up to that point where the VMP = wage. We see in Figure 13–3b that a

$25 wage will only equal a $25 VMP when the fourth man is hired. Therefore, one point on Chester's labor demand curve would be a $25 wage combined with four workers.

If, for example, the going wage were $50, Chester would hire up to and including the third man (remember that Steve's VMP was $50). Chester would thus have a second point on his labor demand curve.

Finally, with a wage rate of $150 it would obviously be worthwhile to hire only two people. This would make the third point on the labor demand curve. In Figure 13–4a we have plotted this information. When the three points are connected as they are in Figure 13–4b, we have Chester's complete demand curve for labor.

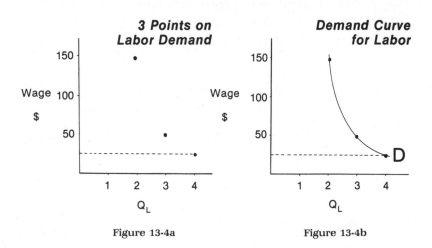

Figure 13-4a   Figure 13-4b

It should be no surprise that Chester's labor demand curve looks precisely like the VMP curve for labor in Figure 13–3b. In fact, as long as Chester maximizes his profits where VMP = wage, *the VMP curve becomes the labor demand curve!* The VMP curve is, in turn, a monetary representation of diminishing MPP.

Why then does the demand curve for labor slope downward? We now know it's because of declining MPP, or more simply, because of diminishing returns! This conclusion is true for any resource that we choose to be the short-run variable; the demand curve for capital or land is the same as their respective VMP curves. Thus, the other resources also have downward-sloping demand curves that reflect their compliance with the law of diminishing returns.

So much for resource demand curves. Now what about the supply curves for these resources? If we are to discover the origin of resource prices (in order to understand the nature of costs), we must develop a supply curve to complete our resource market. So let's now take a look at the basics of a single supply curve using labor once again as our primary resource.

The Labor Supply Curve

Labor supply is perhaps one of the most interesting topics in microeconomic theory. This is true partly because it does not lend itself to a simple income maximization process as does labor demand. Instead, labor supply is conceived in man's psychological realm. It's a subject that addresses itself to different types of people and their unique preferences for work and leisure. How, for example, can we possibly explain via simple economic rules one person's tendency to become a "workaholic"? At the other extreme, how can these rules explain another person's ability to take leisure whenever it is wanted, such as the individual in Robert Frost's poem, "Lone Striker." Here the person simply refuses one day to supply his labor to the local woolen mill:

> He knew another place, a wood,
> And in it, tall as trees, were cliffs;
> And if he stood on one of these,
> Twould be among the tops of trees . . .
> He knew a spring that wanted drinking;
> A thought that wanted further thinking
> A love that wanted re-renewing . . .

Obviously, there are all types of work attitudes that must be taken into consideration when discussing an individual's willingness to supply labor. Yet I think the general configuration of most people's labor supply curve would probably be somewhat similar. Let's see if we can figure out what that configuration is.

Let's say you wanted to find out what my labor supply curve looked like. You would probably begin your investigation by asking me a question such as, "Given complete freedom to choose the amount of hours you wanted to work, how many hours would you choose per week if you received $2 per hour?" My answer would give you a single point on my labor supply curve. Next you might ask, "How many hours would you work if the wages were three dollars per hour? Four dollars per hour?" And so forth.

You may wish to inquire about my work preferences even at very high wages. Each time I answer, you note down the desired quantity of labor. No doubt my response to a rising wage rate would be somewhat similar to most people's response. If, for example, the wage were extremely low, I would probably be hesitant to "break my back" working a great many hours, unless I were forced to by necessity. Then as the wage increased, the possibilities for greater income would probably be an incentive to put in more hours. We might call this direct, or positive, relationship (i.e., higher wage rates leading to more hours worked) the *consumption effect*. This implies that the greater wage was sufficient incentive for me to work longer, to enlarge my income, and to significantly improve my level of consumption.

At some high wage level, however, a remarkable thing happens. It suddenly occurs to me that "enough is enough," and that any higher wage after this point will result in fewer hours worked. Apparently I am now looking for a greater amount of leisure in which to enjoy my relatively higher income. When this happens, we say that the *leisure effect*[36] has become more powerful than the consumption effect.

Labor Supply Curve

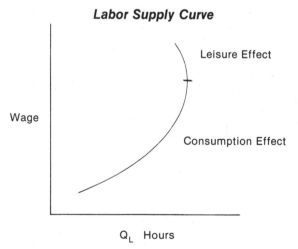

Figure 13-5

What we have then is not just a positive slope on the labor supply curve but also a curve that turns "negative" when the leisure effect takes over. This makes the labor supply curve appear to "bend backward"; hence, economists frequently refer to it as a *backward-bending supply curve* for labor. This configuration can be seen in Figure 13–5.

It is sometimes interesting to experiment with different curve shapes, each demonstrating a variety of work attitudes and work-behavior patterns. Just for fun, let's try three radically different work models: the workaholic, the Henry Thoreau, and the Buddhist economist.

The workaholic's labor supply curve would probably demonstrate high initial work loads that would increase even more as the wage rates increased. Such people seem to need lots of work, and the possibilities for higher consumption levels prod them on as the wage increases. Thus, the leisure effect would be evident only after extremely large quantities of labor had been supplied (see Figure 13–6a).

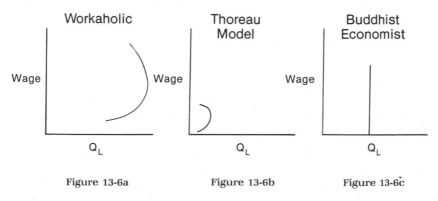

| Figure 13-6a | Figure 13-6b | Figure 13-6c |

Next we will look at the other end of the work spectrum; for want of a better term we will call this work pattern the "Henry Thoreau Model." In *Walden*, Thoreau advocated a simple, low overhead lifestyle. He once said his greatest skill "has been to want but little." This philosophy led Thoreau to something that was not quite voluntary poverty but was close to it:

> I found that by working about six weeks in a year, I could meet all the expenses of living. The whole of my winters, as well as most of my summers, I had free and clear for study.
>
> (From *Walden*)

What then would Thoreau's supply curve look like? Apparently, it would bend back very quickly—such as the one in Figure 13–6b.

A final labor supply model is one we described in Chapter 10—the Buddhist economist model based on E. F. Schumacher's description of an individual who is not motivated necessarily by wages but more as one part of a "dignified existence." Too much work would not be an ideal situation, nor would too little work. Thus, the Buddhist-model supply curve would not have an upward slope or a backward-bending section. It would rise in a straight line at the "ideal" level of work as shown in Figure 13–6c.

You might want to draw an approximation of your own labor supply curve. Of the above three models, which does yours resemble most?

A Labor Market

So far we have examined a single producer's demand curve for labor and a single person's labor supply curve. What we need to find out now is what the *overall* industry supply and demand curves look like. Fortunately, this is not too difficult. For example, to determine the industry demand, all we need to do is ask all the hay farmers the same question we already asked Chester Olson; i.e., "How much labor would you demand at different wage rates?" If at a $4 rate Chester maximizes his profits with x workers, farmer

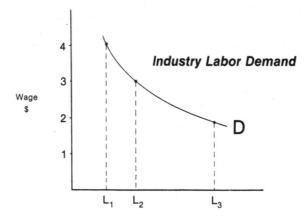

Figure 13-7

Jones with y workers, farmer Smith with z workers, and so on, then we simply add up the total numbers of workers (x + y + z, etc.) at that particular wage rate. This information will give us the first point on the industry demand curve (see point L_1 on Figure 13–7).

At a $3 wage rate, we would go through the same addition process to obtain another point (L_2) and the same for a $2 rate (L_3). Connecting these three points, we thus have an *industry labor demand* that can be represented by the curve in Figure 13–7.

The supply curve for labor is determined in a similar way; i.e., we add up the total amount of labor that all workers (in that particular market) wish to put forth at different wage rates.

In Figure 13–8 we combined the industry labor supply curve with the industry demand curve. Together they form our first labor market—a unique supply-demand situation that generates an equilibrium price (i.e., wage W_1) and an equilibrium labor quantity (L_1).

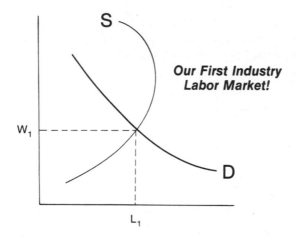

Figure 13-8

So much for the labor market, but what about the other resources of land and capital? What do their markets look like, and how do we determine their prices? We can apply a similar kind of analysis to both land and capital. The demand curve for land, as we noted before, is land's VMP curve. It slopes downward for the same reason that labor's demand did—diminishing returns.

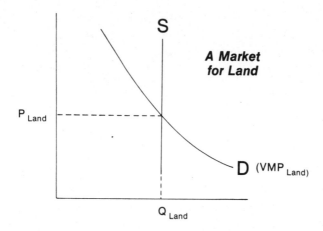

Figure 13-9

The other half of the land market is land's supply curve. We know that by definition the supply of land is fixed; i.e., there are only so many land resources no matter what the price. Thus, land's supply curve is simply a vertical line at the fixed quantity of land resource. The combined supply-demand market for land would look something like Figure 13–9.

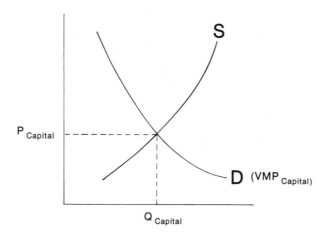

Figure 13-10

Finally, let's look at capital. Capital's demand curve is also its VMP curve, and capital's supply is determined by the available capital stock at any one time. The resulting equilibrium price is often expressed as a rate of interest. We will, however, simply use the designation "P capital." Thus, a short-run market for capital would be similar to Figure 13–10.

We have now reached a useful conclusion for our chapter. We traced short-run production theory from the law of diminishing returns through simple resource markets, and we understand how resources are priced. And it is from these prices that we determine a producer's costs of production!

In the next chapter we will combine these costs of production with the concept of producer revenues. This knowledge will, in turn, lead us to an understanding of our final goal, i.e., the product supply curve.

Chapter 14

COMPETITIVE SUPPLY

Before moving on, let's take a minute to look back and see how far we have come. Keep in mind that one of our primary objectives in microeconomics is to build a model of a simple market. We began by exploring the origins of the familiar supply and demand curves that make up a typical competitive product market.

From chapters 11 and 12, recall that our analysis was of the product demand curve. The origin of demand, we learned, can be traced to the law of diminishing marginal utility and the consumers' desire to maximize utility within a limited income. In seeking the origins of the product supply curve (chapter 13), we found that we had to go back a step to first learn about a producer's costs of production. These, in turn, are based on the markets for economic resources (land, labor, and capital). We also discovered that the resource demand curves were explained primarily through the law of diminishing returns combined with the producer's desire to maximize profits.

What we have yet to do is make the important connection between these costs of production and the actual supply curve *for a product*. This is, therefore, our major objective in this chapter. By chapter's end we should have a bonafide product supply curve, which, when combined with the product demand curve, will complete our model of a competitive market.

The Idea Of Costs

Based on our work in the previous chapter let's now derive Chester Olson's costs of production. First, we determine the going industry resource prices by observing the equilibrium of supply and demand within the respective markets. In Figure 14–1 we redrew these markets and the resulting price for each of the resources (P_{land}, P_{labor}, $P_{capital}$).

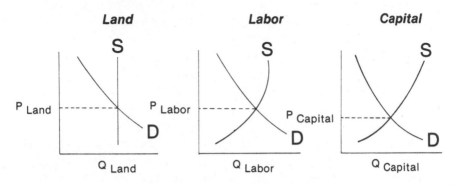

Figure 14-1

Once these prices are known, we can then use them to understand a variety of cost concepts. Let's begin with *fixed costs*.

Fixed Costs

Fixed costs result from the fact that land and capital are not allowed to change in the short run. The total cost (to Chester) of these two resources will therefore be the going industry price (P) times the quantity (Q) of the fixed resources that Chester decides to use. To illustrate this point we'll say that his fixed costs are the following:

$$P_{land} \times Q_{land} = \$50$$
$$P_{capital} \times Q_{capital} = \$50$$

Adding these costs together, we have fixed costs of $100. Of course, we are greatly simplifying our illustration. In reality, Chester would have many kinds of fixed or *overhead* costs on his farm. Land rental costs, tractor, wagon, baler, barn depreciation, insurance, and taxes are just a few of the fixed costs for a typical farm.

Variable Costs

Chester's variable resource has always been labor. Therefore, his *variable costs* would be the industry wage rate times the amount of labor that Chester decides to use (based on the procedures out-lined in the last chapter).

Again, in reality a farmer's variable costs are far more extensive than just labor. They also include expenses like fuel, seed, fertilizer, and so forth. In general, any input that is directly connected with output would be considered a variable resource.

To summarize Chester's situation, his total costs so far are the $100 fixed cost (FC) plus the variable costs (VC). Thus, his total costs = FC + VC. In our example, these are the "obvious costs" to Chester and will involve an apparent outlay of money. Such costs are often called *explicit costs*.

There may, however, be another kind of cost—a cost not so obvious—which also should be included as part of Chester's overall production costs. Economists call them *implicit costs*. Let's look at some examples.

Implicit Costs

Frequently, a single operator like our friend Chester Olson forgets to consider his own labor as part of his costs. Or perhaps, he will simply undervalue the long, long hours that he spends working on his farm. This is also true of the many "ma and pa" stores, single proprietorships, and partnerships that often fail to fully recognize the value of the total hours spent on the job. Logically, these kinds of implicit costs should be included as part of the overall produc-tion costs.

How do we estimate an implicit labor cost? In Chester's case, we could ask how much he might be able to earn elsewhere for working the same number of hours. An alternate method is for Chester to assess how much he would have to pay someone else to replace him. Note that if these implicit labor costs were added to Chester's other expenses, they would reduce what Chester thought were his profits.

Another implicit cost that Chester has probably not fully accounted for is some fair return on his land and capital invest-ments. If, for example, he has invested $50,000 in farm assets, he is foregoing a certain rate of return he could be earning on this money if it were invested elsewhere.

Thus, when economists look at costs of production, they should include both implicit and explicit costs.

Social Costs

Another category of costs that should be included (but usually are not) is what are called *social costs*, i.e., the financial sacrifices that society pays as a result of production. These sacrifices usually take the form of direct or indirect pollution costs. A good example can be seen when Chester Olson pollutes his neighbor's water supply by overusing nitrogen fertilizer. When Chester's neighbors discover their water is unfit for drinking, they must drill a deeper well.

The economist looks at this situation and says that the financial cost of drilling a new well is really a legitimate cost of production for the farmer, and Chester should be made to pay the extra well drilling expense. Our economy, however, has a long way to go in recognizing the logic of social costs and of forcing producers to bear the burden of these costs themselves. (For more details, see Chapter 4.)

Let's call the sum of these costs, the total economic costs:

Explicit costs + Implicit Costs + Social costs = Total economic costs

Marginal Costs

Assuming (for simplicity sake) that the social and implicit costs are zero, let's now look at an example of how costs change as Chester's output increases. We will also assume that Chester can hire both part-time and full-time help so that he can figure out precisely how much extra money it will cost him to produce one extra load of hay. Economists call this extra cost of producing one more unit of output the *marginal cost* (MC).

Output Quantity (loads)	Total Costs $	Marginal Costs $
1	110	--
2	130	20
3	140	10
4	146	6
5	150	4
6	170	20
7	210	40
8	270	60

For example, we might now say that the "MC of the fourth load is $6," or the "MC of the fifth load is $4." Once you know the total costs, the MC is simply the increment between the various loads of hay. In the chart on page 197, you can see how these costs are calculated.

The next step is to graph the MC curve using the data from the chart. Chester's MC curve can be seen in Figure 14–2.

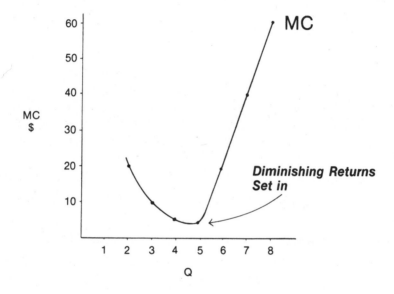

Figure 14-2

What does the MC curve show? At a glance, it shows how much extra money it will cost Chester to produce any particular load of hay. One thing that stands out about the MC curve is its interesting "U" shape. Marginal costs first go down, and then around the fifth load of hay they begin to go up. This common configuration implies that Chester must pay more and more money for extra loads of hay after the fifth load of hay. What do you think causes the MC to go down and then up?

You have probably guessed correctly; it's our old acquaintance, the law of diminishing returns. Recall that when Chester hired me, I brought the total daily production up to 5 loads. My marginal physical product (MPP) was 3 additional loads compared with Chester's MPP of 2 loads; in other words, up to load 5 we were in the stage of increasing returns. My higher productivity, therefore, led to lower marginal costs.

To get an extra load after the fifth load of hay, however, becomes a very expensive proposition for Chester. Remember that Steve's MPP was only 1 load due to diminishing returns; but Chester must still pay Steve *the same wage that he paid me* ($20 per day). This explains why Chester's marginal costs literally "shoot up" after this fifth unit and continue to rise rapidly from that point on. In short, the MC curve begins to rise at that point where marginal physical productivity begins to fall, i.e., where diminishing returns sets in.

It should be emphasized that after two chapters on the nature of costs, we have at last arrived at our most important cost concept so far: the derivation of the MC curve. It is, as we just noted, a cost concept that has its roots in the law of diminishing returns. Its resulting "U" shape will, in turn, become the basis of the product supply curve.

But we still have one more idea to pursue before we are able to put product supply together completely. We need to know something about Chester's revenues in order to assemble his total "profitability picture." What then does our microeconomic theory tell us about revenues within the setting of a competitive market structure? Let's answer this question by reviewing what we mean by the term "competition."

Competition

The competitive market structure can perhaps most easily be remembered as a marketing situation precisely the opposite of a monopoly. Monopoly, as we noted in Chapter 2, is the most concentrated market structure; competition is the least concentrated. A monopolist is a single seller of a product with virtually no close substitutes (i.e., a one-firm industry) and therefore has undisputed control over industry price. In contrast, the perfect competitor is just one of many thousands or even hundreds of thousands of sellers; he is simply a drop in "an ocean of suppliers" who all supply exactly the same product. Thus, the lone competitor has virtually no control over industry prices, and any attempt to differentiate his product is obviously not worthwhile.

Competition can be a confusing term. Ask the man in the street to name a competitive industry, and he might respond the automobile industry or the steel industry. Indeed, there may be a lot of *rivalry* between Ford and General Motors, but they are not truly competitive since the auto industry does not adhere to the competitive characteristics outlined above.

In addition, purely competitive industries have one attribute that auto manufacturers would never wish to share: easy entry and easy exit. Thus, to become a single seller in a true competitive market, we assume you can move into the industry without exotic skills or a great deal of capital. In turn, this characteristic of easy entry means that any excessive profit is threatened by new profit-seeking firms which can easily move in, depress prices, and squeeze out existing profits. This is obviously the kind of competition the large auto and steel industries wish to avoid. So what is a good example of pure competition?

Given all of the above characteristics, we find that it is the agricultural industry which best represents a competitive industry.

Of course, there are certain "big-business" farm operations, such as a modern dairy farm, that are not so easy to enter. In addition, the prices of certain grain crops have been supported by government programs, which tends to dilute the pure competitiveness of these segments of American agriculture.

Perhaps the best illustration of farm competition is the hog or hay industry. For example, hundreds of thousands of hog producers (many quite small) can move in and out of the industry with relative ease. Thus, when prices are good they "move in." The cumulative effect of this influx is a rapid increase in supply and hence, a lowering in the overall price of hogs. Once prices drop significantly, many of the more inefficient producers leave as quickly as they moved in.

Let's now return to our earlier question about a competitor's revenues. Exactly how are they determined under competitive conditions? Generally speaking, the revenue situation for a competitor involves multiplying the industry price by whatever the competitor has to sell. For example, a single hog producer might sell 1,000 or 10,000 pounds of pork at the industry price. Thus, no matter how much a single competitor has to sell, he cannot in any way affect the overall market price.

Since the above characteristics also apply to hay producers, let us return to Chester Olson to see if we can work out some general competitive principles.

If Chester can sell all the hay he produces at the going price, what would Chester's hay demand curve look like? Obviously the individual demand curve for Chester would be *flat* (or perfectly elastic), showing that the market will take everything he produces at the industry price. If the overall market price for hay were $60 a load, the demand curve facing Chester would look like that in Figure 14–3.

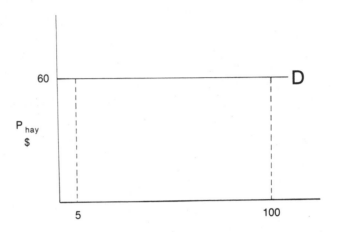

Figure 14-3

Once we know Chester's revenue situation (as defined by his demand curve), we are then equipped with all the necessary information to derive his product supply curve. Let's give it a try.

Competitive Supply

Recall that a product supply curve is a series of points that shows how much output a producer wishes to supply the market at alternative prices. For example, Chester's supply curve for hay would indicate how many loads of hay he will want to supply if the going price of hay were say $60 a load or $40 or $20 or any price in between. The line that connects up these points thus becomes Chester's supply curve for hay.

Obviously, Chester's decisions on how much hay to produce at different prices will be based upon maximum profitability. He will want to produce x amounts of hay at $60 per load because that amount will give Chester the maximum amount of profits at that price. Exactly how will Chester know when he has arrived at that maximum profit quantity?

To find out, Chester must go through a marginal decision making process that is similar to the one he went through when trying to decide how many workers to hire. This time, however, he will be asking himself, "Will the first load be profitable? Will the second load be profitable?" And so forth. As a general rule, Chester should *continue to increase output as long as each additional load adds something toward his profits.*

Assuming, as we did in Figure 14–3, that the market price of hay is $60 per load, would it be profitable for Chester to produce those first loads of hay? He answers that question by comparing the costs of those first loads with the revenues he will receive by selling them. To find out what his costs are, he refers to his MC curve shown in Figure 14–4.

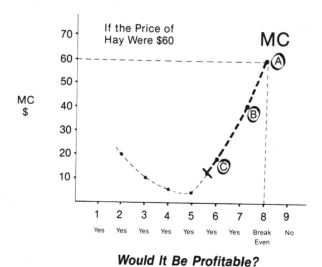

Would It Be Profitable?

Figure 14-4

We can now see that the costs of production of the early loads are significantly lower than the $60 revenue he receives from selling each load. Thus, it is profitable for Chester to produce those first hay loads.

Now let's move along the x axis until we get to the seventh load. Again, Chester asks his question, "Is it profitable to produce and sell unit 7?" From the graph we see that the MC of this load is $40, but the extra revenue continues to be $60; thus the marginal decision is still "yes." Now what about the eighth load? This particular load is obviously a "break-even" situation. With any loads past the eighth, however, the MC will be greater than $60, and Chester should not produce them. Therefore, Chester ought to continue producing *up to* the eighth load; to go beyond eight loads, however, the extra costs (MC) will be greater than the extra revenues (P). Our "profitability rule of thumb" would therefore be the following: *Stop producing at that quantity (Q) where price = marginal cost.*

This rule in turn helps us obtain our first point (point A) on Chester's product supply curve. To find another point, we must begin all over with a new price. For example, how much hay would Chester want to produce if the market price were $40? Going through the same marginal decision process, Chester would obviously maximize his profits by producing and selling 7 loads. (Note that the eighth unit now would represent a $20 loss; its MC is $60, but the revenue is now only $40). A price of $40 and 7 loads supplied gives us Chester's second point on his product supply curve (point B).

Finally, if the price of hay were $20, we can easily see that Chester will stop producing with the sixth load (point C).

Perhaps you are noticing what seems to be a consistent pattern: The three points we have derived on Chester's supply curve are *exactly the same three points on his MC curve.* This is no mere coincidence. It should be obvious that as long as we determine profitability points in the above manner, Chester's MC curve *becomes* his supply curve!

We should note, however, that if the industry price of hay falls too low, it may not be worth Chester's while to initiate production, at least in the short run. (In terms of committing resources, remember that short run means that our friend could not get out of paying a fixed amount of costs even if he shut down his operation!) What would this "shut-down price" be for Chester? Using the figures from our earlier example, we can say that the amount of money he would lose by shutting down would be his $100 fixed costs.

Suppose that the price of hay fell so low that Chester's revenues wouldn't even cover his variable costs. This would mean that poor Chester would lose not only his fixed costs ($100) but also *some* money from the variable costs that were not matched by sufficient revenue. In this case it would be wise for him to shut down and minimize his losses ($100) that derived from the unavoidable fixed costs.

In summary, we can say that Chester achieves his shut-down price when the revenues generated from total sales do not quite cover variable costs. Chester's product supply curve can therefore be defined as *his MC curve above the shut-down price* and would look something like the curve in Figure 14–5.

Chester Olson's Supply Curve for Hay

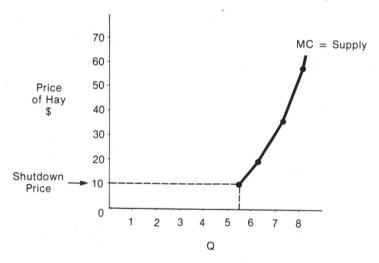

Figure 14-5

With the derivation of Chester's supply curve, we are now near the completion of our journey. All we must do now is work out the so-called industry supply curve. In our example the industry would include *all* producers of hay in that particular area. Therefore, to find the industry supply all we do is add up the total quantities of hay that all producers wish to supply at the different prices. The other producers' supply curves would probably look very much like Chester's because of similar MC situations.

The only major difference between an individual's supply curve and the industry curve would be quantities of hay at the different prices. Instead of 8 loads at $60, the industry might produce, for example, 8 million loads, yet the slope of the industry supply curve would look very much like Chester's positive-sloped supply curve.

Building A Market

So far we have used Chester's hay-baling example to demonstrate the fundamentals of production. We moved along with Chester from the basic law of diminishing returns, to resource pricing, to profit maximization and on up to the derivation of the industry supply curve. Obviously, Chester and his fellow hay producers are just simple illustrations of what goes on behind the scenes with all competitive suppliers. Thus, in *any* short run competitive market, the product supply curve reflects rising marginal costs and therefore slopes upward to the right.

Similarly, in previous chapters we derived a simple product demand curve. In the case of demand, our starting point was the law of diminishing marginal utility, which eventually contributed

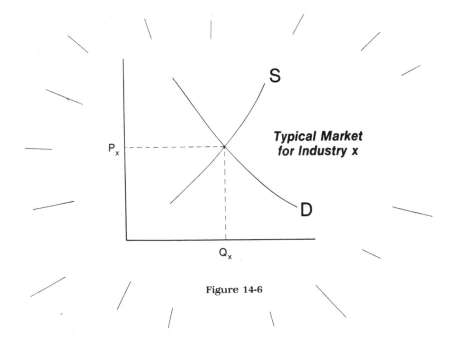

Figure 14-6

to a downward-sloping demand curve. We can now say that *all* product demand curves have a similar downward-sloping shape.

With both these theories of supply and demand behind us, it now seems appropriate to draw a more generalized market using a typical supply-and-demand curve from virtually any competitive market. We'll call it simply "industry x." This sample market is shown in Figure 14–6.

We have thus completed our major objective for the first half of our microeconomics section—i.e., the building of a complete product market. Now as we look at this "basic building block" of our market economy, we can appreciate even more the many principles and concepts that lie behind those simple lines.

Chapter 15

USING THE MARKETS

One of the rewarding things about microeconomics is that after we have made the effort to develop the concept of economic markets, we then have at our disposal some highly useful tools that are more than abstract theory. These markets now become useful instruments to help us understand real-life issues and problems. This chapter explores some of these possibilities.

The material is divided into two sections. Section I examines a typical labor market. Specifically, we'll learn how labor markets can help us in understanding the problem of income distribution. Section II uses our understanding of product markets to learn about the American farm problem. By chapter's end, I hope you will have gained a greater respect and appreciation for the versatility and usefulness of market models.

SECTION I—INCOME DISTRIBUTION

Who receives the fruits of economic activity? Why do some individuals get more than others? What mechanism divides up society's income? What part of the economic pie will the labor resource get compared with capital or land resources? These questions relate to the issue of *income distribution*. Indeed, they are questions that have not always been easy to answer in relation to a modern market economy.

In the older traditional economic systems where production and distribution were based upon well-established patterns, the question of "who receives the output?" was fairly easy to answer. Once you understood the culture's traditional source of power

(which was often based on land control), you pretty much understood how the income was distributed.

But what about our present market system? If traditional patterns do not determine who gets the fruits of production, what
does? A precise answer to this question—based on resource
markets—was formulated around the turn of the century. The
solution became known as the "Clark Theory of Distribution,"
named for the American economist John B. Clark.

In its simplest form, Clark's theory attempted to demonstrate
how much of the total economic pie went to labor resources compared with that which went to land resources. His conclusion was
fairly simple, once one understood what a labor market was. To
demonstrate, let's redraw a typical labor market. Recall that the
labor demand curve was largely a representation of worker's value
of marginal product (VMP). We will simplify labor supply by using
a vertical line as in Figure 15-1.

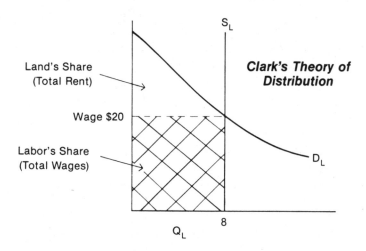

Figure 15-1

Clark observed that each worker will receive a wage equivalent
to the last worker's VMP. In Figure 15-1, the eighth worker's VMP
is $20. It is at this point that supply crosses demand; therefore, *all*
workers will receive a wage that is equivalent to the eighth (i.e., the
last worker to be hired) worker's VMP. Notice that workers one

through seven contributed *more* than their $20 wage, but they still only received $20. Labor's total share will therefore be $20 × 8 workers or $160 (represented by the shaded rectangle).

This only satisfies labor's piece of the economic pie; what about land's portion? According to Clark's analysis the landowner would receive what looks like a *surplus*, represented by the area under the demand curve that is not shaded. This unshaded triangle can be viewed as a value to which workers one through seven contributed but for which they did not get paid. In a pure market economy, the unshaded triangle represents a kind of *rent* or return to the owners of the land resource.

It should be obvious that labor's wage rate (and its share of the total economic pie) will generally depend *on the positioning* of the supply-and-demand curve. This knowledge, in turn, can help us answer some intriguing questions about what takes place in our market economy, e.g., why do very hard working individuals frequently receive the lowest wages? Let's look at a typical example of this problem: the case of the waitress and her dentist.

The Waitress and Her Dentist

Marilyn Jones, a waitress at the Bixby drive-in, had to see her dentist, Dr. Franklin, last week. When she received her bill in the mail, Marilyn was at first surprised, then angered to discover that in thirty minutes her dentist had completed $50 worth of work or the equivalent of three full days of her waitress wages. "How in the world could my dentist make forty to fifty times my own hourly wage?," she wondered.

This large differential in wages can be explained in part by simple resource market analysis. To demonstrate, we have drawn a separate market for both dentists and waitresses (see Figure 15-2).

Let's look at the waitress market first. In Figure 15-2b, you can actually see how the supply-demand positioning works to the detriment of Marilyn Jones's wage rate. This, however, does not explain why the labor supply is so great and the demand so small. Some possible explanations for the large labor supply are:

- Too many relatively unskilled individuals who are willing to do this kind of work.

- Relatively free entry into the waitress labor market, i.e., no unions, no licensing, no certification, etc., required.

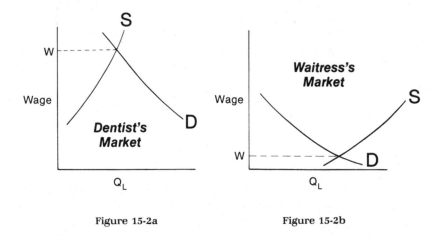

Figure 15-2a   Figure 15-2b

The waitress labor market also suffers from low demand. What could cause this? Possible reasons, based on our knowledge of labor demand, are:

- The value of a waitress's marginal product is low, especially when compared with a dentist's VMP, because waitress work is labor intensive with little use of technology or capital.
- The demand for the final product (a restaurant meal) is generally low.

On the other hand, Dr. Franklin's labor market (see Figure 15-2a) has a more favorable supply-demand configuration—a high demand for dentist's labor and a relatively low labor supply. We should note that high wage rates come about as a result of *both* supply and demand being in favorable positions. What are possible explanations for this situation? First, consider the reasons for the low supply:

- There are relatively few qualified dentists because of long and expensive training.
- There is restricted entry into the field. Entrants are approved by the professional associations that control licensing exams, certification requirements, etc.

On the demand side, dentists benefit from the following factors, among others:

- Dentist's productivity (VMP) is relatively high because of expensive dental technology: high-speed drills, x-ray equipment, etc.
- There is relatively high demand for dental health care.

Now if, by some quirk of fate, the waitresses in our above example had imposed stiff schooling and licensing requirements, while dentists had opened up their profession by building more dental schools and lowering barriers to entry, then the gross wage differentials between these occupations would undoubtedly be reduced.

The above analysis includes only the *market reasons* why wages might differ. In the real world there might be other explanations why one occupation, or one individual, might suffer in relation to another. For one thing, waitress work has usually been considered "women's work," and traditional female occupations, such as teaching, library work, nursing, etc., are generally poorly paid. Other social factors that might enter into a particular individual's wage include race, ethnic origin, religion, age, or perhaps whether that person was fortunate enough to have wealthy parents who could pay for expensive professional training. Also, "who you know" or "just plain luck" can play an important part in determining any particular individual's lifetime earnings.

Unions

Another area where we can apply our understanding of resource markets is in explaining the economic impact of *unions*. Generally speaking, unions are formed because of an inherent weakness of individuals in dealing with very large, powerful, and often impersonal employers. Where single workers might be unsuccessful in promoting individual interests, a unified group—with the power to strike—can often promote the group's interests quite effectively. What is often overlooked when discussing unionization is how this organizational power can "manipulate" labor markets, usually for the express purpose of raising wage rates. We now have an excellent background to understand how this is accomplished.

There are basically three methods by which organized labor can raise wages. Let's begin with those policies that can shift the labor supply curve to the left (see Figure 15–3).

As we saw before, stiff barriers of entry (or, simply, "upgraded" entry requirements) erected by any organization can often shift

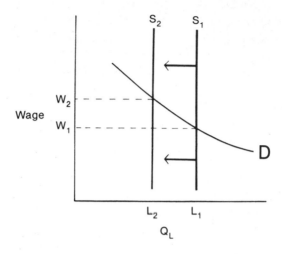

Figure 15-3

labor supply to the left. A variety of professional organizations, including barbers, doctors, teachers, accountants, etc., insist on apprenticeships or years of schooling before individuals can begin work. Adam Smith recognized over 200 years ago the true intent of many of these occupational "regulations" when he wrote:

> The intention of both regulations is to restrain the competition to much smaller number than might otherwise be disposed to enter the trade. The limitations of their number of apprentices restrains it directly. A long term of apprenticeship restrains it more indirectly, but as effectually, by increasing the expense of education.[37]

Smith was therefore unhappy that many of these artificial barriers (apprenticeships, long schooling, licensing, etc.) prevented individuals from freely exercising their skills and entering into productive relationships with a potential employer:

> The patrimony of a poor man lies in the strength and dexterity of his hands; and to hinder him from employing this strength and dexterity in what manner he thinks proper without injury to his neighbor is a plain violation of this most sacred property. It is a manifest encroachment upon the just liberty both of the workman and of those who might be disposed to employ him. . . .
> To judge whether he is fit to be employed may surely be trusted to the discretion of the employers whose interest it so much concerns.[38]

Note that the same restrictive impact can be accomplished by simply establishing *fixed quotas* on the number of workers who are allowed to join a union. The more direct technique of quotas characterizes many of the building trade unions. Unions also may support legislation to limit foreign immigration of certain workers who might compete in their particular labor market, thus indirectly restricting entry.

For the union, a leftward shift in labor supply does indeed result in higher wage rates, but at the same time it also reduces the number of people who can enjoy that high wage. Note in Figure 15–3 that the number of workers employed was reduced from L_1 to L_2. For the rest of the economy these barriers and restrictive policies may reduce the efficiency of the overall economy by preventing individuals from entering the more specialized job arena. In turn, the price of the final product to the consumer becomes higher than if a free-entry situation were in effect.

Another method of increasing wage rates is by expanding the demand curve, as shown in Figure 15–4.

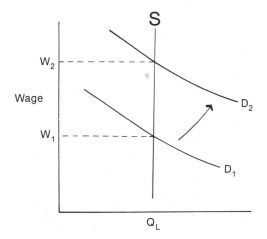

Figure 15-4

How would an upward shift in the demand curve be accomplished? Recall from our earlier discussion that labor demand reflects the VMP curve. Therefore, any increase in productivity by working harder, by adding more capital, or by utilizing more advanced technology will eventually shift labor demand upward. This is the major reason why wage levels in the "capital-intensive"

Western countries are significantly higher than those in less developed Third World countries.

Another method of raising the demand curve would be for the union to encourage the purchase of labor's output (for example, Ford autoworkers buying Ford cars). This strategy recognizes that the VMP curve (i.e., the labor demand curve) reflects not only productivity but also *the demand and the price of the final product*.

Some unions help advertise their product (i.e., "buy the union label"), while others tend to put their promotional energies into political channels. For example, construction workers often push for lower mortgage rates, auto workers lobby for the construction of highways, and textile workers urge for further restrictions on imports. These are just a few examples of how unions aid in shifting demand upward to the right.

A final method of raising wage rates reflects the sheer collective power of the union. Firms can agree through collective bargaining on a "higher-than-equilibrium wage rate" in order to avoid a strike. In Figure 15–5, the equilibrium wage is at W_1, but the agreed-upon wage can reach up to W_2.

The raising of wages to level W_2 appears to defy the labor market; it looks as if the union is getting something for nothing. But as with most economic benefits, there are costs involved. What is the major drawback to this situation? Notice that in Figure 15–5 this higher wage rate intersects the labor demand curve at L_2, which indicates a lower quantity of labor demanded than the old equilibrium labor quantity of L_1. In practical terms, this means that some of the people who were formerly working would lose their jobs after the hike in wage rates.

On the other hand, it is often asserted that nonunion labor in equivalent or similar industries frequently benefits from the union wage rates. Employers attempting to prevent unionization, in some cases, may offer higher wage rates than they would have without the existence of unions.

From the topic of income distribution and resource markets, let's now turn our attention to the subject of product markets—with particular emphasis on the farm problem in the United States. I chose the agricultural industry because of the ease with which we can apply our knowledge of competitive supply and demand as developed in the previous chapters.

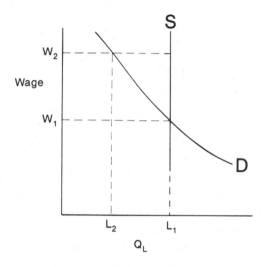

Figure 15-5

What then is our "farm problem"? How did it begin, and what are some of the possible solutions? Let's take a look.

SECTION II—THE FARM PROBLEM

Although there is no example of perfect competition in real life, farming does indeed come closest to our definition as outlined in the previous chapter.

For example, competition is usually considered healthy for the economy. In theory, a competitive industry operates at peak efficiency and provides relatively low prices for the consumer. Indeed, these characteristics are beneficial to all of us. Yet from the viewpoint of the producer, American farming has greatly suffered from its inability to control both output and prices—a characteristic that is especially unfortunate when we consider that most American industries *do* have some control over their prices. This imbalance has often worked to the disadvantage of the farmer.

To see more clearly how this situation works against farm producers, we must go back to the "root problem" of agricultural prices. Economists have looked at this price dilemma from two vantage points—the historical problem and the short-run problem.

Let's now use our supply-demand tools to help us understand the historical difficulties farmers have faced over the years.

The Historical Problem

American farmers are incredible food producers. Through the exploitation of natural resources and the intensive use of energy, farm chemicals, large-scale machinery, hybrid seeds, etc., our agricultural producers have amazed the rest of the world with their productivity and the sheer magnitude of their output.

One average farmer, for example, can feed himself and about *seventy* other people. Yet, ironically, this amazing and enviable productivity is also a source of the historical farm problem. How can "too much" be a problem?

Our high state of farm technology has, in effect, shifted the food supply curve far to the right of the historical supply demand market. America's historical food demand, however, has not kept up with this large shift in supply. Indeed, our population has grown as have our incomes; but these increases have simply not matched the potential food production.

Recall that food is generally an *income-inelastic* product. From our earlier reading (see Chapter 12), we learned that if one's income increases a certain percentage, the corresponding increase in consumption of an income-inelastic product (like food) would not be proportionately as large. Thus, food demand does increase over time, but it has not increased enough to match the large increases in supply. Nor did the population growth rate make up the difference. The ultimate result, therefore, is *depressed agricultural prices relative to prices elsewhere in the economy.*

A final factor compounds the problem: recall that agricultural products are *price inelastic* (see Chapter 3), i.e., the quantities demanded are relatively insensitive to a change in price. Inelastic demand curves, in turn, have a rather steep slope, rendering the possibility for low farm prices (see Figure 15-6). In summary, agriculture's historical problem stems from:

- A large rightward shift in supply (technological advance)
- A relatively small shift in demand (income inelasticity)
- A steep demand curve (price inelasticity)

When we put all of these factors together on our historical graph, we can easily visualize the farmer's price problem as it developed over the years.

In Figure 15–6, P_1 is the equilibrium price from an earlier period. Over time, supply and demand curves shift to positions S_2 and D_2 giving a new lower equilibrium price of P_2. Admittedly, this example is somewhat exaggerated. The absolute prices of agricultural commodities have not actually fallen. What has happened is that farm prices have dropped *relative* to the prices of goods that farmers pay as consumers as well as the prices of farm inputs such as land, fertilizer, seed, and machinery.

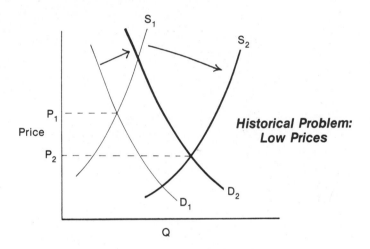

Historical Problem: Low Prices

Figure 15-6

This relative price disadvantage is sometimes referred to as a *parity problem*. A poor parity situation, for example, means that it now takes more bushels of a given commodity (wheat, corn, soybeans, etc.) to purchase a certain bundle of consumer or producer goods than it did in years before. To bring farmers up to some higher level of parity, such as 90 or 100%, requires government subsidies, primarily in the form of price supports. We'll examine price supports and other government programs a little later. Now, however, let's take a look at the so-called short-run agricultural problem.

The Short-Run Problem

If deteriorating parity summarizes the farmers' historical problem, then their short-run problem might be summarized as *unstable farm prices, output, and income on a year-to-year basis.*

Obviously, no farmer knows ahead of time what his year-end production will be, nor does he know how the industry (involving all suppliers) will come out in terms of total production and market price. There are simply too many variables: lack of rain, damage from insects, fungus, an early frost, and so on. These factors may result in higher prices for that year, but at the same time they may have left the farmer with very little to sell.

On the other hand, perfect growing conditions can result in a *bumper crop*, which, ironically, can be just as much of a headache as too little output. How so?

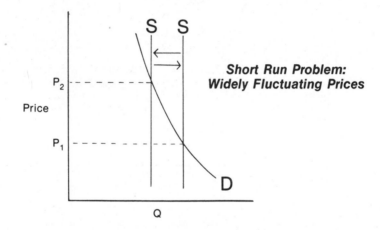

Figure 15-7

This can perhaps best be explained in terms of your home garden. Has your family ever experienced a true bumper crop? Perhaps there were times when you had not only twice as many beans or tomatoes as you needed, but five times as many. Unfortunately, everyone else is probably in the same situation at the same time. Hard as you try, you can hardly give those tomatoes away. Now imagine that your yearly income is dependent on the price of your beans or tomatoes!

Figure 15–7 summarizes these short-run pricing problems. Notice the wide variation in price in Figure 15–7; the major causes of this situation are widely-fluctuating supply and inelastic demand (steep slope).

Price instability leads to income instability. Even small changes in commodity prices, a few cents up or down, can have dramatic effects on the farmer's annual income. When nonfarmers hear the "noon price report," they probably wonder why anyone would be interested in fractional changes in the price of corn, wheat, hogs, or any other commodity. Yet these small changes can easily make the difference between profit and loss for the average farm producer. Few industries face an equivalent situation of income uncertainty on a year-to-year basis.

Our discussion of the two related farm problems leads us to ask what (if anything) can be done about them? Unfortunately, no one has yet discovered a sure-fire, low-cost solution for either the historical or the short-run problem. There have, however, been various government programs to help the American farmer. Looking at these programs with the aid of our supply and demand tools, we'll examine how they work and also note their strengths and weaknesses.

Farm Programs

Let's look first at the government's *crop-restriction* (or *soil bank*) program. In essence, the crop-restriction program pays the farmer (either in cash or in surplus grain) to keep a certain amount of his land *out of production*. Once we see that much of the farm problem stems from oversupply, it is easy to see the logic in restricting the number of acres that farmers are allowed to plant. If we look at the impact of this program on a graph (see Figure 15–8), we note that crop restriction shifts the supply curve backwards (i.e., to the left) and thus brings about higher agriculture prices.

Besides receiving a higher price for the farm commodity (P_2), the farmer also receives greater total revenue for producing less output. How do we know this? Note in Figure 15–8 that the total revenue lost (as represented by the smaller shaded rectangle) is smaller than the total revenue gained (the larger shaded rectangle). This will always be true whenever we deal with a price-inelastic demand curve (see Chapter 3 for more details). In sum-

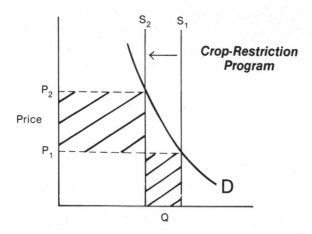

Figure 15-8

mary, the farmer's benefits from crop restrictions are (1) extra money from the government for keeping his land out of production and (2) high commodity prices and greater total revenue.

This program, however, has some major drawbacks for both taxpayers and consumers. These disadvantages include (1) higher taxes to support the crop-restriction program and (2) higher prices and less food available for consumption.

In another form of intervention, the *price-support program*, the government attempts to deal more directly with the price and income instability problems. Basically, price support does two positive things for the farmer: it increases *and* stabilizes commodity prices above the normal equilibrium price. In Figure 15–9, the government's support price is P_s, a price well above the original equilibrium price P_e. This higher price too will give the farmer greater total revenue because of the inelasticity of the demand curve. The higher support price has also cut back the quantity demanded (i.e., from Q_2 to Q_1), but supply will remain constant at the original level. The inevitable result of this situation is the creation of a surplus that must be bought up by the government at the support price. The quantity of this surplus is the difference between Q_1 and Q_2, and the cost of the surplus is represented by the shaded area. When the government buys up this surplus it is a bonus income for the farmers, but it is also a headache for taxpayers. Along with the cost of purchasing surpluses, taxpayers face the additional expense of storing the surplus, and as before, the consumer winds up with higher food prices.

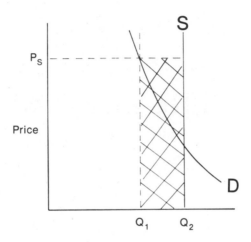

Figure 15-9

And, finally, we've had our government intervene in an attempt to enhance the *demand side* of the market. The large Federal Food Stamp program is one example of this. Also, high on the list of U.S. foreign policy objectives is to create a favorable international climate to sell our agricultural commodities (and sometimes surpluses) overseas. Such efforts, if successful, will improve prices for the American farmer.

Of course we still have a way to go before our deep-seated farm problems are solved. Yet whatever the approach, it should be clear that an understanding of basic supply and demand will be essential in our search for solutions.

Chapter 16

BACKGROUND TO THE LONG RUN

Until now our discussions of competitive supply have been primarily concerned with the short run. Recall once again our hay-baling friend Chester Olson whose resources were fixed except for the one variable resource of labor. It was out of this strict condition that the idea of diminishing returns evolved.

But what would happen now if we suddenly dropped this strict condition? What if we allow Chester the opportunity to expand or contract the amount of land he farms or to add more capital or to alter some other resource? If we give Chester this kind of freedom, we will be in what economists call the *long run*. The long run, therefore, is a "whole new ball game," and its analysis involves a somewhat different approach than that of the short run. Let's see how it works.

The Long Run

I find it easiest to think of the long run as a time period that is long enough to *allow all resources to become variable resources*. In the short run, Chester could not get out of paying for things like land costs, insurance, depreciation, taxes, etc. In the long run, however, we are assuming he can reduce or expand any resource that was formerly fixed.

Thus, at one extreme the long run allows a producer the opportunity to leave farming altogether (if he cannot meet his economic costs), and at the other extreme it means he has the opportunity to

purchase entire new farms, to double or triple the size of his operation if that's what he wants to do. Economists use the phrase
"changing the scale of operation" to indicate an enlargement or
reduction of all resources.

To show the long run on a graph, we must therefore have some
method to indicate scale changes. Economist's do, in fact, have such
a technique—one that is surprisingly similar to the indifference
curve-budget line system that we developed in our chapter "Background to Demand." This technique is called the *equal-product-
curve budget system*. The similarities between these two systems
will be pointed out as we move along.

The Equal-Product Curve

Note, for example, that the curve in Figure 16-1 looks very much
like our earlier indifference curve. This time, however, instead of
two goods on the x and y axes (hamburgers and milkshakes), we
have two resources: capital (K) and labor (L). On the old system, we
had an "indifference curve" that showed a constant level of utility.
Our new curve, however, shows a constant level of output, thus
explaining its name, the equal product curve.

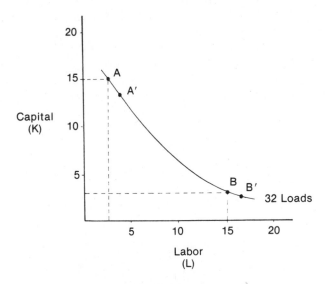

Figure 16-1

Assume, for example, that Chester's equal-product curve, shown in Figure 16–2, represents an output of 32 loads of hay per day. Such an equal-product curve thus indicates *all the combinations of capital (K) and labor (L) that would generate 32 loads of hay.* For example, at point A the combination of 15 units of K and about 2 units of L will give Chester 32 loads, but so will point B, which represents 15 units of L and about 3 of K. Any points between A and B will generate precisely the same output!

Both the equal-product curve and the indifference curve from the theory of demand are "convex to the origin" (note the way this line bends *away* from the lower left-hand corner). This means that if Chester wants to maintain 32 loads of hay and move from say point A to A', he will have to give up quite a bit of capital. On the other hand, if he is at point B and wishes to move to the more "labor-intensive" situation of B', the necessary reduction in capital won't have to be as great as before. Thus as Chester moves from A to B, this apparent "falling rate of substitution" of capital for labor will give rise to a curve that shows a progressively-falling slope as seen in Figure 16–2.

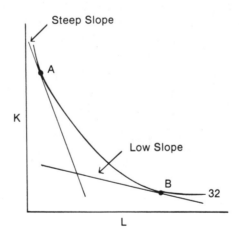

Figure 16-2

We can establish other similarities too between the indifference and the equal-product curves. For example, in the long run

Chester has the opportunity to move onto higher and higher equal-product curves, just as the consumer (in Chapter 11) could move onto higher indifference curves. Each new equal-product curve (moving upward to the right) will therefore represent higher levels of output. When a number of curves are placed together on one graph, we have what is called *a production map*, or *production function*, showing us the thousands and thousands of resource combinations that will produce any given level of output. Figure 16–3 shows a partial production function with three possible levels of output. One might, of course, enlarge the graph and draw in other possible levels as well.

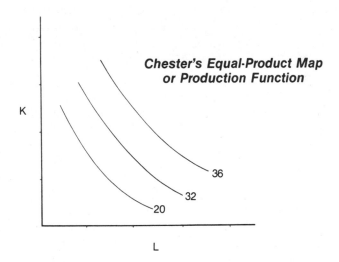

Figure 16-3

The budget line is another point of similarity with our consumer analysis. In Chester's example, the budget line represents a certain budget to pay for production costs. The producer's budget line is drawn in exactly the same fashion as it was for the consumer. (You may wish to reread the explanation on pages 164–166 if you feel uneasy about how these lines are derived.) Once a budget line has been drawn for any specific budget, we are able to see exactly where Chester *maximizes output* with a given budget (just as the consumer maximized utility with his budget). Of course, when we say Chester is "maximizing output with a given budget," we are also saying that he is minimizing costs when producing that many loads of hay.

Let's assume that Chester is given the opportunity to spend a fixed amount, say $300, and then we will see how he maximizes output on a fixed budget. In Figure 16–4 the budget line represents $300.

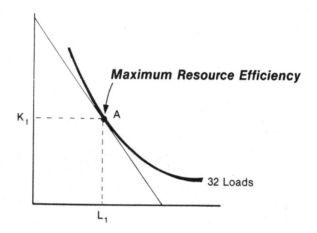

Figure 16-4

The point of maximum efficiency is really no surprise; the solution is indeed similar to the one we obtained earlier in demand theory. Here, however, the producer maximizes output (or minimizes costs) at the point where *the equal-product curve is tangent to the budget line.* In Figure 16–4 that "optimal" point is obviously at A. Once we find the tangency, we can dot over to the K (capital) axis and then down to the L (labor) axis to find the best or most efficient combination of resources Chester would use to produce his thirty-two loads of hay. The ideal resource mix would therefore be K_1 and L_1.

One reason we are taking pains to make all these comparisons between the theory of demand and the theory of production is to show the amazing similarities between consumer behavior and producer behavior. Both the consumer and the producer are trying to maximize their individual objectives under financial constraints: The producer attempts to maximize output, while the consumer tries to maximize utility, with their limited budgets.

The major difference between producer and consumer theory, however, is that the producer is not just seeking an efficient use of resources, he also wants to maximize long-run profits. Profit maximization, in turn, makes our discussion of supply somewhat more complex than that of demand, as we will see a little later in this chapter.

Chester Goes To India

Let's again return to Chester's efficiency position as seen in Figure 16–8 and try an experiment. Let's transfer our hay baling friend to a labor-intensive, capital-poor country such as India.

India has an extremely large labor supply that contributes to a situation of depressed wages. On the other hand, India's capital shortage means relatively high capital prices compared with the United States; these resource prices will therefore force Chester into a different pattern of production than he had in the United States. We can easily see how this works using the equal-product curve.

First, we must realize that equal-product curves in India will probably be the same as those in the United States. The "mix" of resources that can produce a certain level of output is more or less a "mechanical arrangement," where so much input anywhere in the world will result in the same output. So what is the major difference between India and the United States?

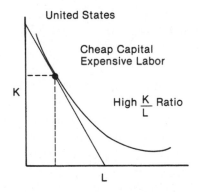

Figure 16-5a

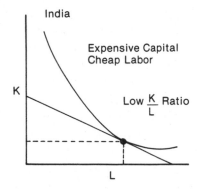

Figure 16-5b

Figure 16–5 shows this difference between countries to be *the slope of the budget line*. For example, a $300 budget in India can obviously buy a great deal of labor because of India's relatively low labor costs. However in that same country, Chester can't buy very much capital because of its high cost. The resulting budget line for India would therefore be a low sloped line. Figure 16–5 shows a budget line comparison between the United States and India. Note that there is a relatively steep-sloped budget line for the United States because of our high labor cost and our relatively low capital cost.

What is so interesting about these two diagrams is that they clearly show the dramatic impact that difference resource prices have upon the way a country will produce its products. *Production efficiency* in the United States, for example, is defined by a resource mix that represents a high capital-to-labor (K/L) ratio. Indeed, this is really no surprise as we frequently see businesses using more capital intensive methods in an economic climate of relatively high labor costs.

Efficiency in India is just the reverse. There, Chester will produce the maximum output in India with low K/L ratio, i.e., a very labor-intensive technique. One might jump to the conclusion that because India winds up with a labor-intensive method of producing hay, its system is necessarily less efficient than the U.S. capital intensive system. This may not be correct, however. To find out which country's production method is more efficient, we need to compare the overall costs of production. If we assume that Chester is operating on the same budget and producing the same output, then the two countries would be equally efficient.

The Expansion Line

Let's now bring Chester back to his original farm in the United States and offer him what we originally promised—the chance to use a wide variety of budgets and the long-run freedom to change any or all of his resources. Then we can watch him expand his scale of operation while we note the points of tangency between equal-product curves and the new budget lines. We will then connect the points of tangency with what is referred to as an *expansion line*. The expansion line will show Chester precisely which combinations of capital and labor will most efficiently produce a large variety of output levels.

Figure 16–6 illustrates a sample expansion line using five equal-product curves.

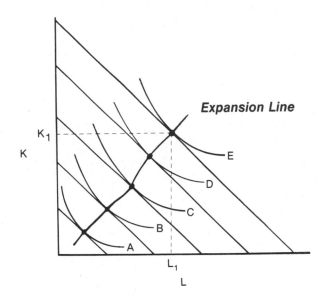

Figure 16-6

With the expansion line in place, it is now possible for Chester to choose *any* level of output, then find the point of tangency and dot over to the horizontal and vertical axes to determine the most efficient combination of capital and labor. For example, at output level E in Figure 16–6, Chester would find that L1 and K1 turn out to be the most efficient resource mix.

From the expansion line we can also see how our present long-run situation differs from the short-run conditions in our earlier discussion. Note how Chester is now changing *both capital and labor!*

Long-Run Average Cost

We are now in a good position to discuss what is perhaps the most important idea of this chapter—the derivation of Chester's *long-run average-cost (LAC) curve.* You might be wondering why we are so interested in discussing another cost concept; after all didn't we earlier spend a lot of time and energy developing the important idea of marginal cost?

Indeed, marginal cost is still a crucial idea as it helps us to determine where a producer maximizes his profits. The LAC curve, on the other hand, will be our best measure of output *efficiency*. Although we analyzed "efficiency" when we discussed the point of tangency, this was only one kind of efficiency, i.e., the best combination or mix of resources in which to produce an A, B, C, D, or E level of output.

What we don't yet know is *which of the different levels of output* is the optimum level. As an example, level A may be only one load of hay per day (see Figure 16–6). Although we now know the "best" combination of resources to produce that one load, there nevertheless may be certain *efficiencies of size* if we go to some higher level of output (i.e., large-scale operations can often produce more cheaply than small-scale operations). These size efficiencies are

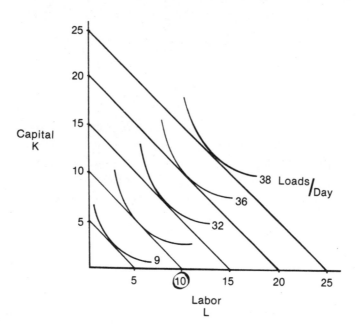

Figure 16-7

referred to as *economies of scale*. Which level of output (A, B, C, D, or E) will maximize these economies of scale? We can find out by calculating which level of output will give Chester's lowest average cost. Let's look at some examples.

For simplicity's sake, we'll assume that a unit of capital costs $20 and that a unit of labor is also $20. We now have sufficient data to find Chester's average costs. To start off, let's give him $100. At $20 per unit for labor the maximum potential labor quantity with this budget would be 5 units. Thus, the budget line would strike the labor axis at the 5-unit level. On the other hand, if Chester spent all of his $100 on capital and none on labor, he could buy 5 units of capital. This budget line is shown as the smallest budget in Figure 16–7.

Next we will give Chester $200 and work out a budget line for that amount. Then we will give him $300; $400; and, finally, $500. Each new and higher budget is represented by an expanding budget line in Figure 16–7.

Finally, we will draw the relevant equal-product curve that's tangent to each of these budget lines and note the output that is associated with each equal-product curve. From these figures we can derive our long-run average costs.

Let's work out a specific example using the above information. Look carefully at that particular budget line which strikes the labor axis at 10 units (note that the number 10 on the labor axis is circled). Remembering that labor is priced at $20, we know that this budget must be worth $200 (i.e., $10 \times \$20 = \$200$).

Next, we read off the maximum output that is possible for this $200 budget as represented by the equal-product curve tangent to this budget line. It's worth 20 loads of hay, right? Thus, the average cost of producing 20 loads of hay is:

$$\$200/20 \text{ loads} = \$10 \text{ per load (Average cost)}$$

Using the same method, we can go on to figure out the average costs at the other points of tangency as well. Each average cost (in relation to a particular quantity) is thus one more point on Chester's LAC curve. Rounding off to the nearest half dollar, we get the average costs shown in the chart on the next page.

$$\frac{\textbf{Budget}}{\textbf{Loads}} = {}^{\$}\textbf{LAC}$$

(Rounded to the Nearest Half Dollar)

1 $\dfrac{\$100}{\text{9 Loads}} = {}^{\$}11\Big/\text{Load}$

2 $\dfrac{\$200}{\text{20 Loads}} = {}^{\$}10\Big/\text{Load}$

3 $\dfrac{\$300}{\text{32 Loads}} = {}^{\$}9.50\Big/\text{Load}$

4 $\dfrac{\$400}{\text{36 Loads}} = {}^{\$}11\Big/\text{Load}$

5 $\dfrac{\$500}{\text{38 Loads}} = {}^{\$}13\Big/\text{Load}$

Finally, using the data in this chart, we're able to graph 5 points on Chester's LAC curve in Figure 16–8.

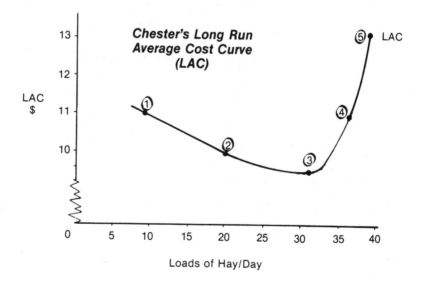

Figure 16-8

This LAC curve has a special shape to it, which raises some interesting questions. Why do you think it first turns down, and then at about 32 loads (point 3) begins to turn up? What do you think is the optimal level of output? And finally, how does this curve relate to the process of profit maximization?

We will be taking a close look at these and other questions as we move on to the next chapter.

Chapter 17

LONG-RUN SUPPLY

In the preceding chapter we derived Chester Olson's long run average-cost (LAC) curve from his equal-product curves. Now we are going to look much more closely at the *shape* of his LAC curve, in our continuing quest to understand the nature of economic efficiency. And later on, we will be asking the important question, "How does Chester maximize his profits in the long run?" Our answer, in turn, will lead us directly to the long-run competitive-supply curve.

To begin our discussion, it will be helpful to look again at Chester's LAC curve in Figure 16–8. Note its U-like shape—the curve drops steadily to its lowest point at 32 loads of hay, and after that it rises fairly sharply.

What is behind this U shape? Are we again experiencing a situation of increasing returns and then diminishing returns? No, not this time; recall that diminishing returns always requires all productive factors except one to be fixed. Chester is now in the long run, a time period in which he can vary all resources. What actually causes this drop and rise of LAC is called *economies and diseconomies of scale*. Let's take a close look at these twin ideas.

Economies And Diseconomies Of Scale

Returning to Chester's hay-baling operation, we see that when he produces only 9 loads a day, his average cost per load is $11. As he expands production, however, he is able to reduce his average costs. They then drop to a low of $9.50 per load as his scale moves to 32 loads. This drop, as we mentioned above, is because of the economies of scale. What then are these mysterious economies?

Economies of scale are various cost-cutting efficiencies that are brought about as the scale of operation grows. Certainly the most common one is a result of specialization and division of labor. When workers specialize, they learn to do their specific jobs quicker and more accurately than a worker who shifts around from job to job (as Chester did when he was baling by himself). In addition, you have probably experienced the difficulty in "getting going" on a new task (studying for an exam perhaps?) or moving from one project to another. Adam Smith once described the problem this way:

> A man commonly saunters a little in turning his hand from one sort of employment to another. When he first begins the new work he is seldom very keen and hearty; his mind, as they say, does not go to it, and for some time he rather trifles than applies to good purpose.[39]

Returning to Chester's situation, we find that when he enlarges the scale of his operation, he is now able to increase not only the number of people but also the number of tractors, wagons, and so forth. Thus one man can specialize in loading hay, another in driving the tractor with the baler, another in taking loads back and forth, another in unloading, and so on. After a while, Chester's baling crew will be able to operate much like an assembly-line operation.

Also, consider the possibilities for larger machinery. A baler that costs $1,000 might easily be *more than twice as productive* as a $500 machine. You can see these economies of scale at work on many large farms with their large tractors, plows, and other machinery.

Economies of scale can also be observed in other industries. For example, if someone tried to produce automobiles on a scale of 100 cars per year, their average cost per car would obviously be extremely high. If, however, they are able to "up the scale" to 30,000 cars per year, they will soon discover many, many little efficiencies that work to bring average costs down. In addition, large businesses often operate dozens of separate plants that are able to take advantage of specialized expertise at the management level, as well as efficiencies in purchasing large quantities versus small. Good examples of such businesses are the McDonald's restaurants and the K-Mart retail stores where we see economies passed on to the consumer in the form of relatively lower prices. From Henry Ford's original assembly line to large-scale farming to McDonald's restaurants, the average consumer has benefited from production techniques based on economies of scale.

We should, however, recognize some of the drawbacks as well. Large-scale concerns often take on an impersonal dimension for both the employees and their customers. In addition, workers on the bottom may frequently suffer from chronic boredom as a result of overspecialization. Indeed, the LAC curve of a business may continue to fall as the organization gets larger and more specialized; keep in mind, however, that the LAC curve represents monetary costs only.

If it were possible to have some simple measurement (like dollars) for the psychological costs, we might find that organizations reach their "optimal" efficiency long before the average monetary costs reach their minimum point. Figure 17–1 presents a comparison between average economic costs and average "psychic" costs for a sample large-scale system. This system could conceivably be a business, a factory, a government agency, a hospital, a school, or even a city.

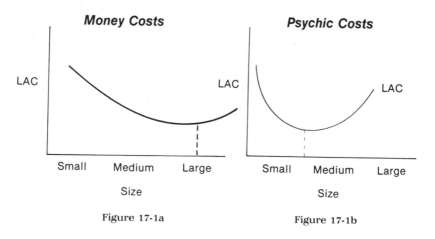

Figure 17-1a

Figure 17-1b

If the situation shown in Figure 17–1 is in fact true, we would note that as a system gets larger, its average economic costs drop; i.e., it would be less expensive to build a car, to treat a hospital patient, to educate a child, or to administer a city. On the other hand, the "nonmonetary diseconomies" would become a growing problem much earlier.

Yet even without the problem of psychic costs, long-run average monetary cost curves *eventually will turn upward on their own.* In Chester's example, his LAC curve began to rise after approximately thirty-two loads of hay. When LAC starts to rise, it means that production has reached a point where diseconomies of scale tend to outweigh the economies of scale. Sometimes it's interesting to assess what these diseconomies might be for different organizations. Let's look at some examples.

In Chester's case, diseconomies probably begin to emerge when he finds himself wasting time and fuel hauling his tractors and machinery around his enlarged farm operation. Another diseconomy becomes apparent when he discovers additional difficulty in *coordinating* all the diverse factors (people, machines, etc.) that must be accurately synchronized to maintain efficient production. Related to this is the increasing problem of *getting accurate information* on what is happening around the farm as the size of the operation increases; without good knowledge of what is going on, Chester finds himself making decisions based on inadequate information—decisions that cost him money. In addition, his large machinery may mean more costly repair work, and "one sunny day's breakdown" will become far more expensive to him than it was when he ran a smaller operation.

For large businesses, diseconomies frequently crop up in the form of *bureaucratic red* tape and the layers and layers of hierarchical decision making. Upper level management people in large businesses often have difficulty knowing what is going on at the lower levels; some organizations are simply too big and too spread out. In order to get the information they need, middle and upper level management people find themselves spending more and more time in meetings and conferences. They also need the opinions of a growing army of management specialists, and yet these hour-to-hour sessions of highly paid executives take their toll in costs. Smaller companies, on the other hand, can frequently avoid some of these information gathering inefficiencies.

Larger companies may also be *more rigid* about certain policies, such as approving new ideas or hiring particularly gifted employees. Perhaps you can think of certain types of jobs that relate specifically to large companies—jobs that would probably not exist if the organization were smaller. (Possible examples might be security personnel, parking lot attendants, or legal and public relations departments.)

Of course, these are often little diseconomies, but they do add up. And at some point they begin to outweigh the more commonly known economies of scale. When this finally happens, the LAC curves begin to rise.

Double Efficiency

Let's now summarize and tie together what we have learned about economic efficiency. We discovered that Chester Olson will experience economies of scale as he enlarges his operation up to a certain point—32 loads of hay per day—and it is only at that quantity that he can produce hay for the lowest possible average cost of $9.50 per load. Thus, 32 loads is that special scale of output where Chester's economies are in full force. This, in fact, would be the correct capacity for *any* producer who is using the same baling technology as Chester. We thus have one kind of efficiency—*the efficiency of scale*—that is represented by the bottom point on an LAC curve.

This low point on the LAC curve also represents another kind of efficiency, i.e., *the right mix of resources.* This is represented by the tangency of the equal-product curve with the budget line.

There is therefore a kind of "double efficiency" that takes place at the bottom of the LAC curve. In Figure 17–2 we have combined these two efficiency ideas in order to show how the two systems relate to each other.

In summary, the 32-load level of output and the $9.50 average cost represent double efficiency because (1) it's the most efficient mix of resources (for that output) and (2) it's an optimum output or scale (considering all outputs).

Now, if this double efficiency point on Chester's LAC curve is such an ideal situation economically, will Chester, in fact, operate there?

Before we can answer that question we need to find out how he will go about maximizing his profits. Only if the point of efficiency is the same point as profit maximization can we be sure that our competitive model works to promote the best use of resources in the long run.

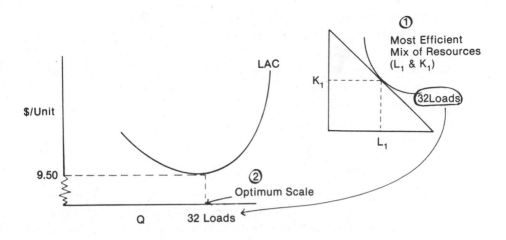

Figure 17-2

Efficiency And Profits

Fortunately, we have already worked out a technique for determining profit maximization. Recall our general principle that Chester should increase his output as long as the marginal cost (MC) is less than the price of a load of hay. Only when the extra costs exceed the value of a load of hay should he stop adding to his output. We therefore concluded in Chapter 13 that Chester will reach the maximum profit position when the MC equals the price.

Nothing has changed this theory even though we are now in the long run. We do have one problem, however; we have not yet worked out what Chester's marginal cost (or more specifically, his *long-run* marginal cost *LMC*) curve looks like. Our only long-run information is summarized by the LAC curve that we developed earlier, and without knowing LMCs we have no way to calculate profitability. It is possible, however, to roughly work out LMC from his LAC curve.

One of the best methods of seeing how "marginal" and "average" relate to each other is to look at a topic closer to home to most students—grade point averages. The secret to connecting average with marginal is to recognize that one's grade point average is made up of many, many marginal grades. In fact, it's the marginals that raise or lower an average.

For example, let's assume that you take economics as an "extra" course, and you get an "A." But your overall average grade for all of your courses is a "C." The "A" is your marginal grade; that is, it is the grade you get from taking an extra course. Now if your marginal grade is *above* your overall average, *it will pull the average up*. Of course, that marginal "A" will not lift your overall average to an "A," but it will pull it up to some degree. On the other hand, if your marginal grade was a "D," it would obviously pull the overall average down.

Now let's return to the world of economic costs. If the above analogy holds, we know that if the average (i.e., the LAC curve) is falling, it means that the MC is below it. Just as very low marginal grades pull one's average grade point down, very low MCs pull the average cost down. On the other hand, if we are at levels of output where LAC is moving upward, then we can be certain that MCs must be above LAC (just as your "A" grade pulls up your average).

One important characteristic of this relationship is that as soon as LMC is a fraction of a dollar above LAC, *it begins pulling LAC up*. This, in turn, means that LMC must strike through LAC *at the bottom of the LAC curve*, i.e., at the most efficient scale of output. When LMC, which is the guideline to maximum profitability, is equal to LAC at its most efficient point, it is indeed a good omen. We can see this unique relationship in Figure 17–3:

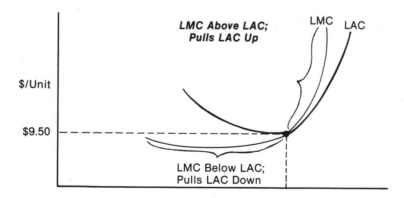

Figure 17-3

But, as you can see, there are many other points on Chester's LMC curve as well. If the price of a load of hay happens to be above the $9.50 level, or below it, then Chester will maximize profits at some "nonoptimum" point. What we need is some kind of guarantee that the overall industry price of hay will settle at the $9.50 level. Chester will then equate price with LMCs (maximum profit point) at that place which coincides with the bottom of his LAC curve (maximum efficiency point).

Is there any unique characteristic of a competitive market that will guarantee this "correct" price? Fortunately there is. The key characteristic is easy entry, easy exit. (Recall our discussion in Chapter 14.) The fact that small competitors may easily enter or leave the industry guarantees the $9.50 price because that is the only price where there will be no excessive long-run profits. Let's look at an example.

Suppose the price in the short run were $12, a price that would give hay producers a temporary profit because it is greater than average costs. This profit, in turn, will be a "signal" for a swarm of small producers to move in increasing overall supply. (Remember the earlier hog example?) The result will be to drive the price back down to the only *no-excess-profit* point of $9.50 (where price equals average cost).

Perhaps you object to the fact that Chester is going to wind up at a break-even situation in the long run even though he is "pursuing maximum profits." Keep in mind, however, that we are assuming that all of Chester's economic costs are being met.

Therefore, a "no-profit" situation means that Chester is paying himself a fair wage and earning a decent rate of return on his investment. Outside of these returns, though, he has virtually no control over other hay producers moving in if the price of hay goes above average costs. In the short run, therefore, there might be extra profits (since it is not a long enough period for new producers to enter), but in the long run we must assume they will move in. And, if the price is right, they will.

This situation operates in reverse too. For example, if the price should happen to dip below the $9.50 level, there will be some losses within the industry because the price will be lower than average costs. Again, the long run is a long enough period of time to allow some of the losing operators to move out of the industry.

This will cut back overall industry supply and eventually increase the industry price to the \$9.50 level. What is important to see is how the easy entry, easy exit characteristic of the competitive market model *forces* the suppliers to operate where we want them to, i.e., at that quantity where the LAC curve is lowest and the maximum economies of scale are in effect (see Figure 17–4a).

Therefore, in the long run we have a rather strange-looking supply curve for a perfectly competitive industry (Figure 17–4b): it is a horizontal line emanating from the y axis at the very lowest possible point on the LAC curve. Of course the possibility exists that if an industry's output grows *too* large, it may take more money to attract additional resources. If we find basic industry costs rising, we can expect (at some large output level) an eventual upward turn. This situation is represented by the dotted line in Figure 17–4b.

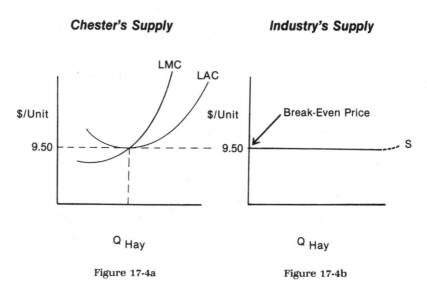

| Chester's Supply | Industry's Supply |

Figure 17-4a

Figure 17-4b

In conclusion, we can say that purely competitive industries in the long run will supply as much output as needed at the lowest possible cost. Not only is our long-run competitive solution good for the economy in terms of efficiency, it also offers the consumer a product for a price equal to the lowest average cost possible.

These are the major reasons economists find the competitive model so attractive.

Competition Versus Monopoly

Farming is a good illustration of competition partly because its ideal scale is relatively small compared with the overall demand for the product. As an industry, agriculture can accommodate thousands and thousands of small, efficient operators. This then is an ideal setting for a highly competitive industry, as can be seen in Figure 17–5. (Note the change in the x axis from 32 loads to 320,000 loads.)

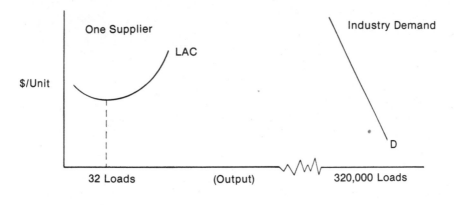

Figure 17-5

But what would happen in some other industry that *had to have* a very large scale so as to take advantage of all the scale efficiencies? An extreme example of this is the electric utility industry where the regional demand is usually insufficient to meet the optimal scale requirements of more than one seller. We have graphed this situation in Figure 17–6.

Note that in this example we have a continually-dropping LAC curve, indicating "room" for only one producer in the market. This situation is precisely the opposite of our competitive model. What we now have is an environment that is made to order for a monopolist. The above situation, in fact, is called a *natural monopoly* because *even one* additional supplier would be economically unnecessary.

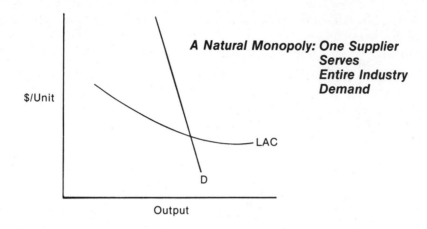

Figure 17-6

How then do these monopoly industries operate in regard to pricing and efficiency? Are monopolies good or bad for the overall economy? These and other questions will be examined as we zero in on the monopoly market structure in the next chapter.

Chapter 18

MONOPOLY

To get a perspective on the subject of monopoly, let's first look at the broader concept of *imperfect competition*. As you undoubtedly realize, most of the industries in the United States are not really competitive according to our strict definition of a competitive market. As noted before, some industries need such a large scale of operation that there is room for only one seller. Other industries, such as auto, steel, or television manufacturers, also require large-scale facilities, but their industries can accommodate a number of firms, although not the thousands and thousands needed to call it competitive.

In addition to the scale requirement, we also find situations where potential rivals are discouraged from entering the market by existing firms. Barriers, such as patent protection, monopolization of raw materials, brand name recognition, or aggressive price cutting, are often erected to ward off newcomers from entering the industry.

Thus with these entry barriers, we move into the "real world" economic environment that was briefly examined in Chapter 2. Adding to our former list of noncompetitive models (i.e., monopoly and oligopoly), we will also be looking at a new model called *differentiated competition*. Let's take a look at how all these markets (including pure competition) relate to each other in their degree of concentration (Figure 18–1).

Thus, if we are going to get an accurate picture of how our economy actually functions, we must now go beyond pure competition. Fortunately, this does not mean that we have to begin all over again with resource pricing, deriving cost curves, etc. Our

Levels of Concentration

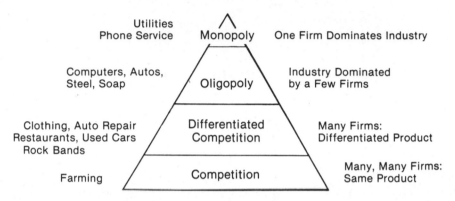

Figure 18-1

production theory for noncompetitive systems is pretty much the same since *all* firms (in any of the four market structures) have similar-looking long-run average-cost (LAC) and long-run marginal-cost (LMC) curves based on their production functions. So what is the difference between the competitive market structure and the three noncompetitive structures, monopoly, oligopoly, and differentiated competition?

The major difference between these markets is reflected in the *individual firm's demand curve*. The demand curve, in turn, is based upon the firm's relative *control* over the industry market. The monopolist, for example, has the entire industry demand to himself. The oligopoly and differentiated-competitive market structures have unique demand situations that reflect their respective ability to control the market. We will be taking a look at the latter two models in the next chapter, but for now let's focus our attention on the pure monopolist.

A Definition Of Monopoly

I find it easiest to remember a monopoly as simply a *one firm industry*. Recall that, in theory, there are no close substitutes for the monopolist's product; the consumer, therefore, has no choice—

either you buy from him, or you don't get the product or service. As we learned earlier, the monopolist might attain his unique status by scale requirements alone; that is, the market cannot logically contain more than one seller (such as an electric utility). If this is the case, it's called a *natural monopoly*.

On the other hand, there have also been cases, such as the formation of the original Standard Oil Company, where the monopoly attained its dominant position by ruthless price cutting practices undertaken to "freeze out" the competition. Economists would call this a *predatory monopolist*.

Monopolies can also be formed through the exclusive use of new or secret technology, the exclusive control of raw materials, and other techniques. But no matter how it is formed, the monopolist always winds up with the entire industry demand.

Of course, there are some limits to the monopolist's power. Even though he has considerable price control, he must still operate within the confines and constraints of the industry demand. Thus, if he decides to charge some outrageous price, the monopolist will discover (as in any other business) that nobody will show up to buy the product.

Nevertheless, price control does work to the monopolist's advantage in that he is able to "fine tune" the industry price to gain a maximum amount of monopoly profits. Certainly no other market structure enjoys so much flexibility.

To show how a pure monopolist uses price control to maximize profits, let's devise a new example. Let's pretend that Chester Olson, now fed up with the risks and uncertainties of baling hay, decides to become a manufacturer of hay baling equipment. Let's further assume that after extensive research and testing our friend comes up with a new, improved, revolutionary hay-baling machine.

The other hay-baler companies are shocked to discover this simple farmer has invented a new baler that is so efficient, it makes all others virtually obsolete. Despite some start up problems, Chester establishes a huge baler factory and successfully markets his baler nationally. Farm trade journals, in turn, praise Chester as "the new Henry Ford" of hay balers.

As an effective monopolist, Chester now finds himself in a much more favorable position than as just plain "Chester Olson,

competitive hay supplier." In the old days he had to abide by the industry price, no matter what it happened to be. Now Chester can set his own price geared to make maximum profit within the constraints of market demand and costs of production. Just how does Chester choose this "ideal" price?

The procedure is not much different from his earlier method of maximizing profits. What he first looks for is the correct output associated with the greatest profits. Thus, he will continue to produce balers as long as the extra cost (marginal cost, MC) of producing a baler is lower than the extra revenue (marginal revenue, MR) of selling that baler.

Notice our new term *marginal revenue*, defined as "the extra revenue gained from selling an extra unit of output." When Chester was a competitive hay supplier the MR was exactly the same as the price of hay; if he sold an extra load of hay, he would receive an additional amount of revenue equal to that price. Now, however, because Chester is dealing with total industry demand (as a monopolist), he is undoubtedly facing *a downward-sloping demand curve*, which, in turn, has a marginal revenue something different from the price. To understand this point clearly, let's work out a simple illustration. Our example will also help show us how Chester chooses the "ideal" quantity and price to maximize profits.

First, let's figure out Chester's industry demand curve. We will say that if Chester charges $1,000 for a baler, he won't sell any, but at $900 he will sell one. If he drops his price to $800, he'll sell two; $700, three; and so on. In the following chart the first two columns show Chester's demand-curve information.

$ Quantity	$ Price	$ Total Revenue	$ Marginal Revenue
(Q)	(P)	(TR)	(MR)
0	$1,000	$0	--
1	900	900	900
2	800	1600	700
3	700	2100	500
4	600	2400	300
5	500	2500	100
6	400	2400	-100

To work out the total revenue Chester carefully multiplies price times quantity (third column).

From the total-revenue column Chester can now calculate what his additional revenue will be from selling an extra unit, i.e., his MR. For example, the MR of the second unit is $1600 (total revenue from selling unit 2) minus $900 (total revenue from selling unit 1) or $700, while the MR of say the fifth unit would be $2500 minus $2400 or $100. Note the interesting relationship between the MR of a given unit and its price. MR in each case (except for the first unit) is lower than P.

Next, by graphing Chester's MR curve against the demand curve we can actually see these relationships (see Figure 18–2).

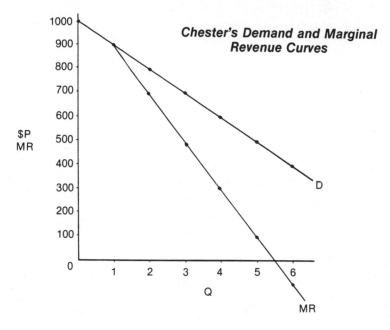

Figure 18-2

OK so far. Chester now knows what his demand and MR curves look like. But to make profit-maximizing marginal decisions, Chester must find out what his marginal costs are. In Figure 18–3, all the relevant curves (including LAC) can be seen on the same graph.

Figure 18–3 provides our hay-baler monopolist with all the information he needs in order to maximize his profits via the old marginal-decision-making approach. Thus, the first question he asks is, "Is the first unit profitable?" Since we can see that the first unit gives him far more revenue that it costs him to produce, the answer is a resounding "yes." The second unit is also profitable, but this time there will be a smaller marginal profit since MR is rapidly dropping. The third unit is obviously the quantity where Chester ought to stop. Past unit three, there is no hope for any more profitable units; the MR is dropping too fast while the MC is speedily climbing.

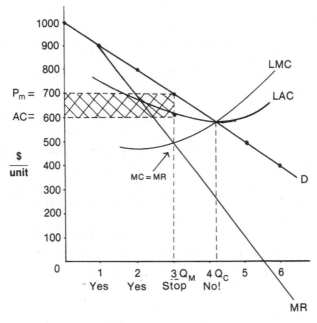

Figure 18-3

While this example shows the logic of marginal decision making, there is no reason why we can't simplify the whole process by saying: *maximum profits are achieved at that quantity where MC equals MR.* Therefore, from now on we will simply note where MC crosses MR and then "dot" down to locate the Q that's associated with maximum profits.

Pricing And Efficiency

Once we find out that Chester maximizes profits at 3 units (Q_m), we can then trace all the other important information concerning monopoly operation. From Figure 18–3 we can work out the following:

- Monopoly price—Dot up from Q_m to the demand curve, then go straight over to the price axis; monopoly price (P_m) in this example: $700 per unit
- Average cost—Dot up from Q_m, but this time stop at the LAC curve, then go over again to the price axis; average cost: $600

- Per-unit profit—Each unit sells for $700, average cost is $600; per-unit profit: $100

- Total profit—Selling three units and making $100 per unit; total profits (shaded-in area): $300

Figure 18–3 also shows what the output and price would have been in a long-run competitive situation. From the last chapter we learned that a competitive market forces a long-run price equivalent to the lowest possible average cost (lowest point on the LAC curve). Using Figure 18–3 we see that the competitive price would have been just under $600; the competitive quantity—Q_c or just a little more than 4 units—can be found by dotting down from the low point on LAC.

Thus, the competitive model has some advantages over monopoly: Competition offers a lower price to the consumer and also forces a larger output that is more in line with the optimum scale of production. The monopoly, in turn, often creates an "artificial scarcity" while simultaneously charging a price higher than the competitive price. The net result is a misallocation of the economy's resources.

What often irritates people about monopoly behavior is that monopolies seem to make unusually large profits simply because of the company's considerable control of the market. What might surprise you, however, is that monopolists sometimes do not make such excessive profits. How could this be?

It's because profits are dependent upon a favorable average cost situation in relation to the demand curve. As an example, it's *possible* that Chester could become so complacent as a businessman that he would allow his average cost curve to creep up above the market price of the baler. If this happened, monopolist Chester Olson would actually lose money (an unusual situation, but still possible).

Yet assuming that Chester does in fact earn a significant monopoly profit, can we say that these profits are unjustified? Some people would probably answer affirmatively, but there may, in fact, be reasonable justification for large profits for both monopolists and other businesses operating under imperfect competitive situations.

For example, it is generally acknowledged that profits can be a legitimate return on *innovation*. In Chester's case it is difficult to argue that Chester did not deserve some financial reward for his superior hay baling machine. In addition, Chester should probably receive some kind of monetary reward for the *financial risk* that was involved in undertaking this hazardous venture. Finally, economists generally recognize the need for a certain amount of profits as reward for effective coordination of resources, that is, for *entrepreneurial skills*.

Nonetheless, economists still worry that any degree of monopoly within a market, compared with a more competitive situation, will ultimately result in a less efficient use of society's resources. Furthermore, monopoly profits are not always a result of innovation, risk, and efficient resource coordination. They often come about when new firms are, in one way or another, barred from entry into the industry. Illegitimate profits can also appear from the formation of a *trust*, *cartel*, or *shared monopoly*, where producers get together to carve up markets, to fix prices, and thus to act as if they were a single monopolist:

> "People of the same trade seldom meet together, but the conversation ends in a conspiracy against the public, or in some contrivance to raise prices."

This statement is perhaps as true now as it was when Adam Smith first composed it two centuries ago; yet we know that profits resulting from such collusion are neither fair nor justified. Recognizing that monopolies can be a problem for society, it is therefore important to ask what can be done to eliminate them or reduce their harmful effects.

Dealing With Monopoly

Perhaps the easiest type of monopoly to recognize and to deal with is the natural monopoly. As we learned earlier, a natural monopoly comes about because of scale requirements; thus, a phone or electric company can be allowed legal status as a monopolist as long as it consents to *regulation* by some publicly appointed commission. The regulators can then establish a price and quantity more in line with what would have been true under competitive conditions.

Another method of eliminating unjustified monopoly profits is to "tax them away" with a fixed or lump-sum tax. If, for example, the government had deemed all of Chester's monopoly profits as unjustified, it could tax him the full $300 profit, raising his LAC curve by $100 and making it a no-profit situation with price equal to average cost. The drawback to this "solution" is that it leaves Chester's old MR = MC intact; thus he will continue to produce at the artificial scarcity level of Q_m (see Figure 18-3).

For cartels and predatory monopolies, we have a slightly different situation. These monopolies are often difficult to recognize, but once detected, the government must legally prove their anti-competitive behavior under our antitrust laws. Firms violating these laws may be penalized with stiff fines, and the individual executives responsible for the illegal decisions could possibly be sentenced to jail terms.

Other types of monopolies are even more difficult to deal with than those mentioned above. In *Tools for Conviviality* Ivan Illich identifies what he calls *radical monopolies*, which involve the dominance of large product systems:

> I speak about radical monopoly when one industrial production process exercises an exclusive control over the satisfaction of a pressing need . . . Cars can thus monopolize traffic. They can shape a city into their image—practically ruling out locomotion on foot or by bicycle in Los Angeles.[40]

Illich has also written about radical monopolies in schools (*Deschooling Society*) and modern medicine (*Medical Nemesis*)—monopolies so powerful and pervasive that they leave us with very few practical alternatives. If Illich's conclusions are correct, radical monopolies may pose greater problems for an economic system than industrial or corporate monopolies. Indeed, this is one important area that needs further research.

I also believe that the understanding of an economic monopoly can help us deal with this problem in other guises; e.g., a political dictatorship or a one-party state is a form of monopoly. One might also look at the parent-child relationship as a monopoly, a theme that is explored in John Holt's book *Escape from Childhood*.

Yet, however we look at the monopoly concept—whether in purely economic terms or in its broader context—it is usually bad news. It involves a no-alternative situation for the consumer. It's a situation where often the competitive system of checks and balances is absent, allowing the monopolist to magnify man's tendency to hurt and exploit others in pursuit of profits and power.

Chapter 19

OLIGOPOLY AND DIFFERENTIATED COMPETITION

Rounding out our discussion of the imperfectly competitive market structure, we're now going to take a look at the oligopoly and differentiated-competition systems—certainly the two most prevalent industry structures in the United States today. We will again have the benefit of our earlier production and cost analyses as well as the tools we developed to find maximum profit via the marginal decision approach. Nothing will change in these areas. What does change as we shift from one system to another is the relative control that an individual firm will have in its specific market. This difference in turn gives rise to different demand curves.

Oligopoly

Recall from our discussion in Chapter 2 that an oligopoly market structure is one in which the entire industry *is dominated by a few firms*. In most cases, the oligopolist markets a product that he considers different from his rivals and tries to promote this product not so much by offering the lowest price possible (i.e., by *price competition*), but by a variety of techniques that are lumped under the title *nonprice competition*.

Nonprice competition includes things like stylistic differences, brand name recognition, advertising, service, quality (real or imagined), special location, and so on. This kind of competition can be as honest as a "five-year unconditional warranty" and "true craftsmanship-like construction" or as devious as linking up the buyer with an improbable image of sexual or financial success. Price cutting, however, is generally frowned upon, as it would have the effect of disrupting the industry as well as destabilizing corporate earnings.

We also know that oligopolies (like monopolies) maintain their market position through a variety of *entry barriers.* You might review the possible obstacles you would face in attempting to start up a new automobile company or in marketing a new breakfast cereal or in manufacturing and selling over-the-counter drugs. Besides the problem of large scale manufacturing requirements, you would also need to gain access to and get the confidence of money lenders, researchers, specialized production experts—on through the stages up to distributors and ultimately the consumers themselves. At each stage you would probably face great difficulties as you attempted to chisel into the existing industrial edifice— breaking down corporate rigidities, rearranging traditional patterns, and fending off the skilled defensive activities of the dominant producers.

Another characteristic of an oligopoly is *mutual interdependence*, a concept that can be best explained by making a comparison with the pure competitor. Recall that Chester Olson as a farmer competitor did not really care what his neighbor farmers were doing. Sure he might be curious, possibly envious, if Jones bought a new tractor or built a new barn; but what Farmer Jones did (or what any other single competitor did) would not in any way affect Olson's economic situation.

In contrast, the oligopolist is extremely concerned about what his fellow industrial rivals are doing in terms of pricing, styling, advertising, and so forth. At times, this interdependence becomes as complicated as a chess game and, in some cases, as serious as warfare.[41]

Interdependence, in turn, makes it difficult to design an appropriate oligopoly theory that is as predictable as the models for perfect competition and monopoly. A good analogy can be drawn with a football game. While it is possible to develop a theory to predict an opposing team's strategy, it would probably be accurate only *some of the time.* So it is with oligopoly: the best of our models are only partly accurate. One of the better of these models is called *oligopoly under a kinked demand curve.* Let's see what this model says about oligopoly behavior.

Kinked Demand Curve

Why is there so little price competition among oligopolists? Why do these industries tend to display rigid pricing policies? Can we actually prove that price inflexibility is consistent with profit maximization? The kinked demand curve helps answer these questions.

Let's assume that over the years Chester Olson loses his monopoly position as manufacturer of hay balers. New baler companies have now moved into the market with a similar product, and the old stand-bys, like John Deere, New Holland, etc., reestablish themselves. Chester is now one of a half dozen or so oligopolists within this particular industry.

Since we no longer have a monopoly, we will assume that the overall industrial price for balers is established first by the dominant company (say John Deere), the *price leader*. The other firms, in turn, follow right along. We will call this established price the *administered price* (P_A).

Given the existence of an administered price, how might this affect Chester's own demand curve? If Chester, on his own, *raises* his price, the rest of the producers probably won't be too concerned; the industry will gladly watch Chester lose a lot of his old business by unilaterally raising his price. The very fact that he will lose a large part of his market share implies that he is on an elastic demand curve; we will call this elastic portion "Chester's own demand curve." Naturally, our friend should think twice about raising his price.

Another strategy for Chester would be to *lower* his price in the hopes of capturing a larger share of the market for himself. Indeed this plan might work as long as the rest of the industry left him alone. But they probably won't because they simply aren't willing to lose their market shares to the "Olson Baling Co." Thus, if Chester lowers his price, the other sellers *will follow right along*, forcing Chester to move onto the industry demand curve; this curve, in turn, will be much less elastic than Chester's own demand curve. Chester might gain a few more sales from lowering his price, but it won't be a substantial increase since all the other producers will be lowering their prices as well.

Chester is therefore facing two distinctly different demand curves. In summary, the demand curve above the administered price will be very elastic, while the one below will be less elastic. When these two curves are combined on one diagram, it results in a "kinked" demand curve representing the total price quantity options for Chester (see Figure 19–1).

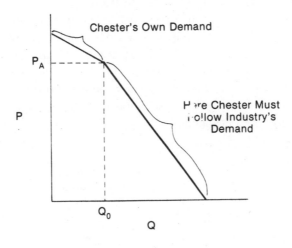

Figure 19-1

Perhaps you already have a feeling as to why Chester would be reluctant to make a price change. Indeed, our instincts tell us there is no practical reason to raise or to lower the price. But we have yet to *prove* (via profit maximization) that our instincts are correct on this point. Let's now see what our theory will tell us specifically about profit maximization.

Profit Maximization

To find out where our oligopolist friend maximizes profits, we will once again refer to our system of marginal decision making where profits are maximized when the marginal cost is equal to the marginal revenue (MC = MR). What does Chester's MR curve look like in relation to his kinked demand curve?

His MR curve will appear quite similar to what we developed for "Chester the monopolist," implying that the MR will lie somewhere below the demand curve. The only difference is that now we are dealing with two demand curves and will therefore have two MR curves, each falling below their respective demand lines and also reflecting the different demand-curve slopes.

In reference to Figure 19–1, we can say that up to Q_0, the relevant MR curve is that one associated with the relatively elastic demand curve, and after Q_0 the relevant MR curve is associated with the less elastic industry demand curve. In Figure 19–2 we have drawn the two MR curves and added some sample MC curves to help us find where Chester might maximize his profits. Note that because the kinked demand curve has two distinct slopes, it causes a *discontinuity* in the two separate MR curves, i.e., there is a long break in the curve directly under the kink and above Q_0. It is this discontinuous section that provides us with the basis for price rigidity in oligopoly markets.

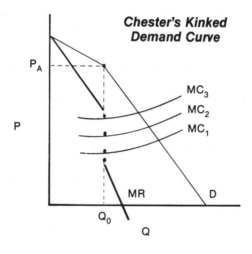

Figure 19-2

Note that wherever the MC curve intersects within the discontinuous section of MR, Chester will achieve his maximum-profit position (MC = MR) in the same vertical plane (see Figure 19–2). Chester then moves down to the x axis to find the maximum profit quantity and then up to the demand curve and over to the y axis to find the maximum profit price.

In each case the correct quantity turns out to be Q_0, and the correct price is P_A (the industry leader's administered price). Maximum profitability is therefore consistent with a large degree of price rigidity. In short, price competition usually doesn't pay.

Thus, in many of our oligopolist industries we find pricing policies that are much closer to the monopoly model than to pure competition. Certainly there is fierce rivalry in design, workmanship, packaging, advertising, and service among the oligopolists; but very rarely will the consumer benefit from good old-fashioned price competition.

We are now approaching the end of our microeconomics section. There is, however, one more market type that needs to be examined. It's an industry that often goes under the title *monopolistic competition*. The term, however, may lead the reader to believe it is closer to monopoly than to competition. Actually, these industries are much closer to the decentralized competitive market, and because of this we will use a slightly different name—*differentiated competition*—reflecting more accurately its true nature.

Differentiated Competition

I always enjoy discussing the differentiated competitive model because it typifies the small operators—the "little guys"—who strike out on their own in an attempt to become "their own boss." It is partly a romantic notion reminding us of the old "free enterprise ideal." Nonetheless, it is a value that continues to be deeply ingrained in the minds of many Americans.

Who exactly are these differentiated competitors? They are the small restaurant and resort owners, the barbers, the beauticians, used-car salesmen, or repair shop owners. They are also the struggling artists, rock bands, freelance photographers, poets, craft potters and painters, and small publishers. A seller in this kind of market will usually share the industry with dozens and dozens, perhaps hundreds, of other sellers.

These industries share with their pure competitive cousins the characteristic of easy entry, easy exit; thus, scale requirements are usually not an important factor in entering one of these markets. Easy entry also implies that differentiated competitors face an uphill struggle to achieve anything more than a "normal" profit in the long run (if they're lucky!). Indeed it is these little operators who contribute disproportionately to the overall business mortality statistics.

I have discovered that many of my students look forward to starting a business via the differentiated competition route to become restaurant managers, artists, photographers, fashion merchandisers, and so on. They like the idea of controlling their own fates, and they dream about the possibilities of taking an entrepreneurial "fling" at the universe—risking their savings, working twelve-hour days, and often bringing in their families for extra help.

Perhaps you are thinking that this market sounds a lot like pure competition: many, many sellers; easy entry and exit; high risk; and little, if any, extra long-run profits. However, within the name "differentiated competition," we find the major difference. In this market, each seller has a *slightly* different product, service, or location. There is almost always some difference between Frank's and Joe's barber shops (or bars), "Super Sam's Roast Beef" and "The Village Cafeteria," or between the many makers of designer clothes. In short, differentiated competitors have an identifiable product or brand name that attracts some degree of consumer loyalty.

Consumer loyalty, in turn, means that the seller has a *slight* amount of control over the price. Recall for a minute that a competitive seller of corn can't get away with selling his product even a penny above the industry price. In contrast, the differentiated competitor usually has a *small amount of price flexibility*. Yet if prices increase too much, even the loyal customers will turn away and seek one of the many alternatives.

Therefore, if we were to draw a differentiated competitor's demand curve, it would probably be quite elastic, but because of product differentiation it would not be perfectly so. A sample curve can be seen in Figure 19–3. Note that the differentiated competitor can raise his price from P_1 to P_2 without losing all his customers; people will continue to patronize the seller because of their brand name or an individualized product or service.

To return to the odyssey of our friend Chester, rumor has it that he sold the Olson Baling Co. He "bailed out" after he heard about a firm developing a revolutionary new baler technology— just as he had done years before.

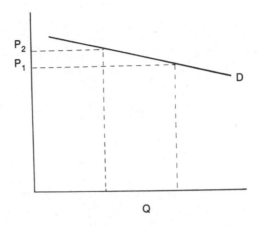

Figure 19-3

In the meantime, Chester has grown a beard. He also read a book called *Zen and the Art of Motorcycle Maintenance*, which inspired him to think about a new line of work. Thus, he is now a skilled motorcycle (and bicycle) mechanic in Missoula, Montana. Our friend has indeed made the rounds—from competition to monopoly to oligopoly—and now he has settled in a differentiated competition market. Since we have already approximated a demand curve for this type of market (see Figure 19–3), why don't we simply call this one "the demand for Chester's motorcycle tune-ups." How then will Chester maximize profits this time?

First, he would figure out his MR curve. As in our earlier example, MR would be a straight line that falls below the very elastic demand curve. Next, Chester computes his long-run marginal-cost (LMC) curve. In Figure 19–4, we have an approximation of both of these curves.

Where then does Chester maximize his profits? Like a broken record, repeating itself over and over, "Profits are maximized at that quantity where MC = MR." Thus Chester's profit-maximizing quantity is Q_1. We then dot up to the demand curve to find out what price will be charged, and reading off the y axis, we discover that our friend would charge $33 for his comprehensive tune-up.

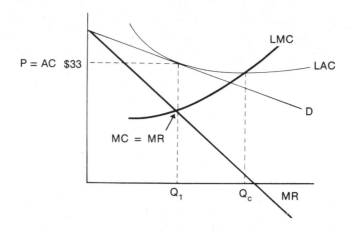

Figure 19-4

Next, let's look at the extent of Chester's profits. Our standard procedure to determine profits is to dot up to the LAC curve to find average cost and then compare this average cost with the price. When Chester does this, however, he is stunned to discover that his average cost *equals* his price leaving him no long-run profits. What characteristic of this market structure denies sellers a long-run profit?

The answer is "easy entry, easy exit," as it was for the pure competitive model. This "no excessive profit situation" still implies, though, that Chester is earning a fair wage and is receiving a reasonable rate of return on his investment. Just as when our friend was in the hay-baling business, there is no way he could keep other firms from easily moving in. For all those who are interested in getting into a market of differentiated competition, the easy-entry characteristic ought to raise a red warning flag! As the saying goes, one should "hope for the best, but expect the worst."

There is, however, another more optimistic side to this model. It is the possibility of creating a unique product—a fantastic restaurant, a gas station with unequaled service, an incredibly good repair shop, or such popular poems or songs—that will reap "quasimonopoly" profits and yet still belong in the market of differentiated competition. But don't count on it! Those who make it big against the competitive odds are few and far between.

Now if this model has some pluses and some minuses from the producers viewpoint, how does it fare in terms of overall economic efficiency? To find out we must look back at Figure 19–4. Notice on this graph that Chester's output is not the ideal-scale output, which is represented by the bottom of his LAC curve. The optimum quantity is Q_c or the quantity that prevails under purely competitive conditions.

Firms in differentiated competition may build a less than optimally efficient plant or operate their plant something under optimal capacity. This conclusion is not surprising when we actually observe workers in gas stations, barber shops, bars, and other small businesses spending many hours of the day relatively idle. Even when this condition is obvious, or seems obvious, we often notice some "brand new" seller coming onto the scene because of easy entry, thus diluting the market even more.

This type of industry does not offer the consumer the lowest price possible as does pure competition, but due to the highly elastic demand curve, the price will not be too different from the purely competitive price. You can easily verify this point in Figure 19–4.

To sum up, differentiated competition tends to have (in theory) the following long-run drawbacks:

- No extra long-run profits for the producer
- Chronic underutilization of resources
- A price that is slightly higher than the competitive price

However, let's remember that this type of market has some advantages too. For one thing, it offers us a variety of suppliers. Indeed, who, for example, would like to have only two or three possible restaurants from which to choose? Particularly in large urban areas, these little businesses add a considerable degree of interest, variety, and novelty to city living.

The other advantage alluded to earlier is *symbolic*; it stems from the free enterprise dream. Unlikely? Yes, but still possible.

What we have here is a group of industries that provide the opportunity to escape from a hierarchical existence, from large bureaucratic offices, or from the suffocating boredom of the factory—if that's what one wants to do. It's like a small slot within our basically concentrated economic system where you can still organize your own resources, where you can test your own entrepreneurial strength, and possibly, just possibly, not only survive but prosper.

Part III

THE WORLD ECONOMY

Chapter 20

THE BENEFITS OF TRADE

Why do countries like the United States, Japan, Mexico, Germany, and the U.S.S.R. trade? What's in it for them? What's in it for us? How do we benefit? Let's look at some possible answers.

Perhaps the most obvious reason to trade is to get essential or highly desirable raw materials that cannot be obtained domestically. For example, the United States must import most of its bauxite (used in aluminum smelting), chromium, manganese, and cobalt and, to a lesser extent, oil, potash (used in fertilizer), zinc, nickel, and tin. Add to this list some nonessential (but desirable) food imports, such as coffee, tea, bananas, and cocoa, and you can begin to see how important international trade is to the United States. And what is true for us is even more true for most other countries that are less endowed with the basic raw materials for industrial production.

Another obvious benefit from trade is that it *promotes competition* in our highly concentrated industries. Consumers almost always benefit from having more choice among products as opposed to less. Imported products usually offer us more variety, sometimes better quality, and frequently lower prices. Of course this kind of international rivalry may annoy, even hurt some of our domestic industries. Yet in the end, healthy competition can only improve the consumer's overall standard of living.

Also remember that *trade is a two-way street* and thus benefits our own export industries. Consumers and businesses in foreign countries purchase tremendous quantities of American agricultural commodities as well as many of our manufactured products including computers, plastics, farm machinery, chemicals, and aircraft. When discussing the pros and cons of trade, we should never forget that approximately one out of every eight American jobs depends somehow on on healthy trade arrangements with the rest of the world.

International trade also creates a sense of *interdependence* among world nations and can have the side effect of enhancing world peace. "We need you and you need us" is the unspoken theme as a continuous flow of imports and exports ties countries together with invisible threads of mutual benefits and sometimes mutual trust. Free trade among the formally antagonistic Common Market countries (Germany, Britain, France, Italy, etc.) is a good example. The "binding effect" of trade, however, is sometimes no match for the explosive forces of nationalism. The 1979 Iranian anti-Western revolution is a good illustration of where trade's mutual benefits were not able to overcome deep seated Iranian hostility and mistrust.

Mutual interdependence has sometimes been criticized as cre-ating an unhealthy dependence, especially on critical imports, such as those related to defense. This problem is compounded when the essential import is controlled by a monopolist country (i.e., the sole supplier) or, in the case of oil, by a cartel (OPEC). Thus the huge increase in oil prices during the 1970s alerted us to the need to promote conservation and to develop our own alternative energy supplies. We should keep in mind, however, that such a monopolistic situation is unusual and should not distract us from recognizing the general benefits of free trade.

Perhaps you are still not convinced; running through your mind may be the following thoughts: "Sure trade is a good outlet for our own surpluses and yes, it provides us with some essential raw materials; it may even create some healthy rivalry in certain industries. But what about the situation where the United States is obviously good at producing certain products, yet over a period of time we find ourselves losing out to imports at the expense of American jobs; how can you then argue that free trade is a good thing?"

It's a good question, one that is often on the minds of workers, businesses, and elected representatives. The answer, surprisingly, is, "Yes, free trade is still a positive force in the long run, even though there may be short-run difficulties." This discovery was made about 150 years ago by British economist David Ricardo, who first began to wonder about the benefits of trade as he noted a growing volume of imports and exports between his home country of Great Britain and nearby Portugal. Ricardo observed that even though both Britain and Portugal had relatively good capabilities for producing both wine and cloth, the countries still began to specialize over time, resulting in short run unemployment in the weaker industries. Ricardo intuitively felt that both countries were better off because of the new free trade arrangement. He then set out to prove his intuitive judgment, and out of these observations and analysis came his famous *theory of comparative advantage*. Let's take a look at his discovery.

The Theory Of Comparative Advantage

Instead of Britain and Portugal, let's see how Ricardo's theory might pertain to trade between Japan and the United States; and instead of using wine and cloth, let's use television sets and rice. I hardly need remind the reader that Japan is quite good at manufacturing TVs (especially the small, inexpensive, black-and-white variety), but what may come as a surprise is that the United States is quite efficient at producing rice. In fact, rice is one of our major food exports!

Let's assume that both countries have the capabilities to produce both products (which they do have). We could even assume that in terms of price, Japan has a slight edge (i.e, an *absolute advantage*) in both products, and yet, as we shall see, they will both still benefit from specialization.

To determine which country ought to produce what, we have to examine a simplified version of each country's production possibilities (PP) curve (remember our old "guns and butter" curve from Chapter 1?). In Figure 20-1 we have drawn a straight line PP curve for both countries using TVs and rice.

First let's look at the United States. Notice that the domestic trade-off is 1 for 1; i.e., if the United States wants to produce an additional ton of rice, it must give up 1 TV set. For Japan the trade-off is 1 for 2; i.e., if the Japanese want to produce that additional ton of rice, they must give up 2 TV sets.

Obviously each country is capable of producing both products, but their *opportunity costs* are significantly different. For example,

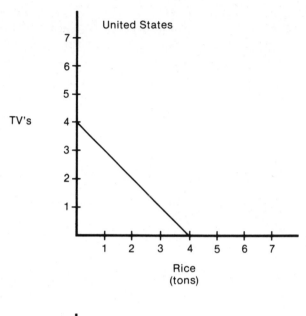

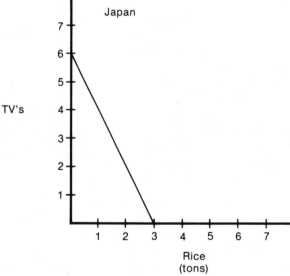

Figure 20-1

we might say that rice is *relatively cheap* in the United States (costing but 1 TV set), whereas TV sets are cheap in Japan (costing but 1/2 ton of rice). Were David Ricardo looking at these data, he would say that the United States has a *comparative advantage* in producing rice, while Japan has a comparative advantage in the production of TV sets.

Now it should be obvious that both countries have something to gain by producing their own specialty product and trading it with the other country. Looking first at Japan, wouldn't Japan literally jump at the opportunity of taking 2 TVs to the United States and getting 2 tons of rice? Recall that before trade, these 2 TVs would be worth (domestically) only 1 ton of rice. Similarly, the United States, in envying the Japanese domestic terms of trade, would leap at the opportunity to take a U.S. ton of rice to Japan and get 2 TVs—a much better deal than the 1 for 1 U.S. trade-off. But now you're probably wondering: "Hmmm, there's something wrong here; exactly what advantage would there be to having each country make exchanges using their own internal trade-off ratios? For example, what's in it for the United States if it gives Japan the *same* terms of trade (1 for 1) that it can get for itself without trade . . . and vice versa?"

Were Ricardo here to consider this situation, he would probably say, "Why not compromise with some international terms of trade, i.e., something between 1 for 1 and 1 for 2." A likely candidate for the compromise (depending on the demand for each product) would be perhaps 1 ton of rice for 1½ TV sets (or the equivalent ratio of 2 rice for 3 TVs). Now the United States can take 2 tons of rice and get 3 TVs (better than 1 for 1!), while Japan need give up only 3 TVs (instead of 4) to get its 2 tons of rice.

We'll assume that both countries find this compromise satisfactory, thus obtaining some very positive end results. For example, the United States now has the potential to increase its total TV consumption by 50 percent (note that if the United States wanted to export all its rice, it could import as many as 6 TV sets), while Japan's total rice potential has increased by 33 percent (i.e., if it exported all the TVs, it could enjoy as much as 4 tons of rice instead of the original 3). These new trade possibilities can be shown on an *expanded production possibilities curve* for both countries (see Figure 20–2).

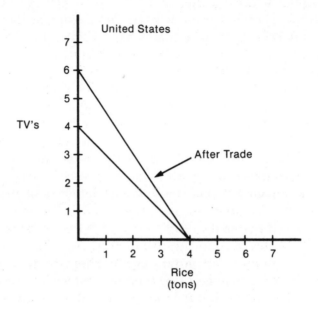

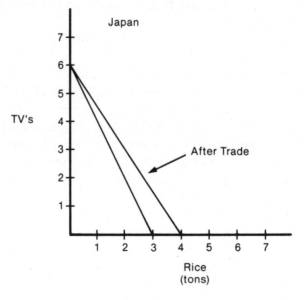

Figure 20-2

An expanded PP curve means that the consumers in each country have the opportunity to enjoy *more* of both products. Their standard of living has indeed improved, but not through an enlargement of the resource base; they are simply using the original resources more efficiently by specializing in those areas where they have a comparative advantage.

For David Ricardo, free trade gave countries this unexpected bonus. He was therefore not saddened when he saw the British cloth industry grow at the expense of its wine industry, nor did he think it unfortunate when the cloth industry in Portugal declined and wine production expanded. Though certainly causing short-run dislocations (unemployment, bankruptcies, etc.), the net long-run change was positive as each country pursued its comparative advantage.

Actually, the benefits of international trade are really no different than the benefits from trade of any kind. Think, for example, about the obvious advantages of trade within the United States. There is a significant difference, however, between international trade and domestic trade in that the dislocations caused by foreign imports are usually a *more potent political issue* than the dislocations caused by purely domestic trade. This issue, in turn, brings us to the heart of a very sensitive subject—*protectionism*.

Trade Protectionism

One of the best ways to illustrate the pressures to restrict imports (but without losing sight of the benefits from trade) is to draw up an exaggerated example involving trade between two states.

Imagine that once upon a time the state of Wisconsin was like a small, self-reliant country; i.e., it produced most, if not all its essential economic requirements. Let's further assume Wisconsinites had an unusual craving for citrus fruits. Thus, over the years there grew up in Wisconsin a thriving orange and grapefruit industry.

Perhaps at this point you might want to interrupt and ask, "How could Wisconsin, way up there along our northern border, grow citrus fruits?" The answer, of course, is that if the domestic demand were great enough (i.e., the people of Wisconsin were willing and able to pay high prices for citrus fruit), then it would be profitable to grow oranges and grapefruit in artificially heated greenhouses. Let's say that fruits grown under these conditions would have to be priced around $3 for an orange and $4 for a grapefruit.

Now let's assume that once Wisconsin established its large and thriving citrus industry, some enterprising individual discovered that the state of Florida could grow an orange for 10¢ and a grapefruit for 15¢. Adding another 5¢ for shipping, our entrepreneurial friend found that he could make a good profit selling these fruits in Wisconsin at a fraction of the old Wisconsin industry prices.

Certainly it does not take any imagination to guess what would happen after the "cheap imports" began rolling in. First there would be shock and dismay among the Wisconsin growers. Undoubtedly a powerful trade association would be formed (very likely called the Wisconsin Citrus Growers Association *WCGA*) that would immediately begin exerting political pressures to help save the industry. Horror stories would circulate concerning corporate bankruptcies, loss of tax revenues, and long unemployment lines. Soon the political machinery would begin to respond by undertaking measures to promote Wisconsin fruit consumption and to discourage the importation of Florida fruit.

The first measures would probably take the form of *nontariff barriers*, subtle methods of dealing with the import problem without resorting to the more common tariffs and quotas. For example, in the beginning there might simply be massive advertising campaigns praising the virtues of "domestically" grown fruits—with perhaps the implication that some of the "cheap Florida imports" have been found to be unhealthy. We'll assume, however, that the Wisconsin consumer finds "imported" fruits just as tasty and wholesome as the home grown variety. Possibly the next tactic might be to pass a law stating that all imported fruits must be colored a dark blue. But even that strategy doesn't work—the price is simply too good.

Sooner or later the Wisconsin growers will probably convince their legislators to take more drastic steps such as setting tariffs and quotas. We will be examining these measures in greater detail, but first let's take a look at what we learned about the real world from this example.

The first lesson is that cheap imported products will almost always bring some degree of economic suffering to those industries directly affected. From the perspective of the workers, assertions of

Hi, I used to own the largest orange growing hot house complex in Wisconsin. We grew our oranges even during the harshest Wisconsin winters. Sure they weren't cheap because of high fuel costs. But they sure tasted great!

One day my neighbor Chester Olson Jr. came back from a vacation in Florida with a load of oranges which sold for a tenth as much as mine. He sold out in hours, then went back to get more. Well that got us Wisconsin orange growers thinking. Soon we had a law passed that required all Florida oranges to be dyed blue.

We did this for our customer's convenience, err . . . that way they wouldn't accidently buy inferior Florida oranges. Well that didn't help too much so we tried to reduce our costs by putting cows in our hot houses (the cows seemed to generate quite a bit of heat).

Even that didn't help our orange business. Then one day Chester Jr. came by asking if he couldn't buy some of my milk to take back to Florida. He says milk there costs $10 a gallon while I can sell it to him for a dollar a gallon. Hmmm, maybe I really ought to be producing milk instead or oranges.

Sure enough, my cows were producing milk cheaper here in Wisconsin because they seem to like the cooler Wisconsin weather and our rolling pastures. This makes is possible to ship my cheap milk to Florida. By the way, those inexpensive Florida oranges aren't really that bad after all.

Well that's about it. I'm now a prosperous Wisconsin dairy farmer. One thing I wonder about though . . . why does Florida make me dye my milk green?

"comparative advantage" give little comfort to those workers who have lost their livelihood and incomes. Their first reaction is almost always shock, then perhaps intense anger. Consider the following story from a St. Paul, Minnesota, newspaper:

> Workers at the Teledyne Wisconsin Motor firm, which was playing host to Japanese businessmen, hauled down a Japanese flag in front of the plant and raised an American flag on the same pole.
>
> They sang the "Star-Spangled Banner" as the American banner was raised.
>
> One worker tried to burn the Japanese flag but could not ignite it. He then slashed it with a pocket knife, took it across the street and shoved it down a sewer opening.
>
> John Claffey, president of Local 283 of the United Auto Workers, said . . . the transfer of the so-called Wisconsin Robin engine business to Japan had cost "50 percent of our engine business" and that 350 people had been laid off at the West Milwaukee plant as a result.[42]

These intense feelings are understandable. Compasssion tells us that workers adversely affected by sudden shifts in international trade arrangements need help: not so much help through protectionist measures but, instead, help in softening the pain of sudden unemployment and in aiding workers and businesses to shift their skills and resources to new industries where they have a comparative advantage.

This point brings us to the second lesson from our illustration. It should be clear that despite the economic hardship, Wisconsin really *has no business growing grapefruit and oranges.* Its land, resources, climate, etc., are far more ideal for producing dairy products. Once their specialization takes hold and Wisconsin begins to trade dairy products for inexpensive Florida citrus fruits, it's obvious that both Wisconsin and Florida will be able to enjoy a higher standard of living compared with the days before trade.

Thus the most productive reaction to the import threat would be for Wisconsin to start promoting a dairy industry. To facilitate this change, it may be necessary for the state government to offer temporary low-cost loans for certain types of farm investments, to set up research facilities, or to help seek out potential markets for dairy products. Indeed, it would be folly to attempt to hold onto the citrus production at all costs. Such a reaction *would lock Wisconsin's resources into the wrong industry for years and years.*

Strong protectionist reflexes are, however, far more common than attempts to adjust to new economic realities. We therefore need to take a closer look at the nature of these restrictions, to see how they work and how they affect the consumer.

Tariffs And Quotas

Certainly the most common strategy for fending off imports is to levy a *tariff*. This is nothing more than putting a tax on a specific imported good. Although a tariff is sometimes justified by the claim that it will generate tax revenues, the real intent is almost always to choke off foreign competition. Indeed if revenues were the issue, there would be no point in discriminating against only foreign manufacturers and levying such taxes just on them.

The economic effect of a tariff is the same as that of putting an excise tax on any product; i.e., *it lifts* the supply curve precisely the amount of the tax. How much would the consumer get hurt? That depends upon the demand elasticity as shown in Figure 20–3.

In illustration (a) we see a fairly elastic demand for Mexican tomatoes and in (b) is an inelastic situation for Canadian natural gas. In each example we have moved the supply curve a vertical distance the amount of the tariff—50¢ per unit. But because of the different elasticities, the tariff on the tomatoes increases the final price to the consumer only slightly while the same tariff for natural gas translates into a large price increase. The explanation for this can be traced to the fact that imported tomatoes are a "non-necessity" product, and there are also substitutes in the form of other vegetables. Natural gas, however, is definitely a necessity with few substitutes. The consumer, therefore, has no choice but to absorb most of the 50¢ tariff.

Perhaps of even greater concern to the domestic industry (the one who pushed for the tariff in the first place) is how the tariff affects the quantity of imports. In the tomato market (with elastic demand) the import "choking-off" effect is obviously greater than in the inelastic natural gas market. Generally speaking, we can say that *the greater the elasticity of demand, the more a tariff will help the domestic industry achieve its goal of keeping out foreign competition.* When the tariff approach is not effective, however, a second and more extreme protectionist strategy can be used. It's called the *quota.*

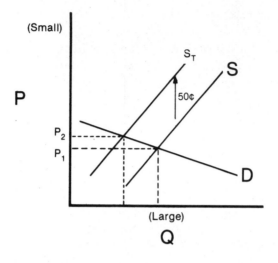

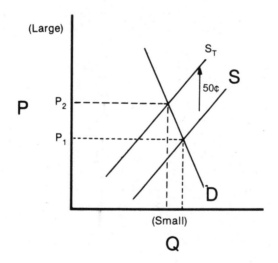

Figure 20-3

The import quota simply puts a physical limit on the quantity of imports. There is no worrying about cheap goods "flooding" the domestic market because only so much is legally allowed to enter the country. The impact of a quota can be seen in Figure 20–4.

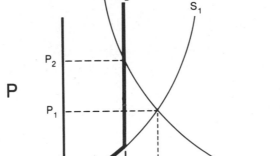

Figure 20-4

Although economists dislike protectionist measures in any guise, they perhaps dislike quotas most of all. At least with a tariff, it is possible to get additional quantities of a product if you're willing to pay the tax. But the quota is an *absolute barrier* once the legal limit has been reached. In the above example the foreign car quota was set at 3 million, whereas the normal trade equilibrium would have been 5 million. Also notice that the restricted supply (S_2) forces those who want the product to bid the price up from P_1 to P_2.

If there is one thread running throughout this discussion, it is that protectionist measures usually hurt the consumer and ultimately diminish the efficient use of world resources. Yet we still continue to use them.

A major reason for this is, of course, the sheer political power of those workers and businesses that are affected by foreign competition (recall the Wisconsin citrus-growers example). What is sometimes difficult to understand, however, is when the *public itself* expresses some of these seemingly "logical" arguments for trade restriction. We will now examine some of the arguments that are most frequently put forth by both the vested interest groups and the general public.

Arguments For Trade Protectionism

A friend once said to me (quite sincerely I believe) that we ought to restrict foreign imports because it's important "to keep our money in the country." This argument has an irrefutable ring to it—how could we *not* want to keep our dollars at home?

Upon further reflection, though, it actually doesn't make any sense. Indeed, my friend should recognize that trade is a "two-way street"; that is, our dollars that go to Japan for Datsuns or Toyotas come right back to us when the Japanese buy our rice, soybeans, computers, real estate, or stocks and bonds. Thus, if there is a healthy trade arrangement between countries, our money *will* eventually return to us because the Japanese have little use for dollars at home.

Another argument I hear quite often is that we ought to restrict imports because American workers cannot compete with "cheap foreign labor." This is a powerful, often emotionally charged argument—one that shouldn't be dismissed lightly. What it is saying, of course, is that products from low wage countries jeopardize American wage rates, American businesses, and ultimately, American jobs.

Those who use this argument often overlook the fact that U.S. wages are higher than wages in other countries primarily *because U.S. workers are generally more productive*; are probably better educated and more skilled; and, more often than not, use more advanced production techniques. Other less technologically advanced countries have, in fact, sometimes argued for tariffs to protect *their* domestic industries from the "unfair competition" of the "highly productive" American industrial worker or farmer.

Of course there may be certain industries where our wage rates might be out of line with industry's general level of worker productivity. But why should the American consumer be forced, through protectionist import restrictions, to subsidize high American wage rates not matched by corresponding productivity? Or putting it slightly differently, why shouldn't U.S. consumers be allowed to *benefit* from inexpensive products made by low-wage workers? And, of course, why shouldn't foreign consumers benefit from our most efficient industries?

If you scratch beneath the surface of the cheap foreign labor argument you usually discover that it is an oblique admission that a particular industry is no longer efficient according to world standards. In certain cases, some of the producers may not have modernized their factories; in other industries it may be that the wages are out of line with productivity or that product design or quality may not have kept up with foreign competition. Indeed, it would be unusual if we didn't see some domestic industries (or individual companies) lose their competitive advantage over time.

Needless to say, if we begin to erect trade barriers on the cheap foreign labor argument, there is no reason why other countries whose own industries are hurt by U.S. products cannot *retaliate* with their own tariffs and quotas on *our* products. This would be the beginning of a destructive trade restriction war where, in the end, everybody loses out. A good illustration of such shortsightedness was the enactment of the Smoot-Hawley tariffs in 1930, which raised the average cost of imported goods about 60 percent. Retaliation ensued, and the inevitable retrenchment in world trade made the great depression of the 1930s just that much worse.

The popularity of each of these seemingly "logical" arguments should not mask the fact that they simply do not hold up under scrutiny. But perhaps you're wondering, "Are there *any* conditions that might warrant interference with free trade?"

The answer to this question is a qualified "maybe." There are times, for example, when we are confronted with a violation of international morality in which restrictions on both imports and exports may be justified on *ethical grounds*. The United States, for example, once refused to import products from white supremacist (preindependent) Rhodesia. And in the late 1970s, President Carter placed an embargo on grain exports to the Soviet Union after their invasion of Afghanistan. This sanction, however, was later rescinded by President Reagan because of political pressure from American farmers.

It has also been argued that Third World countries should temporarily restrict imports so that new industries have an opportunity to become established; this is usually referred to as the *infant industry argument*. The implications here are that (1) it is desirable

for the less developed countries to diversify their internal economies and (2) temporary restrictions are needed so that the "infant"
can have breathing space to "mature," that is, grow efficient by
world standards, without getting clobbered by the existing international giants. For this argument to be valid, the domestic
industry should be forewarned that the import protection will be
cut off at some specific date. Otherwise, the "infants" will probably
want to perpetuate their protected status. Like the proverbial son
who refuses to leave home, it's equally true that some protected
industries also resist confronting the real world.

Finally, we might argue for temporary protectionist measures
to prevent a genuine "culture shock" in some developing countries.
Not so much an economic argument as an anthropological one, this
point of view recognizes the potential for destroying traditional
handicraft societies when there is a sudden, unexpected influx of
machine made goods. When such an influx occurs, it frequently
affects not only the economic livelihood but also the age-old cultural fabric of the community. Again, this is not an argument for
permanent restrictions but simply an admission that it may be
desirable to slow things down so people have a chance to make
adjustments.

But when the exceptions are noted and acknowledged, the fact
remains that free trade is a good thing. And, fortunately, the
world's major trading partners generally recognize this fact. Since
1947 we have witnessed an attempt to significantly reduce trade
barriers through the General Agreements for Tariffs and Trade. By
the early 1980s various milestones of tariff negotiations (the so-
called Kennedy Round in 1967 and Tokyo Round in 1979) reduced
tariffs to historically low levels. Of course there will always be
domestic pressures to impose protective tariffs and quotas, and
hence there will always be the threat of a worldwide restrictive
trade war lurking in the background. We should be on our guard.

Yet even without a trade war, there are still some knotty problems facing each and every country in the form of periodic
imbalances of trade. It's now time to take a closer look at the age-old
struggle of how countries balance their international payments.

Chapter 21

THE PROBLEMS
OF TRADE

Do you remember our fanciful story from the previous chapter about Wisconsin trading with Florida? One of the key ideas of this illustration was to show that the principles of specialization and comparative advantage apply equally to any kind of trade— between states, between regions, between countries. Why then do we seem to have more headaches with our trading arrangements in the international sphere than we do in the domestic realm? This question leads us to one of the most interesting issues in economics—the *balance-of-payments* problem.

Consider again Wisconsin and Florida. If it should happen that Wisconsin imports more from Florida than it exports, we might say that Wisconsin is experiencing a so-called "unfavorable" balance of trade. Yet, as noted above, nobody gets very excited about it. Why not?

It's simply because the entire United States *uses the same currency*. Thus, if Florida businesses collect a *surplus* of Wisconsin dollars, they can easily spend them in Florida—or for that matter anywhere in the United States. In the case of an unfavorable balance of trade with Japan, however, the Japanese will accumulate extra dollars that, generally speaking, cannot be spent in Japan. If this imbalance continues, the Japanese may decide it is simply no longer worth it for them to trade with us. Thus, unlike the trade between individual states, trade between countries ought to roughly "balance out" over time; otherwise the surplus country will build up quantities of unwanted foreign currencies at the expense of sacrificing real goods and services. What mechanisms or policies are available to bring an imbalanced situation back into balance?

There have, in fact, been three major approaches to dealing with this situation. The earliest solution to trade imbalances is called the *Classical Gold-Flow Model* originally described by philosopher-economist David Hume in 1752. Let's therefore begin by taking a look at Hume's theory.

Classical Gold Flow

In order for the classical model to work, Hume assumed that all the countries involved in trade had to be on an *international gold standard* and also on a *domestic gold standard*.

When trading countries go on an international gold standard, it means that traders from a foreign country who wind up with a surplus of dollars have the right to trade those dollars for American gold. If, on the other hand, traders from the United States wind up with a trade surplus, they would have the right to obtain foreign gold for their surplus currencies.

To be on a domestic gold standard means that every dollar in circulation must be redeemable or backed up by an equivalent value of gold. A country's money supply will therefore depend on how much gold it has. If the United States loses some of its gold to a foreign country, we will then be forced to reduce our domestic money supply because of a lack of gold to back it up. On the other hand, if we enlarge our gold holdings, it would automatically increase the money supply.

Before this model could begin solving a balance-of-payments problem, one further assumption needs to be spelled out: the linkage between money and prices through the so-called *Quantity Theory of Money*. This theory can be summarized quite neatly in the equation:

$$MV = PQ$$

where M equals the money supply, V the velocity of money (the number of times an average dollar changes hands during the year), P the general price level, and Q the physical volume of goods and services.

Classical economists like Hume assumed that both V and Q remain relatively constant *leaving M and P to rise or fall together*.

Hi! I'm David Hume. I would like to show you how two small countries can solve an imbalance of trade when they are both on an international and a domestic gold standard.

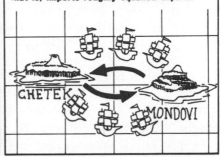

The two islands of Chetek and Mondovi are always trading between themselves. Last year things were pretty much in balance; that is, imports roughly equalled exports.

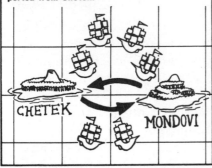

But this year Chetek imported twice as many goods from Mondovi as Mondovi imported from Chetek.

When Mondovi sells more goods, they get a surplus of Chetek currency which they trade for gold. The extra gold increases the money supply and soon pushes up Mondovi prices.

In Chetek just the opposite was happening. A loss of gold reduced their money supply and soon their prices began to go down.

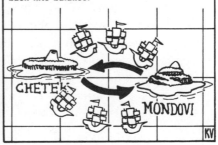

High Mondovi prices therefore discourage Chetekites from buying Mondovi imports and low Chetek prices encourage Mondovians to purchase Chetek products. Soon trade is back into balance.

Thus if the U.S. money supply goes up, it drives prices up too (inflation), or if M goes down, it lowers the price level (deflation). Of course, in our simplified classical world all prices are assumed to have total flexibility, moving downward or upward with equal ease.

The stage is now set for solving an imbalance problem. Assume the United States suddenly finds itself in a serious trade deficit with Japan (U.S. imports greater than exports). As a result, Japanese receive more dollars than they can spend. Under the classical assumptions outlined above, Japanese traders exchange their surplus dollars for American gold, and the quantity of gold in the U.S. treasury falls. A reduction in our gold stock forces a reduction in the money supply. If M goes down, we can soon expect a decrease in our prices. Falling U.S. prices, in turn, make our products less expensive and therefore more attractive to the Japanese. As U.S. exports expand, we find ourselves moving toward a balance-of-payments equilibrium.

We should also note what's going on in Japan. Japan's growing gold stock means more money circulating in their economy. More money (given a fixed Q) will create Japanese inflation. Finally, high Japanese prices will discourage Japanese imports to the United States, which again helps resolve the original imbalance of payments. A summary of the relevant linkages leading to a trade equilibrium can be seen in the diagram on the next page.

Classical gold flow is a neat system, completely automatic and totally reliable. It's an extremely attractive model operating like some self-regulating Newtonian machine that's continually moving the system toward a favorable equilibrium without messy maintenance or outside tinkering. So why don't we use this system today?

First, we are no longer on an international gold standard, nor is our domestic money supply backed by gold (the last vestige of backing went out in 1967). There is simply not enough total gold available to keep up with expanding domestic money supplies and the general expansion in world trade.

More important, though, even if we were on the gold standard, prices would probably not respond with the classical flexibility needed to make the system work. Today, prices tend to go up and up, very rarely down. In fact, the only time the United States has experienced general deflation in the twentieth century was during

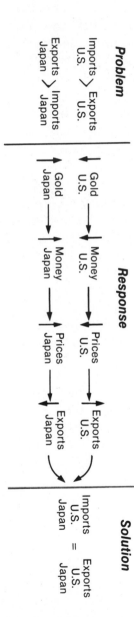

Diagram 21A

the great depression of the 1930s. If a depression is what it takes to get prices down, it's simply not worth it. Indeed, there must be a better way to solve our international balance-of payments problem. This brings us to our second method—a method which in many ways is even simpler than the Classical model. It's called the *flexible exchange rate system.*

Flexible Exchange Rates

The key to understanding flexible exchange rates is to realize that the world's currencies are subject to supply and demand markets not unlike the markets for corn or soybeans. In theory we could draw a demand curve and a supply curve for every country's currency. Perhaps it would be helpful to illustrate this point by choosing one specific currency—the German mark.

We begin by asking the following question: "Why would Americans demand German marks?" There is basically one answer: having a supply of marks will allow us to purchase German products. Thus, the demand for marks will reflect the demand for German imports. If we should suddenly want lots more German cars or cameras, we would therefore need more marks, and hence the demand for that currency would rise.

The second question to ask is: "Why would the Germans want to supply us with marks?" Germany will supply us with marks according to their desire to purchase U.S. products. Thus, if Germans want a lot more American wheat or computers, then the supply curve for marks will increase.

Assuming that there is an equilibrium between German and American trade, there will also be an equilibrium in the market for marks. This example is illustrated in Figure 21–2.

In the market shown in Figure 21–2, we find that the "price" of a German mark (i.e., its *exchange rate*) to be 25¢. We are assuming that at the 25¢ price trade between the United States and Germany is in balance.

Now let's see what happens when Americans suddenly want a lot more German products or perhaps decide to travel more in Germany. We might also be interested in building U.S. owned factories in Germany or in increasing the number of American troops stationed there. Each of these measures will contribute to a short-run U.S. *balance-of-payments deficit* because these actions increase

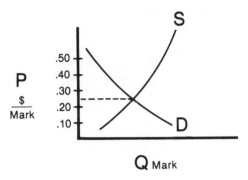

Figure 21-2

our demand for German marks. We will assume that Germany is
not particularly interested in more American products; thus their
willingness to supply marks remains constant. The market for
marks is then altered as the demand increases in relation to a constant supply curve. This change is shown in Figure 21–3.

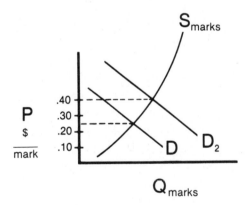

Figure 21-3

What is happening, of course, is that those who want additional
marks must bid up the price in order to get them. This is shown by
a new equilibrium price of 40¢ versus the old price of 25¢. As the
price for marks goes up, we say the dollar is being *depreciated*; i.e.,
our dollars are now worth less in relation to German marks.

In the word *depreciation*, we discover the real key to this particular system. Since the dollar is now worth less, it will take *more* of
them to buy a given amount of German goods and services. If a
bottle of German beer costs 1 mark, it now means that Americans
must pay 40¢ for that bottle as opposed to the old price of 25¢. Virtually every economic dealing with Germany will cost more
proportionately—buying a Mercedes Benz, traveling to Bonn,
building a soap factory in Cologne, or stationing troops in Berlin.
As dollars depreciate relative to the mark, Americans should then
begin to cut back their German purchases, travel plans, etc., thus
bringing trade into balance again.

Note that the change in the currency's equilibrium price is not
only depreciation for the U.S. dollar, it's also *appreciation* for the
German mark. Germany now sees U.S. exports as less expensive (1
mark, for example, will buy 40¢ worth of U.S. goods instead of 25¢)
and therefore will begin to increase their purchase of U.S. products. They may also start to set up factories in the United States
and perhaps travel more to the United States. All of these activities
ought to help regain the original trade balance.

Since the early 1970s we have approximated this flexible
exchange rate system. In fact, the illustration cited above (the
depreciation of the dollar in relation to the mark) took place
during the 1970s and brought about many of the changes that
were outlined. Thus the flexible system (with some minor modifi-
cations) is working today to help realign world currencies that get
out of kilter. Before we discuss current economic policies, we
should take a look at the third method of dealing with world
balance-of-payments problems: the *modified gold-fixed exchange
rate system*, which dominated the international scene for almost
thirty years. How did this system differ from the classical gold-flow
model or flexible exchange rates? Let's take a look.

Modified Gold-Fixed Exchange Rates

The fixed exchange system began at a specific time and in a specific location. It's birthplace was Bretton Woods, New Hampshire,
and the year was 1944.

It was a time when World War II was fast coming to a close. The
war had devastated much of Europe and almost all of Japan. Entire
economic infrastructures (factories, roads, power plants, etc.)
were literally blown apart.

The United States, however, was stronger than ever. Its infra-structure had remained intact; its work force was basically unharmed. It was not surprising, therefore, that the major industrial countries of the world looked to the United States for postwar assistance and leadership.

Assistance was offered in the form of the *Marshall Plan* and the *International Bank for Reconstruction and Development*. Both of these programs poured billions of dollars into European reconstruction. As for international leadership, it was agreed at the 1944 Bretton Woods Conference that the world was henceforth to be on a *fixed exchange rate system* using the dollar as the centerpiece currency. This meant that all the other major world currencies were pegged at some fixed value in relation to the dollar, and the dollar in turn, would be pegged to gold at a fixed rate of $35 per ounce. We were therefore on a *modified gold standard*: those with a surplus of dollars could, if they wished, trade them for U.S. gold. Still, most countries preferred to keep their dollars as reserves in their international "checking accounts." Dollars were, therefore, a kind of world legal tender. These monetary relationships can be seen in Figure 21–4.

Fixed exchange rates had the virtue of inviolable stability—backed by gold, a strong dollar, and an unrivaled American economy. The chance, however, that a country might experience balance-of-payment difficulties still existed. Anticipating such problems, the Bretton Woods officials agreed to set up a fund that could loan deficit countries the requisite amount of dollars (or other currencies) as the need arose. It would be called the *International Monetary Fund* (IMF), and its chief purpose was to help make these short-term loans or perhaps to help make long-term readjustments in a country's basic exchange rate.

Suppose, for example, that some country (for example, Great Britain) kept running chronic balance-of-payments deficits. The British pound (£) then would thus be "overvalued" in relation to other currencies and would eventually have to be devalued. How would Britain devalue? British bankers would approach the IMF and *request* a new (lower) exchange rate in relation to the dollar; instead of $2.60 per pound, they might ask to go down to say $2.00.

This might sound like a case of depreciating under the flexible system discussed earlier, but there are a couple of important differences. First, the flexible system described earlier adjusts

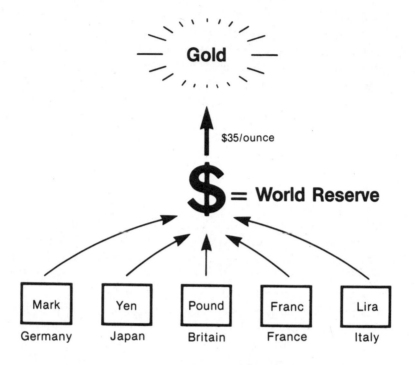

Figure 21-4

automatically to short-run changes in the supply and demand for a currency. In the case of the pound's devaluation, the British *had to ask the IMF for permission to devalue.* The IMF Board of Directors thus ensure orderly readjustments in world exchange rates.

The second difference is perhaps more subtle. After devaluation, the British pound is worth less not only in relation to the dollar but also to *all* other currencies, since the dollar is the major currency by which all the others are valued (see Figure 21–4). To review, depreciation means your currency has been reduced in value with one other currency, while devaluation reduces its value in relation to all currencies.

In general, the fixed exchange rate system worked reasonably well. Yet there was one major flaw: *its overwhelming reliance on the dollar.* For example, what would happen if the United States began to notice *its own* chronic balance-of-payments deficits, i.e., if the dollar itself became overvalued? How would you like to be holding millions of dollars in your international "checking account," believing these dollars would always be worth so much in terms of other currencies (as well as gold), and then, all of a sudden—bang!—have the United States devalue the dollar? This could be done by simply raising the dollar's par value with gold from $35 an ounce to say $70. The value of your dollars—those you've been holding onto with great faith—would suddenly be cut in half. The fixed exchange rate system thus had a structural inability to effectively deal with the possible devaluation of the dollar.

For a long time, however, devaluation wasn't necessary. As indicated earlier, postwar Europe was hungry for U.S. consumer goods and industrial products and therefore wanted lots of U.S. dollars. However, beginning in the mid-1950s and continuing into the 1960s, U.S. trade turned toward problematic deficits year after year.

One quite predictable reason for this was that eventually the Europeans and Japanese would begin to close the "productivity gap" that existed after the war. Their bombed-out infrastructures were, in fact, replaced with the most modern facilities available. Also, the U.S. productivity growth rate fell from a relatively high 3 percent increase per year (the average rate from 1948 to 1966) down to 2 percent (1966 to 1973). And for the rest of the 1970s, we averaged only about 1 percent per year! Not only were Japan's and Germany's productivity growing at a faster pace than ours, but some of the other energetic Asian economies, such as Taiwan, South Korea, and Hong Kong, were expanding their own export production and thus began making significant inroads into U.S. markets.

An additional problem was our relatively high inflation rate that worsened during the mid-1960s. Higher U.S. prices will, of course, tend to discourage foreign buyers and hurt our balance of payments. U.S. military presence overseas was another net outflow of dollars. In addition, the costly Vietnam War undoubtedly contributed to American inflation and trade deficits as well.

Another development that diminished U.S. exports was the formation of the European Economic Community (i.e., the *Common Market*), which promoted free trade within Common Market borders but often set up barriers to the rest of the world (including

the United States). For Americans to compete, it was often necessary to make direct investments within the Common Market countries, which meant setting up our own factories on European soil.
Such direct investments again contribute to a net outflow of dollars and hurt our balance of payments.

Each of these problems added to larger and larger U.S. deficits.
Of course, the modified gold-fixed exchange rate system did have
some techniques (short of devaluation) for coping with the
problem. First, it was possible to exchange gold for the surplus dollars (as originally intended under the Bretton Woods agreement).
Recall that the United States agreed to sell gold to foreign monetary authorities at the fixed rate of $35 an ounce. And indeed there
were countries, like France and Austria, who often insisted on gold
for their dollars. Exchanging gold, however, had its limitations
because of the total U.S. gold stock. Originally worth some $25 bil-
lion right after the war, our gold reserves had shrunk to less than
half that amount approximately two decades later.

Some Congressmen were tempted to solve the imbalance
problem by restricting foreign goods. In the last chapter we saw
that such protectionist policies were self-defeating and could easily
set off a restrictive trade war. Fortunately, the Congressmen's plans
didn't get very far. Legislators did pass laws that helped to a certain
degree. Efforts to "tie" foreign aid, i.e., require that the aid recip-
ient country purchase U.S. products were instituted. We also tried
to restrict the amount of imported goods that an American tourist
could bring back duty free. Again, these and other legislative efforts
did not really solve the basic problem of an overvalued dollar, and
yet we didn't want to devalue unless we absolutely had to.

Perhaps the easiest way to deal with the deficits was to *convince
foreign monetary authorities to hold onto their surplus dollars*. We
mentioned earlier that dollars became a kind of world legal tender.
Many countries kept dollars strictly for this purpose; others
wanted interest bearing dollar assets. Thus, if our interest rates
were relatively high compared with interest rates on alternative
investments, foreigners might be in no hurry to make gold
exchanges.

These techniques, in addition to selling gold and arranging for
assistance from the IMF, helped the United States hang on to the
Bretton Woods' system through the 1960s. But by the early 1970s,

foreign dollar claims were skyrocketing, U.S. gold was dwindling to an all-time low, and still our balance-of-payments deficits continued to grow. It was obvious something had to be done or risk an international dollar crisis. The Bretton Woods fixed exchange rate philosophy was simply not compatible with the current international trade realities.

The dramatic moment finally came on the 15th of August 1971 when President Nixon suspended all gold transactions. In effect, the old system of gold convertibility went out the window. The dollar was now allowed to float, and its future value was to be determined by the forces of supply and demand. By 1973 the dollar had become significantly depreciated against most of the world's major currencies. Prices of many imports—from German VWs to Japanese Datsuns, from Middle East oil to Swiss watches—all went up accordingly. No longer was the dollar in great international demand, no longer was it the paragon currency of the world. A new era had arrived.

Of course the flexible exchange rate system of the 1970s and early 1980s didn't solve all our balance-of-payment problems. Various governments (including the United States) were not shy about intervening against speculators and other "threats" to their currencies, preventing at times proper currency realignments. The United States also found itself hurt by the emergence of an effective world oil cartel (OPEC) whose sudden increase in the price of crude oil in the mid-1970s contributed to a large net outflow of dollars.

In addition, the latter part of the 1970s and early 1980s saw the beginning of an ominous trend toward sluggish U.S. economic performance, inflation, and extremely low (or negative) productivity growth—serious problems indeed for the once unchallenged U.S. economy.

It could be argued, though, that U.S. international economic arrangements were not so terribly bad. First, unlike most European countries and Japan, the United States is not quite so dependent on the foreign trade sector, producing approximately 85 percent of the domestically consumed goods and services here at home. Even in the area of oil, the United States has demonstrated a surprising ability to conserve and develop alternative energy arrangements. In the early 1980s one could hardly pick up a popular magazine without noticing articles on energy conservation, under-ground housing, fuel efficient cars, and the like.

Also, the United States continues to be strong in many of its tra-ditional export industries including chemicals, soft drinks, paper products, aircraft, telecommunications, food and fiber, insurance, banking, farm machinery, computers, TV programming, just to name a few. Finally, we should recognize that even though U.S. pro-ductivity growth has slowed significantly, the American output per worker hour (in absolute terms) is still higher than most other industrialized countries.

In summary, the United States will continue to face various international trade problems in the 1980s, and if certain trends (such as inflation and low productivity growth) become chronic problems, we will be courting trouble in future decades. Yet in relation to those nations where the majority of people live—the Third World countries—we are very well off indeed. Perhaps now it is time to leave our American shores and make a visit to these struggling nations. What is life like in these developing countries? Even more important, what does the future have in store for them?

Chapter 22

STAGNATION AND CHANGE

In the summer of 1974, well-fed Americans didn't seem quite so hostile to the high food prices as they had been the previous year. One explanation might have been the horrifying stories in the major news magazines and on television—horror stories not just of high food prices but of no food at all. During that summer there was very little food for millions of North Africans suffering through their sixth straight year of drought. A million men, women, and children were already dead and an estimated 10 million more were starving throughout the North African famine belt.

Thus, in the middle of the 1970s Americans got their first glimpse of people starving. We could no longer ignore the great suffering—the catastrophe in North Africa was simply too big to be brushed aside.

Of course, this particular crisis passed as others had before. Yet the uneasy feelings around the world would not be completely forgotten when the rains finally came several years later. Frightening talk continued throughout the 1970s and into the 1980s about the very real possibility of a global famine affecting not just millions, but billions of people in the low income countries of the world.

There is no doubt that Americans will have enough food for many years to come. Even under the worst conditions those in the "over-developed" countries will probably continue to eat luxuriously[43] and even to feed protein-rich food to pets. We have the income; we can therefore generate effective demand.

But what about the approximately 3 billion people in the less developed or Third World countries? What will become of them? What are their chances for survival? The problem of mass poverty must be considered *the* major economic issue of our time.

The regions under consideration include Asia (except Japan and Taiwan), Black Africa, and Latin America. Although some of these countries are better off than others, we are essentially talking about two-thirds of the world's population. Let's now take a moment to examine some of the general characteristics that are common to many of these Third World countries.

Certainly one common element in most low-income countries is the problem of *mass illiteracy*. Scarce resources often go toward the education of elite classes who are taught an outmoded colonial type of curriculum in schools which deemphasize the raw skills needed for economic development. For prestigious reasons, students often choose "literate" professions or civil service training instead of farming, trades, or engineering, moving into a world of bureaucratic desks and white shirts rather than to one of farms or factories.

Other students come to the United States, England, or France to receive legal training or to become doctors, eventually to serve an upper-class clientele. Some never return to their homeland. Not only does this kind of high powered training use up scarce public money that could be used for say adult literacy classes or paramedical training, but it also tends to reinforce class consciousness and widen income differentials.

Nutrition is also often a problem. Even without famine conditions, poor countries have always had difficulty obtaining food with adequate protein.

Protein deficiency, in turn, may eventually result in the crippling disease known as *kwashiorkor*. The victims are almost always children, seen in photographs with their large, protruding bellies and thin, reddish hair. Another nutritional disease is *zerophthalmia*, which comes about from a deficiency in vitamin A. This deficiency exposes millions to a bacterial eye infection that can lead to permanent blindness. In addition, there are many other nutritional diseases that in one way or another impair mental and physical performance.

Do these nutritional problems mean that the industrialized countries ought to supply poor countries with free food? Such generosity would, ironically, probably do more harm than good (at least in the long run) by obstructing the evolution of their own agricultural industries.

To illustrate this point, imagine the impact if some "benevolent" country gave free milk to everyone in the United States. In a short period of time much of the U.S. dairy industry would be forced into bankruptcy. Soon we would all be unnecessarily dependent on the charity of this "benevolent" country.

No, what the Third World farmer needs is really no different from farmers elsewhere, that is, *good economic incentives* such as reasonably high and stable commodity prices, access to land, credit, marketing cooperatives, and appropriate farm inputs scaled to the local farmer's needs.[44] Frequently, a successful agricultural industry can get under way by simply *eliminating obstacles* that already exist including elitist land-tenure arrangements or artificially low prices imposed by the government to placate urban workers. Indeed, a successful agrarian base is often the best method of providing food to the masses and thus upgrading nutritional levels.

Also important is the *insufficiency of productive capital resources*—appropriate tools, machines, and small-scale factories. Indeed, the average African or Asian peasant does use a certain amount of low-level capital goods—hoes, wooden plows, pottery for hauling water, etc. But these are extremely unproductive capital goods when compared with those in the industrialized countries.

The key word here is *productivity*. The growth process in the capital-intensive countries goes something like this: First, highly productive labor generates a large amount of output, which translates into relatively high incomes for workers. High wage rates, though, mean increasing costs to the producer; producers, therefore, are forced to mechanize even more, which again increases productivity. The growth sequence thus begins another round.

On the other hand, the less developed country cannot generate high incomes because of the extremely low productivity of its capital resources. What we find is the "vicious circle of under-development"—low productivity, low incomes, and a low level of consumption. The overall productivity in most poor countries is so low that a large percentage of the people live at the subsistence level, producing so little that they are forced to exist just barely above the survival line.

Indeed, it is this living near the margin of survival without prospect of upward mobility that distinguishes the poor of the Third World countries from the poor of the industrialized countries:

> Living poor is like being sentenced to exist in a stormy sea in a battered canoe, requiring all your strength simply to keep afloat; there is never any question of reaching a destination. True poverty is a state of perpetual crisis, and one wave just a little bigger or coming from an unexpected direction can and usually does wreck things. Some benevolent ignorance denies a poor man the ability to see the squalid sequence of his life, except very rarely; he views it rather as a disconnected string of unfortunate sadnesses. Never having paddled on a calm sea, he is unable to imagine one. I think if he could connect the chronic hunger, the sickness, the death of his children, the almost unrelieved physical and emotional tension into the pattern that his life inevitably takes, he would kill himself.[45]

Thus, poor countries are characterized by uncertainty, substandard living conditions, illiteracy, poor health, and hunger, all combined with a traditional economic system based on unskilled labor and primitive technology.

There is, however, another element of underdevelopment that is not as visible as those described above, an element that may be even more harmful to development efforts than the lack of productive resources. This is an area economists call *institutional barriers to change*, which includes adverse power relationships, elitist political systems, cultural traditions, tribalism, and the impact of foreign values. Relevant questions pertaining to institutional problems include:

- How do traditional cultural practices affect development efforts?
- How equal or unequal is the distribution of wealth and income?
- What percentage of those engaged in agriculture are landless?
- What role do foreign values or economic interests play in inhibiting indigenous development?
- How strong is the national feeling? How loyal are the citizens to the state, its laws, and its planning requirements?

Let's begin with the question of traditional culture and its effect on economic development. Many economists feel that the major obstacle to economic betterment is the simple desire to have a large family. In almost every underdeveloped country we find great status (as well as future "social security") given to parents who have many surviving children. Yet such a simple cultural value can create monumental population problems. A 2 percent population growth rate, for example, can result in the doubling of a population in about thirty-five years. Although some Third World countries greatly exceed that 2 percent figure, fortunately the world as a whole averages out to about 1.7 percent. Still, this means that there will be over 6 billion people by the year 2000—up from today's approximate 5 billion figure. Most of the net increase will, of course, be in the poorest regions of the world.

The above numbers may not mean much unless they are put into historical perspective. For example, it took about 2 million years of human history to bring our world population up to its first billion people. The second billion were added in about a hundred years. The third billion took only thirty years, and the fourth took but fifteen years. Now if the 1.7 percent population growth rate figures holds, we will have approximately 8 billion by the year 2015, and 16 billion only a generation later (2055)! Again, most of these increases would be added to the populations of the less developed countries.

These figures are indeed staggering. Such large numbers have to be modified either by increasing overall death rates or, more humanely, by declining birth rates. Indeed, population experts have pointed out that much more could be done in the area of birth control. It is interesting to note that the most successful countries along this line are either authoritarian oriented (mainland China, for example) or have at one time demonstrated rapid economic growth such as Taiwan, Singapore, and Hong Kong. Ironically, the best and least repressive method to reverse people's attitudes about family size is through economic development—helping children survive through better health measures and, perhaps most important, providing outside work opportunities for women. For many of the very poorest countries this appears to be just one more vicious circle: On the one hand, high population growth rates stifle economic development; on the other hand, families will want fewer children only if they actually achieve a higher standard of living. Can anything be done about this dilemma?

Perhaps one answer is economic assistance from the developed countries. But it should not necessarily be the kind of aid that finances impressive capital-intensive projects such as dams, airports, international hotels, etc. Instead, it should be loans or grants for local projects that promote widespread benefits in nutrition, health, education, clean water, population control, housing, and small-scale rural technologies. It's doubtful whether these "people-oriented" investments will increase the gross national product as much as a new steel mill or hydroelectric plant. But a more equal distribution of income and the possibility of reducing fertility rates may well be far more beneficial in the long run.

Consider for a moment the *uneven concentration of power, wealth, and income.* To understand the distribution of wealth and power in the poor countries, we must first grasp the importance of land. Poor countries are usually agrarian societies in which more than three quarters of the population work and live in rural areas (compared with 5 percent, for example, in the United States). In such communities prestige, wealth, and power are measured not so much by capital, money, or material goods but by the amount of land one controls. Think, for example, of the Philippines, a country that has shown some economic growth but little widespread development, where well over half of those working in agriculture are landless. We could also journey to Latin America where the magnificent estates, tens of thousands of acres, are owned by just a few families; to Venezuela where 1 percent of the landowners own more than half of the total land; or to El Salvador where 2 percent of the wealthiest families own about half of the best farmland. We could also find many vast plantations extending for miles throughout fertile regions of Africa and Asia.

These vast acreages and plantations produce tremendous riches for the owners but usually mean continued poverty and dependence for the workers or renters:

> In South America the poor man is an ignorant man, unaware of the forces that shape his destiny. The shattering truth—that he is kept poor and ignorant as the principal and unspoken component of national policy—escapes him. He cries for land reform, a system of farm loans that will carry him along between crops, unaware that the

national economy in almost every country sustained by a one-crop export commodity depends for its success on an unlimited supply of cheap labor. Ecuador needs poor men to compete in the world banana market; Brazil needs poverty to sell its coffee, and so on.[46]

Concentrated wealth, however, is not limited to local landlords and the traditional elite classes. Some foreigners, particularly those who "stayed behind" from the former colonies, also own immense parcels of property. Also, foreign interests often control the corporations that extract vast amounts of raw materials from beneath the earth's surface—tin from Bolivia, petroleum from Nigeria, copper from Zambia and Chile, aluminum ore from Guinea. The list of foreign investments is extensive, and while such investments may bring some temporary employment advantages, the long-run benefits to the poor are questionable when one considers the exported profits, the continued dependency, the strains created by unequal growth, and the tremendous reliance on one or two exports to earn foreign exchange.

This last point takes on even greater significance when we learn that about half of the foreign exchange for a sizable group of developing countries was earned by the export of just one or two raw materials. This means, for example, that Bolivia's ability to purchase imports (capital goods, food, consumer products, etc.) is largely dependent on how much foreign exchange can be earned exporting tin. Under these conditions, a small drop in tin prices could bring tremendous financial problems. Foreign exchange earnings would drop significantly, consumption of imports would be curtailed, the balance of payments would take a turn for the worse, and major development projects might have to be cut back—all this from a relatively small drop in the price of tin.

Manufacturing industries are frequently dominated by foreign interests too. Indeed, our journey to typical Third World countries would not be complete until we visited the industrial parks on the fringes of the major capitals. Here, Westerners would feel much at home with the familiar corporations—Coca Cola, Ford, Union Carbide, Texaco, and Singer, not to mention branch factories of British, German, French, and Dutch firms. These multinational corporations manufacture everything from soap, shoes, and ballpoint pens to bicylces and portable radios. Native manufacturing, in turn, tends to be stifled since the small scale of local operations usually cannot compete with giant foreign companies.

Given the lopsided distribution of wealth and the dominance of foreign interest, there may be little incentive for local economic development. Why build up a rural homestead if you don't own the land and can't benefit from your labors? Why attempt to compete with the giant companies when you are at a disadvantage in all phases of operation, from obtaining raw materials to marketing the product? In summary, institutional barriers can be quite deadening to economic incentives.

So what can be done about institutional problems? Some economists believe that it is necessary to have powerful governments that, over time, can force the necessary reforms and remove the obstacles to economic betterment. The centralized authorities must have the means and the will to radically alter land-tenure relationships, to reduce the enormous inequalities, and to evolve an effective program of population control combined with mass health and hygienic improvements.

Governments must also facilitate the emergence of local entrepreneurs and encourage national savings so there is financial capital available for business loans and essential public services. But they also need to safeguard traditional communities that seek economic self-reliance via their own traditional ways. They must learn to recognize when it is better to keep out of economic affairs and when it is correct to step in.

Indeed, these are difficult tasks for the world's young nation states. Many poor countries presently lack a sense of national legitimacy, unity, and long-term stability needed to institute such changes. In some countries democratic reforms may not be enough. Thus, we should not be surprised to see the rise of authoritarian regimes. Some will be corrupt and antithetical to widespread development efforts; but others will undoubtedly evolve the right mix of intervention and independent action. Indeed, we are bound to witness an era that is certain to have great strife and suffering. Still the prospects are immense:

> Yet if the Great Ascent is slow, cruel, even fearsome, it is also irresistible, stirring, grandiose. It is an avenue of history which, however difficult, leads from an eternity of dark suffering toward the possibility of light and life. That it will surely usher in a period of disorder,

readjustment, even temporary defeat is as true for the fortunate few as for the unfortunate many, but it is also possible to see such a period as prelude to a more distant era in which, for the first time, the potentialities of the entire human race may be explored.[47]

Thus, one of the major problems in economics today is how we, in the highly developed countries, can help bring about the necessary changes in the poorest countries. Only by our understanding, by our sharing of resources and technical know how, and by our willingness to make sacrifices, can we someday hope to reduce the world's gross economic imbalances. This is the challenge facing us all.

NOTES

1. See Vernon Carter and Tom Dale, *Topsoil and Civilization*, (Norman, OK: University of Oklahoma Press, 1974). This is perhaps the best reference I have seen that puts the depletion of the world's topsoil in a historical context.

2. See, for example how this conditioning takes place in children's literature in *Dick & Jane as Victims—Sex Stereotyping in Childrens' Readers* (Princeton, NJ: Women on Words and Images, 1975.)

3. Robert L. Heilbroner, *The Making of Economic Society*, (Englewood Cliffs, NJ: Prentice-Hall, 1962), p. 15.

4. See any issue of *The Mother Earth News* (Hendersonville, North Carolina). See also Stewart Brand, ed., *The Next Whole Earth Catalog* (Sausalito, CA: Point/Random House).

5. North Country Anvil, #4 (Box 37, Millville, MN 55957).

6. George Gilder, *Wealth and Poverty* (New York: Basic Books, 1981). Gilder's path-breaking book gives further commentary on the importance of new, energetic companies to help maintain innovation and create additional employment opportunities.

7. George B. Leonard, "Winning Isn't Everything, It's Nothing," *Intellectual Digest* (1973): 47.

8. Milton Friedman, "The Voucher Idea," *New York Times Magazine* (1973): 23. See also John Coons and Stephen Sugarman, *Education by Choice: The Case for Family Control* (Berkeley, CA: University of California Press, 1978)

9. Maurice Zeitlin, ed., *American Society, Inc.*, (Chicago: Markham Publishing Co., 1970), pp. 513-514.

10. From *The Retreat From Riches* by Peter Passell and Leonard Ross, (New York: Viking Press, New York: 1971), p. 36.

11. George F. Will, "Unpadding the 'Padded Society,'" *Newsweek* (1981): 100.

12. The attempts to increase productivity in some professions—high-speed drills for dentists, clinics for doctors, TV courses for educators— have undoubtedly kept costs and prices from rising higher than they would have without the productivity gain.

13. See Milton Friedman, *Capitalism and Freedom* (Chicago: University of Chicago Press, 1962), p. 150. In his chapter "Occupational Licensure" Friedman suggests that all professional licensing (including medical licensing) should be abolished in favor of a more free entry into the occupations. According to Friedman, this would ultimately lower the cost of professional services for the consumer.

14. For more details on Ehrlich's analyses and predictions, see Paul Ehrlich and Ann Ehrlich, *Extinction* (New York: Random House, 1981).

15. Arthur Schlesinger, Jr., "Neo-Conservatism and the Class Struggle," *Wall Street Journal* (1981):

16. See William Lowrance, *Of Acceptable Risk: Science and the Determination of Safety* (Los Altos, CA: Kaufmann, 1976). This book provides a detailed discussion of how our government views the nature of consumer and worker risks as related to costs and benefits.

17. Saul Pett, "The Bloated Bureaucracy," *St. Paul Pioneer Press* (1981): 4.

18. See Paul Samuelson *Economics* —(New York: McGraw Hill, 1980), p. 143. This text contains a complete breakdown of federal expenditures with an accompanying analysis.

19. *Welfare Myths vs. Facts*, HEW Document No. 392, (Washington, D.C.: U.S. Government Printing Office, 1973).

20. Michael Harrington, *The Other America* (New York: Macmillan, 1962), p. 13.

21. Simone de Beauvoir, *The Coming of Age* (New York: Warner Books, 1971), p. 690.

22. See Scott Burns, *The Household Economy* (Boston: Beacon Press, 1977). If you are interested in learning more about the hidden productive capabilities of the household sector, I highly recommend this text. In addition, Burns has done some interesting work in calculating a "rate of return" for home-production-type investments, which he claims compare very favorably with corporate-type investments. In Scott Burns, "The Economics of Milling Your Own Flour," *Organic Gardening and Farming* (1976): 103. Burns estimated that the rate of return to the homeowner for an electric grain mill was around 40 percent—over three times the return from the average corporate investment.

23. Leopold Kohr, *Overdeveloped Nations* (New York: Schocken Books, 1978), p. 39.

24. Wade Green and Soma Golden, "Luddites Were not all Wrong," *New York Times Magazine* (1971): 40.

The most extreme position I have seen concerning economic growth and man's ecological destructiveness is in the poetry by the late California poet Robinson Jeffers. Many readers have interpreted his poetry to essentially say that "the human race is, in fact, not needed." See Gilbert Highet, *The Powers of Poetry* (New York: Oxford University Press, 1960), pp. 133-134.

25. Irving Crystal, "The Worst is Yet to Come," *Wall Street Journal* (1979):

26. See Peter Passell and Leonard Ross, *The Retreat from Riches* (New York: Viking Press, 1971). This is one of the best books defending economic growth that I have seen. Another thoughtful book that challenges the antigrowth arguments is Wilfred Beckerman, *Two Cheers for the Affluent Society* (New York: St. Martin's, 1974).

27. Mel Ellis, "The Good Earth," *Milwaukee Journal* (1974):

28. E. B. White, *The Points of My Compass* (New York: Harper & Row, 1962), p. 67.

29. Henry Caudill, *My Land Is Dying* (New York: Dutton, 1971), p. 104.

30. See John Galbraith, *The Great Crash* (Boston: Houghton Mifflin, 1961) for a fascinating account of 1929's "Black Tuesday" and the early days of the depression.

31. James R. Adams, "Supply-Side Roots of the Founding Fathers," *Wall Street Journal* (1981):

32. Walter W. Haines, *Money, Prices, and Policy* (New York: McGraw-Hill, 1958) pp. 24-25.

33. Kristen Anundsen and Michael Phillips, "Fun in Business," *Briarpatch Review*, a Journal of Right Livelihood and Simple Living (1977): 30.

34. E. F. Schumacher, *Small Is Beautiful* (New York: Harper & Row, 1973) pp. 54-55.

35. Harold Stewart, trans., *A Net of Fireflies* (Rutland, Vermont: Charles Tuttle Co., 1960), p. 18.

36. Some textbooks call the *consumption effect* the *substitution effect* and use the term *income effect* for what is called here the *leisure effect*. The change was made to eliminate confusion with the use of *income effect* and *substitution effect* in the theory of demand.

37. Adam Smith, *Inquiry Into the Nature and Causes of the Wealth of Nations*, Volume 1 (New York: Dutton, 1910), p. 108.

38. Ibid, p. 110.

39. Ibid, Smith, p. 8.

40. Ivan Illich, *Tools for Conviviality* (New York: Harper & Row, 1973) p. 55.

41. See Michael Maccoby, *The Gamesman* (New York: Bantam Books, 1976) for an excellent discussion of these aspects of businesses and businessmen.

42. "Angry Workers Desecrate Flag in Milwaukee," *St. Paul Pioneer Press* (1981): 1.

43. See Frances Moore Lappe, *Diet for a Small Planet* (New York: Ballantine Books, 1975).

44. It should be noted that a growing number of economists are concerned that the less developed countries are adopting large-scale technology. This is happening because they want to emulate developed countries' production techniques, and because middle or "intermediate" technology is simply not available. One economist who not only described the problem but also started "intermediate technology groups" to develop tools and equipment more suited for poor, labor-intensive countries is the late E. F. Schumacher. See E. F. Schumacher, *Small Is Beautiful* and the follow-up book, George McRobie, *Small Is Possible* (New York: Harper & Row, 1981).

45. Mortz Thomsen, *Living Poor: A Peace Corps Chronicle* (University of Washington Press, 1969).

46. Ibid, p. 173.

47. Robert Heilbroner, *The Great Ascent* (New York: Harper & Row, 1963), p. 158.

INDEX